IMPRESSIONISM IN MUSIC

Music

Editor

SIR JACK WESTRUP
MA, B.MUS, FRCO, HON.D.MUS
formerly Heather Professor of Music
in the University of Oxford

IMPRESSIONISM IN MUSIC

Christopher Palmer

HUTCHINSON UNIVERSITY LIBRARY
LONDON

HUTCHINSON & CO (*Publishers*) LTD
3 Fitzroy Square, London W1

London Melbourne Sydney Auckland
Wellington Johannesburg Cape Town
and agencies throughout the world

First published 1973

*This book has been set in Bembo type, printed in Great Britain
on smooth wove paper by The Camelot Press Ltd, London and Southampton,
and bound by Wm. Brendon, Tiptree, Essex*

ISBN 0 09 115140 6 (cased)
0 09 115141 4 (paper)

To
MIKLÓS RÓZSA
in gratitude

CONTENTS

PREFACE

This is no thoroughgoing examination of the parallels between Impressionism in painting and its so-called counterpart in music, rather a brief general account of the vast corpus of music produced mainly during the early years of this century—and mainly in response to the stimulus of Debussy—which seems to be related in terms both of concept and technique to the Impressionist–Pointillist school. Arriving at a viable definition has been no easy task, and to some the selection of composers categorized in Part Two as 'Impressionist' may seem arbitrary. Why no discussion of Berg or Webern, both (particularly the latter) masters of pointillistic scoring? Why no Messiaen, the roots of whose language delve deep into the Impressionist soil of Debussy? I decided, however, it would be more realistic to limit this survey to those who had actually written impressionistic music *per se* rather than include those who had employed Impressionist techniques to ends often quite alien to the spirit of Impressionism. Part Two I believe encompasses all the Impressionist composers with whom the general reader is likely to come into contact, and a few more besides; space has precluded the mention of minor figures in Portugal, Scandinavia and Latin America, and many interesting people in Canada and North America have had to be by-passed for the same reason. In thus attempting to clarify Impressionism as a self-contained movement I have tended to emphasize its links with the past rather than with the present; and if I omit consideration of such important figures as Ligeti it is in the hope that another study will thereby be provoked, taking over where this one—and the 'movement' as such—left off.

Music examples have in general been restricted to those works to

which the reader is less likely to have access; therefore it is recommended that the introduction be studied with reference to the scores of
Debussy's music. Since the expiry of his copyright in 1968 many new
editions have been published, but the original Durand edition should
be used wherever possible.

For research facilities I am indebted to the staffs of the BBC and
Westminster Central Music Libraries where most of the out-of-print
scores I consulted are viewable, and United Music Publishers and
Universal Edition were also kind enough to loan me music. Of the
many who helped me with advice and criticism I should especially like
to thank Sir Jack Westrup, Dr Gerald Abraham, Dr John C. G.
Waterhouse, Rollo Myers, Lewis Foreman, Lawrence Norcross and
Bernard Herrmann. On the practical side the editorial staff of Hutchinson's have been unfailingly courteous and helpful; Miss J. Tagg and
Miss D. Wilkinson worked wonders with an unruly manuscript;
H. V. Dacombe devoted the better part of a Christmas vacation to
reading the proofs; and my father prepared the index. To all these, and
to Clifford Caesar who drew the music examples, I offer my heartfelt
thanks.

London   CHRISTOPHER PALMER
January 1973

ACKNOWLEDGEMENTS

The author and publisher are grateful to the following for permission to reproduce from copyright material: Boosey & Hawkes Music Publishers Ltd: 'Bredon Hill' (*On Wenlock Edge*) by Vaughan Williams, *Appalachia* by Delius, *Night Piece* by Britten; Chappell & Co. Ltd: *The Garden of Fand* and *Tintagel* by Bax (copyright 1922 and 1923, respectively, Murdoch Murdoch & Co. assigned to Chappell & Co. Ltd); Editio Musica Budapest: 'Floraison' (*Deux Images*) by Bartók, no 2 of Nine Pieces by Kodály; Editions Durand & Cie, Editeurs-propriétaires Paris: 'Après-midi sous les pins' (*Jour d'Été à la Montagne*) by d'Indy, *La Plainte au loin du Faune* from *Le Tombeau de Debussy* by Dukas, *Tristesse de Pan* from *Le Tombeau de Debussy* by Schmitt; Editions Max Eschig: *Jeux d'Eau* by Ravel; Editions Salabert: 'Forêt d'hiver' (*Le Poème de la Forêt*) by Roussel, 'Colloquio di campane' (*Impressioni dal Vero*) by Malipiero, 'Coin de cimetière au printemps' (*En Languedoc*) by Sévérac, 'Sur la falaise' (*Paysages et Marines*) by Koechlin, *Fêtes Lointaines I* and *Cants Magics II* by Mompou; Faber Music Ltd, London: *Enter Spring* by Bridge; Faber Music Ltd, on behalf of J. Curwen & Sons Ltd: 'Neptune' (*The Planets*) by Holst; A. Forlivesi & C.: *Cipressi* and 'Vigneti' (*Tre Poemi Campestri*) by Castelnuovo-Tedesco; Galliard Ltd: 'Fireflies' (*Four Characteristic Pieces*) by Bridge; Oxford University Press: *Summer Night on the River* by Delius; Novello & Company Ltd: 'The reed-grown waters' (*Seven Pastels from the Lake Constance*) by Karg-Elert; G. Schirmer, 140 Strand, London WC2R 1HH: 'Clouds' (*Roman Sketches*) by Griffes; Stainer & Bell Ltd: *London Symphony* by Vaughan Williams; Universal Edition (Alfred A. Kalmus Limited): *Gurrelieder* by Schoenberg; Ann Wolfe: 'La belle au bois dormant' from *The Unknown Goddess* by Humbert Wolfe.

INTRODUCTION

The rise of the school of Impressionist painters in the mid-nineteenth century was a natural outcome of that relentless craving for new forms of sensation, a patrician quest for new subtleties of refinement, which had been dominating the face of French art ever since the early years of the century. Impressionism was concerned above all with sensation. It did not try to render reality as it stood, but rather the individual's sensations in the face of this reality, his personal perception of it. It was interested not so much in an object itself as in the atmosphere with which that object was suffused. As a depiction of reality this is in fact far more effective than any self-conscious attempt to depict 'realistically', since our awareness of a scene or object is always conditioned by our visual reaction to it—we see the object not as it actually stands or exists, but the transformation of it effected by the middle distance, the intangible aura which interposes itself between object and vision—the *atmosphere*. This atmosphere—this consciousness on the part of the painter of some space between him and the object of his painting—is not of course a vacuum. It is filled with matter which may subtly distort the object at which we are looking—dust-particles, mist, raindrops, any of which will refract light-rays and bring about a view of the object which is true for a particular moment in time but which is thereafter constantly changing its shape and substance. Hence the fact that the textures of Impressionist paintings seem instinct with a contained vitality, a sense of mutability and imperceptibly continuous movement, all of which are quite lacking in earlier nineteenth-century art.

The beginnings of a revolt against traditional concepts of representa-

tion in art may be seen in a number of pre-Impressionist painters—
Constable, Delacroix, Daumier and Corot—but it was in the Realist
paintings and lithographs of Manet that new tendencies began to
crystallize for the first time. He and his followers discovered that if we
look at nature in the open we neither perceive every shape and form in
the geometric precision of its every characteristic nor are we aware of
the exact specification of every contour; rather, we receive a generalized *impression* of the scene as a whole: individual details blur and blend
in our eyes and minds. In Manet's lithograph *The Races at Longchamps*,
for instance, a horse-race is depicted impressionistically—we are given
an impression of light, speed and movement in that we are shown the
horses not as fully-fledged figures with every bodily feature carefully
delineated but as a number of vague outlines emerging from a confused
background. This is how such a scene appears to us in reality; we can
never take in all the details of an outdoor scene at once *as* details. A few
salient points will register, the rest will simply be seen as a chaotic
jumble of forms.

Among the painters who joined Manet and helped to develop his
ideas was a young man from Le Havre, Claude Monet, the distinction
of whose mature style was due to two main factors—his insistence on
painting nature in the open air, in the actual physical presence of the
'motif' itself, and (more important since al fresco painting had been
occasionally practised before) an entirely new approach to the inter-
related phenomena of colour and light. It was a picture by Monet
entitled *Impression—Sunrise* which led to the young iconoclast and his
colleagues—Sisley, Pissarro, Cézanne and Renoir in their early days,
and others—being dubbed Impressionists, this being originally a
derogatory term applied to them by a critic of the exhibition at which
this particular painting was on view. *Sunrise* was a picture of a harbour
seen through the early-morning mist, which had the effect of merging
sky and water imperceptibly the one into the other. Effects of mist and
haze became very much a part of the Impressionists' stock-in-trade, for
they found that by filling in their middle distance in this way they not
only obtained a greater sense of reality—since we tend naturally to
perceive objects in this vague indeterminate manner—but also enhanced the sensuous beauty of their representation. This is why so
many of the scenes in Impressionist paintings seem to be in a state of
near-dissolution; wrapped in this relaxed, fluid, constantly-changing,
incorporeal atmosphere they assume the character less of an assembly of
objects disposed in space than of a cuticle or translucent film of reality.

The Impressionists were less concerned with the density and solidity of the world around them than with the constant movement of surfaces and colours. This idea of movement is important. An Impressionist painting may be a transfixation of a moment in time, but it must convey this very transience through a sense of movement-about-to-take-place. In this it is closely related to the central theme of Impressionism, i.e. light. The Impressionist technique and aesthetic were essentially rooted in innovatory concepts of the functions of light and colour which, in turn, traced their origin to the discoveries of contemporary physics—the science of optics and the break-down of the spectrum. A true Impressionist painting presents nature as a mosaic of coloured patches with all the colour split up into a myriad minuscule dabs and dashes, so that the surface may shimmer and throb (a radical development of this technique led to the 'Pointillism' practised by Seurat and his followers). No statement of volume or definition of shape is allowed to impinge upon the more pressing realities of colour, light and air. In Manet's *Gare St Lazare*, for example, the real subject or 'motif' is not the engines and carriages, but the effects of the sunlight streaming through the glass roof of the station and mingling with the clouds of steam and the shadowy forms of objects and people looming confusedly out of the obscurity. It is thus easy to understand why the Impressionists were drawn to scenes not only of mist, fog and haze but also of snow and particularly of water with its reflection of images and consequent sense of unfathomable depths, mystery and dreams. The Impressionists' dream-world, paradoxical corollary of their new concept of realism,[1] is one of the factors which links them not only with Turner but also with certain of their contemporaries in the literary world.

As early as 1816 Hazlitt was describing certain works by Turner as 'abstraction of aerial perspectives . . . pictures of the elements of air, earth and water . . . all is without form and void . . .' Certainly in a picture such as *Venice: the Piazzetta from the Water* Turner dissolves his subject in fluid vibrations of light and colour, and Monet later proved himself equally fascinated by the Venetian lagoons and their effects of colour, space and atmosphere and water. Turner's misty pictures of the Thames with their sudden blazing flashes of sunlight are the immediate precursors of Monet's celebrated series of London views (Whistler's London *Nocturnes*, in their preoccupation with colours and forms rather than with a subject itself are similarly affiliated), and the dream

1. Superior figures refer to end-of-chapter notes.

elements in Turner's work are especially pronounced in such paintings as *Norham Castle, Sunrise, Rain, Steam and Speed on the Great Western Railway, Yachts Approaching the Coast,* and *Snow Storm.* Concerning the latter Kenneth Clark has written:

With our new knowledge of dreams as the expression of deep intuitions and buried memories, we can look at Turner's work again and recognize that to an extent unique in art his pictures have the quality of a dream. The crazy perspectives, the double focuses, the melting of one form into another and the general feeling of instability: all these forms of perception which most of us know only when we are asleep, Turner experienced when he was awake.

This dream-like atmosphere of so much Impressionist art, a natural consequence of the tendency to shroud shapes in mist and blur their outlines, is one of the factors which links the movement with contemporary trends in literature, notably Symbolism. One of the progenitors of the Symbolist movement was Edgar Allan Poe, who evolved from theories of E. T. A. Hoffmann the idea of *correspondances*—the deliberate confusion and intermingling of all sense-impressions—and passed it on to Baudelaire, who in turn greatly influenced Mallarmé and Maeterlinck, both unrepentant Symbolists. Poe dedicated *Eureka* 'to the dreamers and those who put their faith in dreams as the only realities' and many of his stories are in fact disguised dream-tales. In such works as *The Domain of Arnheim* and *The Narrative of Arthur Gordon Pym* we meet again this strange paradoxical blending of dream with reality, precision with vagueness, and a pronounced stress upon *Stimmung* rather than meaning—words being used not so much to express thoughts as to create atmosphere. This verbal Impressionism was related by Poe himself to music:

I know that indefiniteness is an element of true music, a suggested indefiniteness bringing about a definiteness of vague and therefore spiritual effect.

Edward Lockspeiser quotes Edmund Wilson's comment on this statement, to the effect that in Poe's work it is not so much what he actually *says* that matters as what he makes the reader *feel,* and that he had elements in him that corresponded with 'the indefiniteness of music and the exactitude of mathematics'.

The impact of these ideas on Stéphane Mallarmé and, a little later, on Maurice Maeterlinck, was formidable. Mallarmé's professed aims—and those of the entire Symbolist school of writers—were those of vagueness and imprecision, their fields of exploration the fantasy and the dream. Music offered them a perfect analogy for the elusiveness and evanescence of the poetic experience, and they claimed to be trying to take back from music what poetry had lost to it. The great revelation for their age was the music of Wagner, described by Mallarmé as 'la cime menaçante de l'absolu'; they were awestruck by its unprecedented grandeur and sonority. Mallarmé believed that, in Walter Pater's words 'all art constantly aspires to the condition of music', and that he should aspire to the production of an effect in poetry so absolutely aesthetic, so instinct with an untrammelled breadth of pure vision, that the understanding would be almost in abeyance. His aim, in short, was the creation of a world of ideal beauty. The early Symbolist plays of Maeterlinck, e.g. *La Princesse Maleine, Pelléas et Mélisande, La Mort de Tintagiles*, stand even closer to Poe in their invasion of that nebulous twilit zone which separates the material world from the vast uncharted regions of dream, myth and legend; and, moreover, are shot through at regular intervals with nature-evocation of a kind which immediately suggests the Impressionist painters.

Skirting the periphery of this ferociously intense aesthetic doctrine was one of the greatest of all French poets, another master of the fleeting suggestion and changing emotion. Paul Verlaine crystallized his own concept of poetry in the *Art Poétique* of 1874. 'De la musique avant toute chose' was his famous watchword. Prefer suggestion to bald statement of fact, he urges; take time and trouble over your choice of words, for

> Rien de plus cher que la chanson grise
> Où l'Indécis au Précis se joint.

—and he gives as examples of this condition eyes behind veils, the quivering heat of the midday sun, stars twinkling in a pale autumn sky. He extols 'shades rather than bright colours; only then can 'dream be merged with dream and flute with horn'. A plague on eloquence— 'Tords-lui son cou!' Grandiosity and emotional rhetoric are utterly alien to this new world of poetry, a world in which the soul 'takes the wings of the morning and, in an atmosphere fragrant with mist and thyme, soars to the uttermost parts of the heavens'. Such is the message of the *Art Poétique*, and as an artistic credo it is sufficiently akin to that of the Impressionists to render its exponent, together with Mallarmé, Maeterlinck, Turner, Whistler and the Impressionist painters themselves, *personae gratissimae* to the one musician who became an integral part of their world of spiritual and aesthetic ferment—the Impressionist in music *par excellence*, Claude–Achille Debussy.

There never was less of a musician's musician than Debussy. From his earliest days his comrades-at-arms were men of letters and painters rather than musicians, and ultimately it was the keenness and depth of his response to developments in these adjacent provinces of literature and art which led him to his attempt to find their equivalents and counterparts in his own chosen medium; finding the latter as it then stood unsuited to such purposes, he effected a re-orientation and re-constitution of many of its component parts, the repercussions of which are still being felt in western music to this day. It is impossible to overrate the part played by contemporary painting and literature in the formation of Debussy's mature style. There was, of course, the inevitable, ubiquitous time-lag. The first Impressionist work in music, the Mallarmé-inspired *Prélude à l'Après-midi d'un Faune*, appeared some twenty years after the furore occasioned by Monet's *Sunrise*, and by the time Debussy was writing the *Préludes* Impressionism as a movement in painting had long been superseded as the 'in' style and was secure behind the palisaded encampment of official acceptance and academic respecta-bility—which meant that it had long since ceased to function as a vital mature force. Nevertheless much of Debussy's work is undeniably impregnated with the spirit of Impressionism translated into musical terms for the first time. He had a lifelong admiration for Poe and contemplated a number of projects based on Poe's stories (notably *The Fall of the House of Usher*) although not a single one of them was fully realized. From Mallarmé and Maeterlinck he drew the inspiration for two of his most beautiful and original creations; the poetry of Verlaine prompted some of his finest *mélodies*; Turner, of whom he thought most highly, is associated with the genesis of *La Mer*; the starting point of the orchestral *Nocturnes* were Whistler's *Nocturnes*, and the strength of the composer's attraction to oriental art in general and to Japanese prints in particular is evidenced not only by the several pieces with overtly oriental connotations (e.g. 'Pagodes') but also by the fact that he chose a Hokusai print to adorn the front cover of the original edition of *La Mer*.

Debussy's music evinces preoccupations similar to those of the Impressionists, preoccupations which were essentially romantic in origin (musically speaking, Impressionism is very much an offshoot of Romanticism, which explains why so many of Debussy's successors can be described as 'Romantics of the Impressionist school'). 'My desire is to reproduce what I hear', he once said, 'a subject where action is sacrificed to feeling'. Feeling—affirmation of the primacy of the sensual response—was an essential of the Debussian aesthetic. Hence his craving for freedom, naturalness, spontaneity, uninhibitedness— the same yea-saying attitude to life and nature which drove the Impressionist painters out of their claustrophobic studios into the open air.

Debussy's obsession with immediacy of feeling and impact cannot be too strongly emphasized, for in it lies the vindication of all the far-reaching changes in the musical syntax he felt impelled to make. He wished to transfer his sense-impressions directly from his own sensibility to the listener, he did not wish to go through the time-honoured ritual of stereotyped formula and stylized cliché; he wanted a more convincing realism, he wanted to invest music with the power of communicating something of the inner content of a sensation or scene (i.e. what is in point of fact actually perceived by the recipient or onlooker) rather than its outward shape (i.e. what he only thinks he perceives). 'There is too much *writing* of music. Too much importance attached to the formula, the craft'. And elsewhere '. . . it is more profitable to see the sun rise than to hear the *Pastoral Symphony*'.

All of which suggests a man to whom musical analysis, the typical musician's cult of technique as an end in itself, have become utterly abhorrent, and it is certainly noticeable that in the correspondence and reported conversations of those composers most intimately involved with the other arts or faculties of knowledge—Wagner, Debussy, Delius, Scriabin—there is little if any mention, let alone discussion, of the actual craft of musical composition. Debussy would have none of it. His ambition was to make his music sound like a continuous improvisation, so averting the danger of a purely intellectual response. At one of the first rehearsals of *Ibéria* his delighted reaction was 'Cela n'a pas l'air d'être écrit', and this was precisely the effect he was aiming at; for just as life does not exist within rigidly prescribed boundaries and limits and does not conform to any catalogue of arbitrarily pre-conceived definitions, Debussy saw no reason why such restrictions should be imposed upon music. Music should be realistic. Apropos the orchestral *Images* we find with him accustomed flippancy and scepticism repudiating the docket of Impressionism which was being attached to his work: 'J'essaie de faire autre chose, en quelque sorte des *réalités*— ce que les imbéciles appellent L'Impressionisme'. But if *La Mer* gives an incomparably more 'realistic' impression of the sea than, say Rubinstein's 'Ocean' Symphony, it remains, paradoxically, the stuff of dreams—a similar paradox noted in connection with Impressionist painting. How could it be otherwise? Debussy was a supreme poet among musicians, and his mosaic-like conception of form conditioned by pure sensation, his fashioning of his musical textures from the reflexes of fluid sound-shapes—all opened whole uncharted areas of sensibility and emotion none of which had been available, as it were, in musical terms before. This was Debussy's supreme achievement and in this he fully justifies the description of him as the first musical Impressionist—that he empowered music to create atmosphere, to evoke and suggest, to express in coherent though necessarily elusive terms these myriad subtleties and variations of nuance which had previously remained the exclusive preserve of painters and poets. He even maintained that music being an art which existed not in time but in space could approximate more closely to the Impressionist ideal than painting, since in painting the play of light can only be rendered in a static manner whereas music can convey the sense of ever-changing movement, of ceaseless flux, far more effectively. In practice, however, many of Debussy's Impressionist piano pieces are the counterparts of Impressionist paintings precisely in that there is no real movement or progression: they are 'static transfixations of the fleeting moment', on the point of dissolution but 'frozen' in a specific moment in time. We must now look at the innumerable changes he wrought in the substance of music in order thus to translate optical sensations into aural.

The evolution of musical Impressionism is to a very large extent the history of the development of harmony and of new approaches to the concept of timbre—harmony and timbre being the principal means whereby atmosphere is evoked. However before either can be considered we must obviously examine Debussy's melodic reforms, melody being the essential term of reference for any discussion of harmonic innovation. From this point of view there was first and foremost a most pressing need to overthrow the tyranny of the major–minor key systems. One of the main characteristics being this impreciseness, this haziness of definition, no musical counterpart could obviously be found for it so long as every note of every bar proclaimed its whole-hearted allegiance to a definite tonal anchorage. Debussy sought melodic emancipation through a reversion to the very mainsprings of melodic thought themselves— folk-song and plainsong. Thus is most aptly demonstrated the historical truth that music is an art in flux, forever returning to its sources to replenish the energies expended in the pursuit of novelty. Plainsong offered him unstinted use of the old church modes with their many eccentricities of interval-sequence; from folk-music (more specifically that of Russia and the Far East) he gleaned his perennial fondness for the pentatonic scales which were to wield such influence over his harmonic thinking, and by the arabesques of oriental monody are often determined the shape and direction of his wayward melodic lines. Also of oriental origin is that most elusive and evocative of scale formations, that of the whole-tone scale, which never before had attained such pre-eminence in western music.

If a man's melody does not follow the rules laid down by the major-minor key system, neither can his harmony—to harmonize a tune in the Dorian mode on D in D major or D minor would be the equivalent of forcing a square peg into a round hole. So Debussy's harmonic invention may well have been galvanized into action by his early interest in unorthodox melodic systems. But even if it was, one of his most significant achievements was his raising the status of harmony to a level as high and even higher than that of melody. He came to conceive chords as abstract sonorities, self-sufficient entities released from sub-servience to a melodic line, and thus inaugurated the principle of 'non-functional' harmony—harmony which existed not as accompaniment to a melody, but as what the Germans term a *Ding an und für sich*, a thing in its own right. He used freely unprepared and unresolved chords of the seventh, ninth, eleventh and thirteenth both dominant and secondary, added-note chords such as the added sixth and whole-tone chords formed from some or all the notes of the whole-tone scale—used them in fact as *consonances* (hitherto they were regarded as *dissonances* needing preparation and resolution). Debussy revelled in the sensuous opulence of the sound they produced when thus allowed to come into their own, and exploited to the full their wonderful evoca-tive resonance.

No less iconoclastic was his attitude towards common chords. He juxtaposed unrelated major or minor triads in root position to breath-taking effect, and meandered at will in sequences of open fifths or, more frequently, chords built of superimposed fourths and fifths. These harmonic procedures may derive from a knowledge of the practices of medieval organum; from a knowledge of acoustics and the functioning of the overtone series; from a natural feeling for the pentatonic scale, the constituent notes of any formation of which will, if sounded vertically, produce some form of added-note chord. What-ever the source, there was always a single judge to discriminate between right and wrong—the ear, and its decision was final. Lockspeiser quotes a fascinating exchange on the subject of the theory of harmony between Debussy and Ernest Guiraud, his friend and teacher at the Conservatoire, from which the following is an extract:

Guiraud (Debussy having played a series of chords on the piano): What's that?
Debussy: Incomplete chords, floating. *Il faut noyer le ton*. One can travel where one wishes and leave by any door. Greater nuances.
Guiraud: But when I play this [Ex. 1a] it has to resolve.
Debussy: I don't see that it should. Why?
Guiraud: Well do you find this [Ex. 1b] lovely?
Debussy: Yes, yes, yes! There is no theory. You merely have to listen. Pleasure is the law.

Ex. 1a   Ex. 1b

Il faut noyer le ton in order to produce an atmospheric or evocative effect, one which has no validity as artistic expression, unless its appeal is instinctual, directly to the senses. Cézanne once said of Monet that 'he was nothing but an eye, but what an eye!' By analogy, Eric Fenby has described Delius, and Edward Lockspeiser Debussy (quite inde-pendently) as 'nothing but an ear, but what an ear!'

The phenomenal workings of this acutely sensitive 'ear' are mani-fested not only in Debussy's new approach to harmony but also in his quite revolutionary concept of timbre, of texture. For in that Impres-sionism was concerned to evolve a new beauty of sound it had to take into account not only the abstract substance of beautiful sound itself (i.e. harmony) but also the *quality* of the sound, the physical means whereby it was produced. Beautiful orchestral sound, evocative piano sonorities with free use of the pedals, now became ends in themselves— a state of affairs which even Berlioz would have found difficult to understand; for even though colour and special orchestral effects played a much larger part in his work than in those of his predecessors, for him, and for virtually every composer before Debussy, timbre *qua* timbre was of no particular consequence; it was simply a means to an end, the natural method of voicing and communicating a musical thought, and nothing more.

In that he thought orchestrally in terms of the specific quality of each instrumental timbre, Debussy reorientated the process of orchestration. No longer is the orchestra split up into strictly segregated compartments of woodwind, strings and brass with a sum-total of sound produced out of a general anonymity. Every member of Debussy's orchestra has his own individual function to fulfil, and this fragmentation or individualization of the orchestral palette with every player making his minuscule but distinctive contribution to the overall sound-pattern is akin to the *pointilliste* technique in painting. Instruments are deployed with unprecedented regard for their beauty of sound and sensuousness of impact, and a Debussy score has that constant shimmer of glowing sonority, that fleeting, evanescent beauty, that tantalizing elusiveness of detail, which we readily associate with Impressionist painting. Stridency is no longer an inevitable concomitant of brass writing, colouristic instruments such as celesta, glockenspiel, antique cymbals, suspended cymbals and especially the harp are all given their first real lease of life (someone aptly commented on one occasion that in *La Mer* Debussy had made the orchestra sound like a gigantic harp); and the expressive scope of the string body is vastly augmented, with all manner of combinations of *arco* and *pizzicato*, *divisi* part-writing, *sul tasto* and *tremolo*—all resulting in a new variety, flexibility and beauty of string sound. As Edward Lockspeiser has said, 'the miracle of the Debussy or Debussian orchestra is that the most intricate complexity, the most refined and sophisticated instrumental combinations, are ultimately resolved into music of unassailable simplicity'.

Similarly, Debussy's piano style in his mature period stands diametrically opposed to that of Franck or Brahms. Here again the innovations in piano writing stem directly from these preoccupations with complex harmony and beauty of timbre, and reflect yet another facet of his quest for the elusive, the evocative, the Realist–Impressionist; Wilfrid Mellers has happily described Debussy's impressionistic piano pieces as 'a tissue of nerves and sense organs'. An account of the Impressionist conception of the piano will be found in the section dealing with Ravel who inaugurated it in conjunction with Debussy.

Such, then, were the rudiments of musical Impressionism, and as such were they transmitted to those numerous successors of Debussy who qualify for admission to the pantheon of Impressionist composers—the post-Impressionists, as we shall term them. Of course, Impressionist thought-content varies greatly from individual to individual; in one composer the romantic origins of the movement may be reactionarily pronounced, in other its forward-looking tendencies may be emphasized. In one a coldly abstract, impersonal Impressionism may be the norm, in another there may be an intensely personal undertone (*objective* versus *subjective* Impressionism). Every composer who is not a mere Debussy-imitator (a *Debussyiste*) will have his own personal contribution to make to the genre, however slight, for once a style has been perfected by one man it must be cast aside by the next; nothing resembles a great style so little as its imitations. None of the composers discussed in Part Two can be described as a *Debussyiste*, although there is considerable variation in the proportion of Impressionist elements in their work and its importance in relation to their output taken as a whole; compare Delius with Bartók, for example, or Scribian with Roussel.

However, we can isolate certain preoccupations—mainly those of the Impressionist painters—common to nearly all Impressionist composers. First and foremost *nature*: nature in her more romantic and picturesque aspects—mists, sunlight, snow, autumn leaves, winter solitudes, spring awakening, the fullness of summer, raindrops or rivers or streams or the sea, sunrise, sunset, night. *Distance*—the confused hubbub of far-away revelry, the murmurs of distant voices, tolling bells, clarion calls from 'leagues beyond the sunset bars', their echoes and reverberations. *Dreams*—long-forgotten memories rising to the surface, visions, fantasies, mythological stirrings, semi-somnolence. The scene is generally pastoral but it can also be urban or metropolitian, or oriental—the oriental element is more pronounced in Impressionist music than in painting. We may expect the greater percentage of Impressionist music to fall into one of two categories— the dreamy mood-evocation (basically static) or the mosaic-like synthesis of disparate impressions (basically dynamic).

The musical language of Debussy will be the obvious beginning for most composers, but they will adapt and modify it according to the strength and originality of their own personality—in one composer Debussian harmony may scarcely be in evidence at all, another may allot more importance to melodic continuity than Debussy, another may write piano music which is Impressionist in substance but which utilizes a basically nineteenth-century keyboard style. The permutations and variations are endless as we shall also discover when considering the work of those composers who in some way anticipated the Impressionist movement. First, however, we must examine the developments of Impressionist techniques in the principal works of Debussy himself which may be specifically described as 'impressionistic'.

The term 'Impressionism' was first applied to Debussy's music in connection with one of his early *envois de Rome*, the symphonic suite *Printemps*. When submitted to the Academie des Beaux-Arts this august body found cause to condemn 'its vague Impressionism, one of the most dangerous enemies of works of art'. The form in which we today know this freshest and most engaging of Debussy's early compositions is not that originally conceived by the composer. The present version for normal symphony orchestra with piano duet (which does not however play even a *concertante* role) was made by Henri Büsser from the piano-duet arrangement of the original full score, which disappeared in mysterious circumstances even before it could be submitted to the Academy. The interesting point about this original version is that it contained a part for a small choir singing wordlessly with closed lips. Bearing in mind the very early date of this work (1887) we can see here a remarkable prognostication of later developments, since the use of the chorus in this way became very popular among Debussy and the Impressionists. Debussy regarded the wordless human voice not as an agent of the human spirit but simply as an added colouristic resource, a legitimate extension of the orchestral tone palette. It seems a pity that this choral part was not retained in Büsser's arrangement.

The first movement of *Printemps* is indeed an early example of Impressionist nature-evocation. Debussy thought of this as 'a work in a very special colour, covering a great range of feelings', its subject being 'the slow and arduous birth of things in nature, their gradual blossoming and finally the joy of being born into a new life', and we can hear the first sounds of awakening nature in the opening bars with their tentative wisps of melody and repeated delicate poising on chords of the ninth. At fig. 2 muted trumpets sound a fanfare as if from beneath the opening calyx of a flower. As the music grows more animated the textures begin to shimmer and sparkle and a spontaneous lyrical impulse governs the shape of the development in which there are echoes not only of Massenet and Wagner but also of Grieg. None the less an essentially Impressionist conception may be seen in the noticeably piecemeal, mosaic-like overall design: if the first section comes to a full close after the trumpet fanfares described above, the second dissolves in a haze of spread piano chords and a soft cymbal roll; the fanfares again bring the third to a full close and there is a descending chromatic fade-out at fig. B. The harmony throughout is rich and warm with many ninths and added-note chords, and the glowingly scored passage at fig. 17 which contrives the principal climax of this movement offers one of the earliest examples in Debussy of the whole-tone scale, used here to create a sense of wonder and anticipation. The final bars, also, are notably impressionistic with hushed cymbal strokes and harp harmonics which again seem to hint at the awe-inspiring nature of the miracle being celebrated in the music.

On his return from Rome to Paris, Debussy composed a number of works all of which begin to look forward to the first Impressionist *chef-d'œuvre*, the *Prélude à l'Après-midi d'un Faune*—notably the song-cycles to words by Verlaine (*Ariettes Oubliées*) and by Baudelaire (*Cinq Poèmes de Charles Baudelaire*). The first of the *Ariettes*—'C'est l'extase'—is an *Abendstimmung*: cool breezes being wafted from the woods, birds warbling, water gurgling in the stream. In this music many elements of an Impressionist style are beginning to coalesce—the abolition of sustained melody as such, an unalloyed richness of harmony, held as if entranced by its own voluptuousness. The same applies to the third song, 'L'ombre des arbres dans la rivière embrumée' in which this static quality is even more pronounced, and in the beautiful 'Il pleure dans mon cœur'—arguably one of the best of all Debussy's songs—we are given a foretaste of the composer's later Impressionist water-pieces. In all these songs the idiom is still not completely purged of Wagnerian chromatic elements, and these are very noticeably in evidence in the Baudelaire settings. 'Harmonies du soir' and 'Recueillement' have some kinship of feeling with 'L'ombre des arbres' but they are much longer, their harmonic textures more involved; and the most impressionistic song in the set was probably written under the aegis not of Wagner but of Borodin, namely 'Le jet d'eau'.

Water was ever to evoke an Impressionist response in Debussy, and whenever the fountain itself is described—

> La gerbe d'eau qui berce ses mille fleurs
> Que la lune traverse de ses pâleurs
> Tombe comme une averse de larges pleurs

—the music reacts in a totally impressionistic way (Ex. 2). Notice the

Ex. 2
Debussy, 'Le jet d'eau' (*Cinq Poèmes de Charles Baudelaire*)

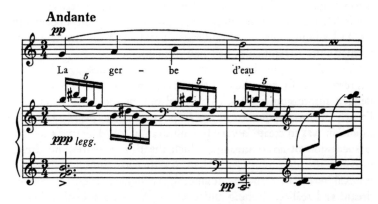

whole-tone scale (bar 1) the 'non-functional' ninth (bar 2) and the equally 'non-functional' major seconds which are a recurrent harmonic feature of this piece—'non-functional' in that there is no reason whatsoever, according to traditional harmonic precepts, why for example the dominant ninth should follow the whole-tone harmony at this point: it is used purely for its own sake, for sheer sensuousness of effect. Water is also the instigator of the only Impressionist passage in the otherwise rather derivative (though engagingly so) *Petite Suite* of 1889. This occurs in the first movement, 'En bateau', where at the end of the middle section there is a whole-tone passage using a little semiquaver pattern 'very like such things in the later music used to symbolize ripples, eddies and whirlpools in water' as Frank Dawes aptly comments. Dawes finds reminiscences of bird-song in each of the *Deux Arabesques* but the flowing triplets which begin at bar 6 of no 1 suggest to me a water-surface, radiant and shimmering in a gentle breeze.[2]

There are many intimations of an approaching stylistic upheaval in other compositions of this period—the distant horn in 'Le son du cor s'afflige' and, at the end of 'L'échelonnement des haies', the magical metamorphosis of the rather dance-like theme to suggest the chiming of distant bells. Both of these songs are to texts by Verlaine, and from the first set of *Fêtes Galantes* the beautiful 'En sourdine' and 'Clair de lune' both distil a quintessentially Impressionist atmosphere (of the second set, written in 1904, only the moving 'Colloque sentimental', reflecting impressionistically the 'vieux parc solitaire et glacé' and emotionally related to 'En sourdine', really qualifies for mention in this context). The texts of the *Proses Lyriques* are by Debussy himself and the music is too rambling and derivative to have any sustained evocative appeal; but in 'De soir' there is an interesting passage of pure gamelan pentatony (at 'Et les bons signaux des rantes . . .') and again the theme is transformed into a crepuscular bell-like ostinato.

These growing tendencies towards a new vagueness and fluidity of expression finally consolidated themselves in 1893 into the first fully-fledged Impressionist work of all, and one of the most beautiful of French creations—the *Prélude à l'Après-midi d'un Faune*. Debussy's intention was to create 'a very free illustration' of Mallarmé's eclogue, 'a succession of *décors* through which the Faun's desires and dreams move in the afternoon heat'. Here, for the first time, is explored in musical terms that strange intangible twilight borderland between dream and reality, sleeping and waking. As Edward Lockspeiser has said 'it reproduces the essentially fleeting qualities of memory, the myriad sensations of forgotten dreams', and here at last Debussy found within his grasp the technique for which he had been groping while working on his early unpublished *Diane au Bois*—a technique which would record the acuteness of the momentary sensation, 'sacrificing dramatic action to the long exploration of inner feelings.' Here for the first time in music there is no thematic development, no thread of logical discourse, but instead a freely sensuous flow of harmony and a new elusive poetry of instrumental timbre, a continuous process of transformation, fragmentation and regeneration of harmonic and melodic particles. In the opening flute solo, exotic in contour, we immediately breathe the air of another planet; rhythmically very fluid and tonally non-committal—unaccompanied withal—it has virtually the effect of a narcotic. It destroys the time-sense, induces a passivity more oriental than occidental, and in so doing impinges itself most prominently on our subconscious minds, inviting us to ask ourselves whether in fact we have heard it or not. The kaleidoscopic shifts of harmony and the harp glissandi do nothing to dispel the dreamlike aura, and how unprecedentedly important is the sixth bar, which is complete silence; in the three following bars the sounds even now produced re-echo hazily, quivering in the afternoon heat of a Virgilian sun. And in these nine bars Debussy cuts the umbilical cord of modern music. When the flute solo returns harmonized for the first time over *sul tasto* strings at fig. 1, it is unequivocally in D major, but upon its next appearance it is just as unequivocally in E major. And so the tissue of dreams is woven, fluctuating, tremulous and incorporeal— erotic fantasy, sensation and mythological evocation on the one hand, a fragrance of flaming Mediterranean sunlight on the other. The harmony is well-wrought and lustrous, the scoring luminous and transparent; at one bar after fig. 3 the whole-tone scale puts in its first appearance. The middle section is more conventionally lyrical and is probably the offspring of Balakirev's *Tamara*, but after a mercurial scherzo-like variation of the flute theme the latter returns at fig. 10 in a recapitulation in which the soporific effect of the shimmering heat can be almost physically sensed. Hazy reminiscences of earlier emotions lead to a final statement of the arabesque, way down on the muted horns, as it were buried deep in the orchestra's subconscious mind. This provokes one final drowsy response from the Arcadian flute, by this time so completely oblivious of any notion of time or space that half the melodic line is simply not brought into focus. One wonders whether Humbert Wolfe had Debussy's music or Mallarmé's verse in his mind when he wrote his beautiful *Belle au Bois Dormant*:

> The silver Faun
> as a leaf drifting sideways, glimmers and goes,
> calling his lovers, clear beyond the dawn,
> and from the dream they had to the dream he is making
> with two notes on a reed, and no one knows
> whether they dream, who follow, or are waking.

Something of this wonder is preserved in the *Chansons de Bilitis*, which again conjure up visions of an Arcadian mythology. Notice the contrast between modal arabesque and triadic juxtaposition in the opening bars of 'La flûte de Pan'; the voluptuously syncopated throb of 'La chevelure' with its subtly-poised added-note chords and wholly emancipated parallel sevenths and ninths under the final vocal phrase; and the Impressionist evocation of a winter landscape in 'Le tombeau des naïades' with its anticipation of 'Sirènes', significantly at the words 'il cassa la glace de la source où jadis nageaient les naïades'.

Hardly had the *Prélude à l'Après-midi d'un Faune* passed almost un-noticed at its first performance in 1894 than Debussy was already at work on what were eventually to emerge as his next Impressionist masterpieces—the orchestral triptych *Nocturnes* and the opera *Pelléas et Mélisande*. The *Nocturnes* were said to be associated in the composer's mind with Whistler's Impressionist *Nocturnes*, but Lockspeiser argues an even greater affinity with the French Impressionist painters themselves:

It is music which is able to convey the precise equivalent of the play of light in Impressionist painting—the soft, whitish-grey light of the Île de France, as in 'Nuages', and in Monet; the dappled, southern light with its fierce contrasts and blinding freshness, as in 'Fêtes', and in Renoir; and the whole universe of light, as in the seascape 'Sirènes', and in Turner.

The main idea of 'Nuages' cannot properly be described as a theme; it is a series of chords, alternating thirds and fifths on woodwind first of all, later a sequence of descending dominant ninths on strings (one bar before fig. 2). A recognizably melodic element is present only in the pungent cor anglais motif over swaying semi-diminished string chords —a passage which returns at two after four with whole-tone harmony and the string body shot through with cannily-located off-beat pizzicati—and in the pentatonic harp and flute motif at fig. 7. The music finally disintegrates into shuddering *sul tasto* tremolos and a minor third drum-roll, with limping dismembered fragments of the two melodic ideas heralding the final moment of extinction. The textures are of a uniform greyness throughout, and all temporal sense is abolished. 'Fêtes' is more squarely built (an ABA format) and is more melodically orientated than either of its companions, and its strongly pictorial suggestions (which have given rise to a deal of interpretative conjecture) are not as instinct with the true Impressionist spirit as the last movement, 'Sirènes'. This beautiful piece is not only among the earliest and best examples of impressionistic sea-music, it is also remarkable for its innovatory use of the wordless chorus (although, as we have seen, the original version of *Printemps* employed a small *bouche fermée* choir). The music reflects the placid rhythmic motion of the waves in pentatonic arabesque, shimmering tremolos and long flowing wordless melismata for the female voices; the key of F♯ major and the tenuous, silvery fabric of the orchestral textures all point to and enhance the changing moods of these moonlit 'Jeux de vagues', the indefinable subtleties of their murmurs and shadows.

Of all Debussy's large-scale works none explores so consistently the uncharted territory in that twilight zone between sleeping and waking as *Pelléas et Mélisande*. The libretto was extracted from the play by Maeterlinck, whose profound affinities with the Symbolists, especially with Poe and Mallarmé, have already been mentioned; it constituted a perfect vehicle for Debussy's concept of 'realism' or 'naturalism' in opera, which involved shaping the vocal lines to the inflexions of the speaking voice in a type of continuous recitative, and underscoring it by a continuous ebb and flow of orchestral sound which provided clear demarcation-lines only between acts, not between scenes or separate parts of scenes. Hence the two cardinal influences on the score are those of Wagner and Mussorgsky, yet, paradoxically, this 'realism' exists almost entirely on the threshold of consciousness. Nothing is really well-defined or brought sharply into focus; the characters, the settings, the action—all is soft-edged, perceptible but dimly and uneasily, the stuff that dreams are made on. Debussy's powers of creating such an atmosphere were unrivalled, and the natural elements which are so important a constituent of Maeterlinck's verses also lent themselves with the happiest results to his flair for evocation and suggestion. To his friend, the music-critic Jacques Rivière, Alain-Fournier, the author of *Le Grand Meaulnes*, commented on the contrast between the sombre-voiced grey 'naturalism' of Maeterlinck's world of dream and legend and the fresh tingling quality of his nature-Impressionism which Debussy had animated in his music:

Le poème empreint surtout de cette poésie flamande si spéciale et si prenante, mais monotone—et la musique la faisant craquer de toute la poésie de l'amour, de la fièvre, des parcs, de la fraîcheur, de la mer, qui y était implicitement contenue. La mer surtout . . .

The preludial music evokes the chilly dampness of a vast forest at the approach of night; there is a timeless quality about the pentatonic theme which rises in the cellos, and the whole-tone scale on woodwind, playing a characteristic Debussian nature-rhythm (cf. 'Sirènes')

over a soft timpani pedal sends a cold shiver through the orchestra. The reedy harshness of the oboe superimposed upon a variant of this rhythm five bars later suggests a misty landscape at evening in exactly the same way as the oboe solo in the second movement of Tchaikovsky's *Winter Daydreams* Symphony, and six bars before fig. 3 the horns sound the first of their wonderfully hushed fanfares which persist throughout this act (indeed right through the opera) like a question-mark. At fig. 3, just before Golaud's entry, the double basses begin their series of murmuring triplets which suggest an ever-deepening obscurity; they form the basis of the first orchestral interlude (from four bars after fig. 21 to fifteen before fig. 22)—which is an evocation of the forest by night.

In the third scene of the first act Geneviève and Mélisande are walking in the castle grounds overshadowed by the great forests with the distant sound of the sea within earshot. The murmuring triplets are still hinting at 'les endroits où l'on ne voit jamais le soleil' but when Geneviève mentions 'la clarté de la mer' there is a sudden and exhilarating burst of sound on '-té'; one looks at the orchestral score and finds with amazement that Debussy has simply given an F♯ major chord to strings, horns and woodwind, accenting the downbeat with a *sforzando* grace-note. It is in such minuscule but telling details that his strength as an Impressionist painter lies; the Impressionist sea-evocation which follows shortly is one of the most sinister in music. A mysterious ship approaches the shore; the voices of its sailors are heard but it cannot be seen because, as Geneviève explains, 'il y a encore une brume sur la mer'. Low strings play in groping tremolos, uneasy rhythmic figures on woodwind and muted horns loom out of the mist for a second and then disappear; the harmony is almost exclusively tritonal and whole-tonal, and the distant sailors' chorus is virtually wordless—the hissing sibilants of their repeated 'Hisse hoë!' if anything inject an added element of menace into the already mystery-laden, electrically-charged atmosphere ('nous aurons une tempête cette nuit', remarks Geneviève). There is a moment of unforgettable beauty at fig. 43, as the darkly-brooding tritonal harmony momentarily gives way to a dominant ninth; Mélisande's theme is heard on flute and oboe as a counterpoint to the distant sailors' chanting and for a brief moment the textures are lit up with a golden autumnal radiance. But the murkiness soon creeps back and barely-distinguishable fragments of the sailors' chorus suggest a sinister calm, the lull before the storm. Debussy closes the act upon an exquisitely suspended ninth at Pelléas's sudden 'Pourquoi partez-vous?', blurted out almost in spite of himself.

Act II opens by a well in the park, glistening with ice-cool, clear water, sheltered from the heat of the sun—a plethora of favourite Impressionist preoccupations which Debussy reflects in music of a crystalline transparent beauty—parallel ninth chords, the diaphanous writing for harp and woodwind and the whole-tone appoggiatura motif which seems to evoke the magical stillness and remoteness of the scene (it recurs later at Pelléas' words 'comme on est seul ici . . .

on n'entend rien'). We can hear the flowing water in the running figure on the strings which accompanies the entry of Pelléas and Mélisande, and later when Mélisande plays with Golaud's ring and loses it in the well, the textures are alive with tremolos and harp glissandi, little shafts of light flickering and darting hither and thither as if following the ring as it flashes in the sunlight and is reflected in the water. After her interview with Golaud Mélisande is sent to look for the missing ring on the seashore with Pelléas, and so the last scene of this act becomes another sea-picture—this time a nocturne. The interlude between Scenes 2 and 3 first of all muses regretfully on the idyllic sunlight-and-water music of Scene 1 but soon merges into the characteristic sounds of a troubled sea at night. Again the murmuring subterranean triplets of the first act are heard, interspersed with a descending passage for tremolo strings muted, in which we can hear the hoarse surging of the sea, sullen and hostile but never openly aggressive—the storm threatened in Act I never actually breaks, at least not over the sea. From fig. 39 onwards, as the couple go into the cave, the music is characterized by a rolling motion which perhaps depicts the sea lapping around the mouth. The entire passage from fig. 41 to four bars after fig. 42 deserves the closest scrutiny; has the sea at night ever been evoked so skilfully in musical Impressionist terms? Notice particularly the lapping motion on bassoons, violas and cellos, the murky tritonal bass on tuba and timpani, and, at three bars after fig. 41, the fanfare-figures on muted brass. At fig. 42 a shaft of moonlight lights up the blue shadowy void for a moment, reflected in horns and woodwind through a haze of up-and-down harp glissandi and shimmering tremolo strings; but soon all is pitch-black again and little glancing blows on the suspended cymbal (a favourite Impressionist device for suggesting the sound of water spray) and timpani fade out the scene. Debussy achieves an extraordinary sense of the obsessive all-pervasiveness of the sea, its vibrancy and potency almost as a living entity. The sea is the true protagonist of the end of this act as it was of the end of Act I, yet this feeling could have never been successfully conveyed but for the composer's evolution of an Impressionist musical terminology.

In Act III, Scene 2, Golaud takes Pelléas to explore the castle vaults (a scene strongly reminiscent of Poe's *Fall of the House of Usher* in its preoccupation with stagnant water and with 'l'odeur de mort qui monte'). To create an appropriately spine-chilling atmosphere Debussy relies, economically and unsensationally enough, upon a prominent whole-tone element in harmony and melody and, in the scoring, divided low strings and bassoons with occasional interjections from muted horns and trumpets. Very skilfully effected is the transition from this Impressionist evocation of a stifling death-bound, decay-ridden atmosphere to one of overwhelming exultation in the blinding midday light with the sea dancing in the sun and sending its fresh salty breeze over the land. This is one of the most celebrated passages in Impressionist music with the characteristically Debussian

rhythmic motif passing through an iridescent haze of orchestral colour which alternates between whole-tone and pentatonic sonority—a gradual accumulation and intensification of orchestral timbre in which the only melodic element is a figure attached to the rhythmic motif quoted above. It matches Pelléas's mood of exhilaration—'et maintenant, tout l'air de toute la mer . . . il y a un vent frais . . . frais comme une feuille qui vient de s'ouvrir sur les petites lames vertes . . .' At fig. 37 he catches the scent of newly-watered roses and greenery (a pentatonic tripping figure on strings and woodwind) and at fig. 38 horns, answered by glockenspiel, sound the midday bells; their parts are so skilfully aligned as to perpetuate the vibrations of each note in a warm hazy sonority (see bars 3–7 after fig. 39). We can also hear the waves laughing and glinting in the sunlight as 'les enfants descendent vers la plage pour se baigner . . .' This subtle blending of scent, light and sound impressions is a conspicuously beautiful example of Impressionist synaesthesia.

Two years after the first production of *Pelléas* Debussy with his *Estampes* for piano inaugurated the series of his unique contributions to the literature of that instrument. In the first piece, 'Pagodes', he turns to his own account the sonorities of the Balinese gamelan he had heard at the 1889 Exhibition, and the result is one of the loveliest of exotic stylizations. Almost entirely based on the Chinese pentatonic scale, the melodic line is extremely flexible and responds acutely to the many minute changes of harmonic and textural detail which are constantly being applied to it. On its final appearance the main theme is accompanied by showers of pentatonic arpeggios with deep sustained semi-breves in the bars to suggest the hum of oriental gongs, and when the melodic movement finally comes to a standstill there is nothing left for the arpeggios to do but to shimmer themselves into silence.

The second *Estampe*, 'La soirée dans Grenade', is another stylization, this time of the Spanish national idiom. Manuel de Falla expressed himself quite adamantly on the subject of the authenticity of Debussy's Hispanicism, and we may ascribe this phenomenon to two main causes—Debussy's intuitive grasp of the evocative power of Spanish music with its exotic, Moorish overtones, and the way in which the natural tendency of the guitar to harmonize melodies in aggregation of fourths and fifths coincided with his own innovatory harmonic concepts. 'La soirée dans Grenade' is not as potently evocative as the celebrated piece of Spanish night-music in *Ibéria*, 'Les parfums de la nuit'; rather is it impressionistic in the sense of assembling and juxtaposing multifarious impressions—for instance, the plaintive oriental melody which begins at bar 7 is interrupted without warning eleven bars later by a strumming of distant guitars, a passage which recurs in a number of contexts. A unifying factor is the constant throb of habanera rhythm and long pedal-points above and below, as if limning a distant horizon; but the thread of the argument is snapped altogether four bars before the end of p. 14 of the original Durand edition, at which point the habanera rhythm and the pedal points vanish, the music loses its languid air and suggests some form of distant revelry. For several bars the two musics alternate one with another; Debussy is here anticipating the cinematic technique of intercutting, where almost completely different sets of images are very rapidly alternated.

'Jardins sous la pluie' is an Impressionist water-piece. There is music symbolic of the patter of raindrops in the outer sections, and a more tranquil middle part where over a murmuring ostinato of major seconds the melody of the well-known French folk-tune 'Nous n'irons plus au bois' is pieced together, rather as if the rain with the sunlight already glinting through were being watched from indoors through window-panes streaming with water. The brilliant coda with its flashes of pentatonic arpeggio tells one that the sun has now finally broken through the clouds and is glistening and dancing on the flowers and greenery in the garden. In its exultant mood this music anticipates *L'Isle Joyeuse* upon which, with *La Mer*, work was begun the following year.

La Mer, described by Lockspeiser as the greatest Impressionist work in music, is probably allied in spirit more to the sea and water pictures of Turner than to the work of the Impressionist painters themselves

since, as we noted earlier, Debussy openly expressed his admiration for
Turner on several occasions, hailing him as 'the finest creator of mystery
in art'. Another influence was that of the Japanese artists, Hokusai and
Hiroshige, both noted for their quasi-Impressionist land- and sea-
scapes. Debussy often spoke of his love for the sea and the 'endless
memories' it aroused in him. Why should he not seek to perpetuate his
impressions using a musical technique akin to that of his favourite
artists?

The first movement evokes the breaking of dawn over the waters.
Over a long pedal-point Debussy savours the characteristically
Impressionist effect of superimposed pentatonic fourths and fifths; the
two cyclic motifs glimmer on the horizon as high tremolo strings
quiver in the nascent light. Momentum gathers in pure pentatonic
sonority which becomes even more pronounced at the entry of the
'modéré sans lenteur'—notice the undulating texture of the upper
strings and the gamelan-like black-note pentatony of the flutes
and clarinets. The interaction of two distinct thematic groups results in
a certain solidity and continuity which renders this movement in
formal terms less strictly 'impressionistic' than the *Nocturnes* or certain
of the *Préludes*; the titanic scale of *La Mer* certainly necessitates this kind
of sturdy though supple structural backbone. But the mosaic-like
orchestration in which instruments are used in so evocative a way as to
seem to merge into or well out of, the natural forces they are representing, results in a classic Impressionist mood-picture of the sea. As an
example of Debussy's *pointilliste* method of scoring, we may examine
the passage beginning three bars after fig. 10. Note the subtle counterpoint of the rhythmic and melodic particles—the heaving motion of
oboe, cor anglais and bassoons

short upward-spurting scalic figures for violins and cellos in unison
seized at their crest by second violins and violas, the bass pointed at
differing intervals by cymbal strokes, the dynamic level constantly
fluctuating between *mf* and *f* but always falling back to *f*—all this is
skilful transmutation into musical terms of the rhythmic colours and
movements of the sea. The coda to this movement is awe-inspiring in
the impression it leaves of mighty elemental forces held in reserve.
Through a fine-spun web of harp figurations the third cyclic theme

—a brass chorale, a Leviathan of the deep—stirs gradually and rises out of the haze to the fore, gradually taking possession of the whole orchestra.

'Jeux de vagues' is a scherzo in which the chromatic flute-patterns of *L'Après-midi d'un Faune* are lifted on to an even more ethereal plane and the textures are more *pointilliste* in their fragmentation (always excepting those of the central section in which sharp-cut string figures in thirds, leaping ever higher, are spurred on to an exhilarating climax via traditional procedures of symphonic development). The penetrating sonorities of solo muted trumpet, glockenspiel and suspended cymbal point a telling contrast with the whole-tone harp glissandi and the somnolently semi-articulate comments they provoke from dream-laden horns between figs. 20 and 21. The calm sea of the coda is wonderfully evoked by muted trumpet and flute as they answer the previous bar's questioning whole-tone oboe by the same phrase now fairly and squarely in a paradisal E major.

The last movement, 'Dialogue du vent et de la mer', starts as a turbulent storm-drama which builds powerfully and insistently upon the first two motto-themes and a new more generously lyrical theme, with prominent use of the impressionistic major second and augmented triad—especially in the apocalyptic clarion-calls which crown the climax and which capture the hoarse cry of the sea-surge. After a lull the brass chorale sounds softly (six bars before fig. 53) and the low string tremolos which lap broodingly around it suggest an object seen hazily through a depth of water. There follows a passage of fabulous textural limpidity in which the lyrical theme is sung by solo oboe and flute over trickling harp figuration and a high harmonic Aβ on first violins—the boundlessly stretching line of the horizon.

La Mer ends upon the same note of pantheistic ecstasy which characterizes Debussy's only Impressionist sea-piece for piano, *L'Isle Joyeuse*, hailed by Mellers as the most wonderful of all Debussy's creations. It combines the sweeping lyrical abandon of *La Mer* with an explosive, incandescent brilliance which, if anything, is even more powerfully suggestive of a Turner canvas. The opening arabesques, marked 'quasi una cadenza', are compound of chromatic and whole-tone elements and are oriental in verve; in fact the influence of *Sheherezade* or *Tamara* can be observed not only in the recurrent triplet motion (the main theme) but also in the dance-like impetus which carries the work along, particularly in the closing stages at *subito p*

(Durand score, top of p. 11). The main substance of the music is essentially conditioned by the original theme with, by way of contrast, an exultant sea-melody marked 'ondoyant et expressif' (the 3/8– 5/8 rhythmic conflict between the hands does remarkably suggest the melody being borne aloft on the crest of a wave and floating up and down) which bursts forth triumphantly at the main A major climax.

The next major Impressionist piano work to be completed was the *Images*—two sets consisting of three pieces each. The first piece in the first set is 'Reflets dans l'eau', the most subtle example of Debussian water-music. Debussy gently disturbs the surface of his pool only to ensure that its patterns of variation are maintained in ceaseless kaleidescopic motion. On the first beat of the first bar the surface is uniformly tranquil but on the third the composer drops three distinct notes one after the other into the water immediately causing the reflections to shiver, expand and sink back. As Frank Dawes has pointed out, at the top of p. 2 (Durand edition) 'reflections are seen in conjunction with the solid objects they reflect, musically depicted in a piece of chordal counterpoint in contrary motion . . . the picture is shattered when a stick or pebble drops into the water, and the reflections go into a tiny convulsion before settling again' (bars 3 and 4). This passage recurs on two subsequent occasions and each time the pattern is subtly varied; on the first occasion the reflections break up into rippling sextuplets, in the second they are reduced to the form of placid triplets. These appearances alternate with the development of a more regularly-shaped melody (bottom of p. 2) which rises through an iridescent wash of figuration and is generally associated with a whole-tone element, although in bar 9 of p. 6 it achieves a miraculous Lydian metamorphosis. The coda is marked 'dans une sonorité harmonieuse et lointaine', but by this time either the onlooker has become so drowsy and bemused by these *visions fugitives* he has been studying in the water that he no longer perceives their reflections, or else twilight has overwhelmed the scene and they are no longer visible. The concluding 'Mouvement' may also be described as impressionistic in that it is a study of the changing play of sound-patterns around a fixed nodal point, the nodal point being the toccata-like *moto perpetuo* ostinato which at the bottom of p. 25 works its way up through the whole-tone scale and disappears into the sky.

The second set of *Images* begins with that classic impressionistic synthesis of tolling bells and rustling leaves, 'Cloches à travers les feuilles'. The bells are first heard tolling in the far distance through the mists of the whole-tone scale, but gradually the atmosphere begins to clear and the ringers gain in confidence, and the culmination is a jubilant peal of sound (p. 5, bar 4). Notice the constant use of the pentatonic scale in the melodic fourths and harmonic seconds. The whole piece is fraught with ambiguity in that it is impossible to distinguish between the sounds of tolling bells and rustling leaves, so sensitively are they here fused. The second piece in this set, 'Et la lune descend sur le temple qui fut' belongs to the world of 'Pagodes'; its discreetly oriental flavour is well captured in Louis Laloy's allusive title. It is an Impressionist evocation of an attic moonlit night in slow swaying chords of pentatonic fourths and fifths (which may be viewed alternatively as common chords with the third replaced by a fourth), parallel triads casting giant shadows and later enveloping a gamelan-like pentatonic melody pointed by grace-notes glancing off the octave above, a folk-song-like fragment in the Dorian mode, and the reverberative hum of a gong (p. 11, bottom line, bar 1). Few pieces are so completely devoid of lyrical or dynamic movement and so evocative of nocturnal stillness. 'Poissons d'or' is a rhapsody of glinting sunlight and fins flashing through orange-tinted water; the music is constantly throwing up impressionistic snatches of tune but all is caught up in a whirl of colour and movement.

Of the orchestral *Images*, three are notably impressionistic—'Rondes de printemps' and, from *Ibéria*, 'Les parfums de la nuit' and 'Le matin d'un jour de fête'. The opening of 'Rondes de printemps' is the mature composer's answer to the opening of the immature *Printemps*—again the slow and arduous birth of creatures and things in nature, but in this case the early spring morning is not warm with the promise of summer but as yet chill in remembrance of winter. Tiny particles of woodwind theme fidget and jostle one another in a manner not unprophetic of *The Rite of Spring*, all above a high tremolo on violins, violas and cello harmonics which suggest the *frisson* of an early morning dew. The music makes a number of attempts to break out of its cocoon but even when the dance is under way in a 'léger et fantasque' 15/8, the textures remain curiously diffuse and fragmented, and at fig. 8 the music begins to relapse into the dream-like state of its opening. Three bars after fig. 9 the trance is once again complete, and there follows a passage of the purest Impressionism. Parallel chords of superimposed fourths and fifths drift downwards on wide-spaced strings; reminiscences of the 'ronde', fractured by grace-notes, wander in and dimly attempt to pierce the veil; and at fig. 11, 'doux et flottant', an intricately worked string-fabric with harmonics, tremolos and an obsessively repeated chromatic figure from the 'ronde', celesta and harp figuration and a soft cymbal roll together form an impressionistic haze through which quasi-improvisatory woodwind skirls and arabesques sound faintly and are underpinned by a syncopated pedal point on timpani and cellos. The impression is of an early morning in spring by the riverside with a faint mist slowly rising, the sunlight just beginning to shimmer over the water and the whole landscape slowly, painfully burgeoning into life. At three bars before fig. 13 Debussy exploits the impressionistic effect of complexes of fourths and fifths in quasi-slow motion, and at six bars after fig. 13 the spring-dance finally begins in earnest.

'Les parfums de la nuit', the second of the *Ibéria* triptych, is the most languorously evocative of Debussy's Spanish pieces. The opening, marked 'lent et rêveur', picks up the various sounds oscillating in the nocturnal atmosphere with almost seismographic precision—a plaintive whole-tone oboe melody piercing a veil of high string pedals, the rhythm of a very distant habanera, borne on the air by bassoons and tambourine. Acutely sensitive to minute variations in the atmosphere the music remains long in a semi-somnolent state with vague intimations and dimly-focused fragments of theme weaving themselves in and out of the texture until at two bars before fig. 45 a new motif in thirds suddenly throbs with life and passion and eventually leads to a climax of great expressive intensity. In terms of Impressionist sound the two bars after fig. 52 have no parallels. In the first bar, over a soft timpani pedal, horns and tubular bells chime to the whole-tone scale in the far distance, the bells (syncopated in rhythm and higher in the scale) almost answering the horns and, enhanced by xylophone (an unusual sound in such a context), create a haze of whole-tone sonority utterly original in quality. In the second bar all is repeated note for note with a distant muted-trumpet fanfare, in dance-rhythm but still in the whole-tone scale, superimposed upon it. The bells and the trumpet motif are in fact the protagonists not of this movement but of the next in this context they are the distant heralds of 'Le matin d'un jour de fête' which eventually floods the scene with revelry and sunlight. This transition, so beautifully managed (the rustle of unseen guitarists marching in the distance is interrupted once by a reminiscence of the bars described above, then the bells and trumpet come ever clearer into focus until the air quivers with their jubilant pealing), is also the transition from one style of Impressionism to another, for 'Le matin' is not a sustained *Stimmung* but a chaotic jumble of light and sound impressions in which desultory fragments of dance tune and song jostle one another in a kind of tonal *mardi gras* with the rhythmically variable whole-tone tolling of the horns and bells ever in the background. Only a detailed analysis would do full justice to the structure of this fascinating little piece, but we may note here that there is no attempt at any sort of motivic organization; the innumerable scraps of theme tumble over and mix promiscuously with one another in sublimely colourful disarray (see for example how the passage for massed 'guitars' has first the whole-tone bells as counterpoint and then, on its second appearance at fig. 64, a ringing trumpet fanfare developed from a segment of a motif which had earlier appeared as a quite inconsequential inner voice and gradually pushed itself more and more to the fore). At one point (one bar after fig. 59) a random reminiscence of 'Les parfums' pokes its head through on the trumpets but hastily withdraws it again, and the passage which follows is an extreme example of the quasi-improvisatory technique which, while tracing its origins to this genre of Impressionism, looks forward to the aleatory procedures of present-day music. At one bar after fig. 60 a troupe of strolling fiddlers seem to be elbowing their way through the crowd; temporarily impeded in their course (two after fig. 60) they finally gain the floor and (fig. 61) push their leader forward who (one bar after fig. 61) is immediately set upon by a band of wind and percussion. By seven bars after fig. 61 a solo oboe has picked up the fiddlers' tune and the troupe is moving on its way, still tuning up noisily. In such a way does Debussy, appropriating the technique of the *pointilliste* painters, seize upon a relatively insignificant but colourful detail and use it as the highlight of a scene.

In the two sets of *Préludes* for piano we find distilled the essence of Impressionism. In these pieces Debussy's ability to crystallize the visual elements and in certain cases the emotional connotations of a scene in terms of musical sensation, in a series of short but telling brush-strokes, is demonstrated to the full; no aspect of the Impressionist aesthetic or technique remains here uncalled into play. No 1 of the first set, 'Danseuses de Delphes' evokes a procession of Greek dancers, their stately hieratic movements mirrored in an interplay of major–minor common chords and augmented triads, laced together by melody basically pentatonic, occasionally inflected chromatically. No 2 'Voiles', is the essence of Impressionism. The very title is ambiguous—

it can mean either veils or sails, but even if we assume the piece to be a seascape in miniature its mystery and remoteness are thereby in no wise diminished. Except for a pentatonic passage at 'en animant' the music is fashioned almost entirely out of the whole-tone scale. The persistent B♮ pedal-point certainly suggests the swell of a calm sea, the opening flourish in thirds the flung spray of 'Jeux de vagues', and the motivic fragment at bar 7 recalls, as Frank Dawes has pointed out, the melody at fig. 4 of *La Mer*. If we are looking at the sea we are doing so through a mysterious veil which is not present in *La Mer* but which lends an added measure of insubstantiality and intangibility to its features; they seem indeed barely perceptible to the naked eye. Such is the effect of this chiaroscuro-like patterning of whole-tone shapes and textures.

No 3, 'Le vent dans la plaine', is a light-fingered toccata, aerial and incorporeal: there is a continuous whirring ostinato composed of minor seconds spread over an octave; a pentatonic motif blows up freshly in the tenor, sinks for a time into a misty area darkly speckled by the whole-tone scale and then returns, eventually leaving a series of semitonally-rising triads seeking to extricate themselves from the midst of the ostinato. The music responds with an Aeolian harp-like sensitivity to the varied inflexions of the wind in the atmosphere. 'Les sons et les parfums tournent dans l'air du soir' is harmonically one of Dubussy's most self-indulgent compositions; the melodic line moves voluptuously and languidly as if weighed down by the sheer opulence of scent and sound with which it has been charged. The ending features the particular Impressionist preoccupation with distance, in this case 'une lointaine sonnerie de cors' exquisitely tinctured by the Lydian mode. No 5, 'Les Collines d'Anacapri', is the first of the *Préludes* to juxtapose disconnected fragments. The opening bars, built of interlocking fourths and fifths, suggest the hum of bells in the atmosphere ('quittez et laissez vibrer', directs Debussy). Although never heard as an isolated sonority again they form a constant counter-point to the Neapolitan gaiety to a stylization of which the remainder of the piece devotes itself—they serve as a transition to the second ele-ment of popular song (a tango), return at the bottom of p. 19 to bathe it in a dream-like haze of blue, and two pages later they become the basis of the main coda, seemingly present in ever-increasing numbers to greet a new sunrise.

'Des pas sur la neige', described by Dawes as 'a study in mono-chrome' is perhaps the equivalent in sound of Monet's 1880 *Landscape with Snow, at Dusk*. It is dominated by a characteristically Debussian rhythmic *tic*, the 'Scotch snap'

which, as the composer informs the player, 'doit avoir la valeur sonore d'un fond de paysage triste et glacé'. This little rhythmic figure (a second, major or minor) is superimposed on a chromatic, kaleidoscopically dissolving harmonic texture, and the slow monotonous throb is interrupted only when a melodic fragment marked 'comme un tendre et triste regret' wanders in over parallel triads, to peter out almost immediately. 'Ce qu'a vu le vent de l'ouest' is by contrast a sea- or rather a storm-piece, a pianistic counterpart of the 'Dialogue du vent et de la mer', although in fact the piano writing is so violent and turbid as to warrant an orchestral setting itself. Debussian features abound—parallel chords, screeching parallel seconds, pentatonic melody, the whole-tone scale—and the composer may well have had Turner's *Snow Storm* in mind, the picture painted as a result of the artist's having had himself lashed to a ship's mast at the height of a tempest, the better to observe it.

No 8, 'La Fille aux cheveux de lin', is scarcely impressionistic at all; in the fresh lyrical flow of its pentatony and the absence of any 'atmospheric' effects this piece belongs really to the world of the *Petite Suite* and the *Deux Arabesques*. No 9, 'La sérénade interrompue', is impressionistic in the manner of 'Le matin d'un jour de fête', with which piece it has a distinct affinity not limited to one of mood or technique. The guitarists' serenade is interrupted once by some unspecified commotion at 'très vif' (p. 34), twice by what sounds like the approach of a distant procession—an almost literal quotation from the massed guitars' music in 'Le matin d'un jour de fête' (cf. fig. 56, p. 88 of the score). 'La cathédrale engloutie' is one of the monuments of Impressionist piano writing. The opening with its superimposed fourths and fifths in rising sequence suggests a calm sea (just like Koechlin's seascape 'Sur la falaise', no 1 of *Paysages et Marines*) with the overtones of distant bells faintly audible; it is marked, most evocatively, 'dans une brume doucement sonore', an apt enough description of the sound of these opening bars. As the sea begins to roll and heave ('peu à peu sortant de la brume') the sound of the bells gradually increases in intensity until the whole atmosphere is thrilling with their vibrations and overtones. At the climactic moment an enormous span of plainsong bursts in upon the scene and only very gradually dies away into the mist, whereupon the bells resume their tolling. In the coda the plainsong is heard as if floating on the sea, on the rim of the horizon, but even this is finally merged into a quivering haze of bell-vibrations sounding from the far distance. We may regard this magnificent prelude as a semi-counterpart of Monet's famous studies of Rouen Cathedral, although there is no element of water in the latter. In fact the legend of the cathedral of Ys might almost have been tailor-made to Debussian Impressionist requirements—water, mists, the innumerable reverberations of bells and an opportunity for introducing, *in statu quo*, the Gregorian chant which already formed a completely integral part of Debussy's musical language.

In 'La danse de Puck' all is fairyland; the texture is of thistledown and gossamer and the music dances nimbly along in dotted rhythm, the only noticeably recurrent feature of the choreography an occasional elfin horncall. P. 47, bars 8–11 anticipate one of the finest of all the *préludes*—'Les fées sont d'exquises danseuses', from the second set. 'Minstrels', the last of the first set, presents impressionistically—as a series of laconic impressions—the various phases of a music-hall act.

Book 2 begins with 'Brouillards', the musical equivalent of a Monet picture of the Thames in which mists and fogs are the protagonists. Debussy's evocation consists of accordion-like common chords offset by flickering bitonal figuration, with every now and then a phrase in octaves suggesting some unidentified object looming murkily into view for a second, then disappearing into the obscurity.[3] 'Feuilles mortes' is a musing on the approaching season of death and decay; the degree of dissonance is more marked than usual and there are intimations of the first of Ravel's *Trois Poèmes de Stéphane Mallarmé* in which a similar landscape is evoked. At one point a spectral fanfare (p. 9, bar 4) echoes and re-echoes for the remainder of the piece until it is finally heard in the bass, *pp lointaine*, harmonized by common chords —the one vestige of life in an otherwise featureless landscape. 'La puerto del vino' is a brief but pungent character-study—'avec de brusques oppositions d'extrême violence et de passionnée douceur'— and it is a wry, rather sardonic Impressionist comment on the Spanish scene; the 'brusques oppositions' are not only of emotions but also of tonality.

'Les fées sont d'exquises danseuses' is perhaps a progenitor of Holst's 'Mercury'; restlessly fragmented, evanescent, will-o'-the-wisp-like

patterns (broken chords, trills, tremolos) alternate with violent outbursts of romantic passion until all is held entranced in a wonderland of
quiet Scriabinesque ecstasy. It is long before the trilling spell is broken.
'Bruyères', like 'La fille aux cheveux de lin', is a piece of breathtaking
diatonic simplicity but its right-hand part is studded with impressionistic arabesques which suggest to Dawes 'the sparkling of dewdrops
caught in the early morning sunshine'. 'La terrasse des audiences au
clair de la lune' is a nocturne in the manner of 'Les parfums de la nuit', a
motif from which is alluded to in the opening bars. Sinuous arabesques
trickle down the keyboard at the beginning and the tiny tinkling
temple-bells of 'Pagodes' are heard at the end; elsewhere the music,
near-static and muskily harmonized, breathes that spirit of subtly refined
sensuality which is a Debussian hallmark in such contexts. 'Ondine' is
a piece of water-music, less elaborately conceived than Ravel's (discussed on p. 117). Again the opening is remarkably close to late Scriabin
and the form and texture of the piece is wholly conditioned by the
rhythm and movement of the running water, its varied plashings and
eddyings, although certain other features (the chromatically inflected
motif in bar 3 of p. 45, the intense melody in thirds over a *murmurando*
triplet accompaniment on p. 46) vaguely suggest an exotic setting. In
'Canope' the sober sustained calm of 'Danseuses de Delphes' is again
invoked, but the organum-like parallel triads soon give way to some
chastely ornamented melodic writing over sustained diatonic harmony.

The final prelude, 'Feux d'artifice', is a piece of considerable pianistic
virtuosity here harnessed in the service of Impressionist evocation. The
opening with its semitonal ostinato suggests the agitation of a great
crowd in the distance, with jabbing semiquavers in the right hand as
spurts of light in the sky. The onlooker draws closer and soon he is in
the thick of the celebrations, where all is a blaze of light and a whirl of
activity. Typically, little is distinctly specified; coruscating pentatonic
and whole-tone elements abound in the Lisztian bravura of the piano-
writing, and after a hectic climax marked by a double glissando down
the black and white notes, all is suddenly engulfed by night except for a
few stray melodic fragments (*La Marseillaise* and the firework motif)
which linger on for several seconds undecidedly and insecurely. And so
the last of Debussy's Impressionist piano preludes ends, literally, 'not
with a bang but a whimper'.

With the ballet *Jeux* and the *Six Épigraphes Antiques* of 1913 we
come to the end of Debussy's Impressionist work, since after the
Épigraphes he abandoned Impressionist haze for the more austere field

of vision represented by the *Douze Études, En Blanc et Noir* and the three sonatas.

Jeux, written to a scenario of singular fatuity which involved, with numerous *sub rosa* erotic implications, the antics of three young tennis-players in a park at sunset, nevertheless emerges as one of the most evocative of Debussy's orchestral scores, for, as Constant Lambert pointed out, 'the dim tennis-players who flit inconsequently through the garden are no more genuine *sportifs* than the croquet players in a fan by Conder, and it is clear that Debussy's real interest is in the atmospheric background where 'les sons et les parfums tournent dans l'air du soir'. This is particularly noticeable in the eight preludial bars in which a descending chordal sequence is sounded 'doux et rêveur' on woodwind under a sustained high B on the strings; each chord contains all the notes of the whole-tone scale and the passage seems to capture all the quintessential *ambiance* of a sultry Parisian summer night. When this music recurs at fig. 5 the slow-moving chromatic counterpoint on strings adds an element of quasi-oriental languor, but it functions most evocatively of all upon its final appear-ance at fig. 81. Here the whole-tone chords are surrounded in an impenetrable haze of soft brass, a timpani tremolo on a major second, and minuscule *murmurando* string figuration, so finely-drawn that only a faint nocturnal whirring or *gazouillement* seems to be perceptible. Here we approach the spirit and technique of Bartókian 'night-music'. For the rest, the scoring and textures are phosphorescent and aerial as never before, and there is little trace of conventional dialectic continuity of musical thought; rather, the music consists in the juxtaposition of innumerable tiny cellular fragments. As David Drew has said, Debussy allows the structure to evolve from a succession of brief sections whose contrasts of tempo and texture provide the variety which animates the motival unity—and in doing so betrays a certain affinity (which we have already noticed in several of the *Préludes*) with one of the most prominent of Russian Impressionists, Scriabin.

The *Six Épigraphes Antiques*—the final distillation of Debussy's Impressionist technique—were developed from matter written some fourteen years previously to accompany a recitation of Pierre Louÿs' *Chansons de Bilitis* and they are suffused in the same mythological afterglow as *L'Après-midi d'un Faune, Syrinx* (a *tour de force* for un-accompanied pan-pipes) and 'Canope'. The first piece, 'Pour un tom-beau sans nom', based almost entirely on the whole-tone scale, has a static, hypnotic quality which is wholly Impressionistic. At only one point does the top line blossom into song in a sobbing chromatically descending lament in oriental style over bitonal chords frozen into immobility by the chill of their nameless grief. 'Pour que la nuit soit propice' is a kittenish nocturne which fuses whole-tone, pentatonic and chromatic elements and disappears in a skirl of arabesque. 'Pour l'Égyptienne' is another Impressionist study in the coldly exotic, whereas the last piece, 'Pour remercier la pluie au matin' with its fluid chromatic rain-ostinato and lack of any pronounced melodic elements constitutes in effect a more impressionistic 'Jardins sous la pluie'.

1. Contemporary interest in early Chinese and Japanese art was largely a result of its perfect naturalness.

2. In the film *Images pour Debussy*, shot in France in 1952, director Jean Mitry took the *Deux Arabesques* and 'Reflets dans l'eau' to make a three-movement interpretation of the composer's work, using images of reflections in the water. The first two sections use landscape and trees with a gentle movement effected by a boat pushing its way through waving reeds. The last piece is set to dazzling images of the sun caught in reflection by rippling surfaces.

3. The piece as a whole was undoubtedly influenced by *Petrushka*, the work in which bitonality burst upon the European musical scene with a vengeance. Not only is the chord sequence reminiscent of Petrushka's accordion, but the upward-shooting arpeggios (e.g. last bar on p. 4) with their dissonant minor ninths are obviously derived from the piano writing in the Blackamoor's scene.

PART ONE

The Harbingers of Impressionism

I

CHOPIN AND LISZT

While there have been individual Impressionist traits in the music of all ages—Gesualdo's madrigals, Elizabethan keyboard-music, Bach's cantatas, Beethoven's *Pastoral Symphony*—it is convenient to locate the earliest crystallization of systematic leanings towards Impressionism in the music of Chopin, not merely because he was a great harmonic innovator (and, as we have noted, the history of Impressionism is to a large extent that of the development of harmony) but also because certain of his ways of thinking and feeling musically influenced the ultimate formulation of the Impressionist aesthetic and conditioned its sensibility.

We noted in Debussy's case that for melodic emancipation he resorted to folk-music of various descriptions. This process began with Chopin in the *Rondo à la Mazur*, op 5, where the Lydian sharp fourth of Polish folk-music puts in an appearance, as it does also in the *Krakowiak*, op 14 (for piano and orchestra). Another Impressionist trait which may be connected with folk-music—the bare fifth—is also to be found here. But no less forward looking is a passage in the same work consisting of four ascending diminished-seventh chords, one resolving into another on a different degree of the scale—in other words the parallel-chord technique which Debussy was to employ extensively with higher-numbered discords. As far as the diminished seventh is concerned there is a precedent for this procedure in the work of Chopin's contemporaries and predecessors, but Chopin treated it with more imaginative resource than anyone else. There is a particularly felicitous example in the 'Là ci darem la mano' variations (p. 843 of the Augener edition, last line), which Gerald Abraham has likened to 'a prism breaking up white light into glittering rainbow particles'. In such passages, momentary though their effect may be in the overall context, the key sense is completely annulled; and as Chopin experimented with the side-slipping of diminished chords in this way (we may assume that in Chopin's case, as in Debussy's and Delius's, harmonic innovations originated in improvisation at the keyboard) the thought doubtless occurred to him that the procedure could quite easily be applied to other chords—so-called 'dissonances' whose natural freedom of movement had been crippled and held in check by all the complex legislation concerning preparation and resolution. Chopin began to agitate in his work for a reform of these laws. From the side-slipping of diminished sevenths he progressed to a similarly cavalier treatment of dominant sevenths in the F minor Ballade (bars 46–53), in the A minor Mazurka, op 17, no 4, bar 9 *et seq.*, and, very strikingly, in the C♯ minor Mazurka, op 30, no 4. Eliminate the square-cut sequential repetition in the melody, the metric stability, and what is left is Impressionist harmony *à la* Debussy. In the Fantaisie, op 49, bar 22 *et seq.*, we can even see a movement toward the use of parallel ninths, although here again conventions of melodic and rhythmic construction serve to camouflage it quite effectively; the characteristic sound of the progression is a little clearer in the D♭ major Ballade, op 47, bars 33–4, but it was never Chopin's intention to call to account the supremacy of melody or seriously to impair symmetry of rhythm.

Chopin's other important contribution to the development of Impressionist harmony lay in his frequent employment of added-note chords. He early acquired the habit of encrusting an underlay of basically simple diatonic chords with all manner of rich florid ornamentation in the form of appoggiaturas, suspensions, anticipations and passing-notes. From this it was but a short step to the use of these heavily embellished chords in their own right. One of the most popular chords in the world, the added sixth, hails from Impressionist harmony, and this is adumbrated on numerous occasions in Chopin's work—in the Fantaisie, op 49, bars 4, 5 and 6 before the end; in the closing bars of the 15th Nocturne; in the opening bars of the 23rd Prelude. An added ninth is included in the final cadence of the A minor Étude, op 25, no 4, and—a celebrated instance—at the end of the 23rd Prelude the seventh partial is left, astonishingly, quite unresolved. It was precisely this kind of ambiguity the Impressionists loved to cultivate, and Chopin showed remarkable prescience in his exploitation of this aural phenomenon. For sheer opulence of chordal sound, however, he never surpassed the ascending sequence of added-note chords in the Barcarolle, op 60, bars 32 and 92.

Chopin was the earliest composer for the piano for whose work Debussy expressed unqualified admiration, and we may be sure that the reason for this was the nature of Chopin's approach to the question of piano sonority and his exploitation of the evocative, atmospheric potential of the pedals. This was one of the earliest manifestations of a concern with timbre which is characteristic of the Impressionists. We may perhaps see the earliest glimmering of this in Field's Nocturnes—the very designation presages a favourite Impressionist preoccupation (Whistler borrowed it from Chopin)—particularly in the seventh, with its suggestion of chimes and dependence on the silvery tone and the special pedal effects obtainable from the early nineteenth-century pianos. Chopin raised the nocturne to a higher level of expressive eloquence through mining still more extensively that vein of pure reverie, pure poetic feeling, already disclosed in Field's Nocturnes. It was above all this poetic sublimation of feeling, a process facilitated by the ease with which experiments can be carried out at the piano, and that instrument's malleability and adaptability (the orchestra is obviously far more unwieldy, and it is deprived of pedals) through which the evolution of a fully-fledged Impressionist idiom finally came about.

Chopin was the greatest pre-Impressionist of his day, the man in whose music harmony and timbre first began to play an important role for their own sakes. The composer most direct in line of descent from Chopin, in this respect at least, was Liszt, who, like Chopin, was first and foremost a pianist and attained mastery of the orchestra only after a long and gruelling apprentice period. As a writer for the piano he continued in the wake of Chopin to open up ever fresh colouristic resources, and since a very large proportion of his orchestral music is pianistically conceived we may assume that his harmonic experiments (especially those of his astonishing last years, by which time, as we shall see, he had left Chopin far behind him) came about as a result of experimentation at the keyboard—as did Debussy's.

The earliest work which suggests a kind of half-way house between Chopin and the Impressionists is no 5 of the *Transcendental Studies*, entitled 'Feux follets' which, Busoni claimed, influenced Wagner in the *Waldweben* and *Feuerzauber* music—both notable examples of pre-Debussian Impressionism. The title itself implies an Impressionist conception, a play of fast-moving particles of light. Much of the interest lies not in melody but in the finely-judged ornamental figuration constantly fluctuating between whole-tones and semitones; the texture is mercurial and kaleidoscopic, the closing bars in which the tiny drops of augmented-triad figuration dissolve in a shimmering whirlpool of light anticipating Ravel's *Gaspard de la Nuit* (compare the ending of 'Ondine'). In 'Feux follets' we can already see glimmering in the distance one of Liszt's greatest pianistic achievements and the one which set the pattern of all Impressionist water-pieces for many years to come, namely *Les Jeux d'Eau à la Villa d'Este*. Not only is this plainly the progenitor of Ravel's *Jeux d'Eau* but it also contains pre-echoes of Debussy's *L'Isle Joyeuse* and *La Mer*. The opening is immediately striking. The main melodic theme does not enter until bar 39. Until then the music is pure Impressionist sonority—arpeggiated chords in ascending and descending sequence, principally secondary sevenths and dominant ninths. Later a phrase of the main theme is accompanied by rising-and-falling secondary sevenths in a manner which obviously attracted Ravel's attention and throughout the piece the textures are coruscating and foaming with trills, tremolos and rippling arpeggio figures. It was left to Ravel to carry further Liszt's experiments here with sonorities in the higher reaches of the keyboard, notably the use of the pedal to create a deliberate haziness of intermingling upper partials (see pp. 113–14).

In fact those pieces of Liszt's in which Impressionist traits are most in evidence are frequently nature evocations of one sort or another, and this allies him more closely than Chopin to the Impressionists. Running water is also suggested in *Au Lac de Wallenstadt* with its basically pentatonic accompaniment ostinato (compare also the closing bars in which the semiquaver movement is passed to the right hand and the pedal sustains the figuration, forming a haze of pentatonic sonority); in *Au Bord d'une Source* with its harmonic emphasis on the seconds, major and minor, and its variety of trickling figures occasionally bringing to mind the *Waldweben*; and in the 1843 setting of Heine's *Im Rhein, im Schönen Strome*—at least in the 'più difficile' version of the piano part, for the alternative simply arpeggiates the basic harmony in conventional sextuplet figuration. In the former a basically pentatonic pattern is maintained throughout. It is instructive to compare this song with a fully fledged Impressionist water-piece such as the central 'river' section of Delius's *In a Summer Garden*. We can see too an early precedent for 'De l'aube à midi sur la mer' in the opening of the first symphonic poem, *Ce qu'on entend sur la montagne* (which, as Rimsky-Korsakov himself admitted, actually did serve as the model for the finest piece of pre-Impressionist sea-music ever written, namely the prelude to *Sadko*). *Ce qu'on entend sur la montagne* (also known as *Berg-symphonie*) is based on a poem from Victor Hugo's *Feuilles d'Automne* in which the poet imagines himself on the mountain-top with the ocean stretching out to infinity beneath him, listening to the confused murmurings of man and nature rising up to him and gradually assuming a coherent shape. In pre-Debussian terms this opening is wholly impressionistic—a soft big drum-roll, a lower string semitonal figure in quivering sextuplets which scales ever greater heights through tremolo strings, harp figuration and horn-calls.

Ex. 3
Liszt, *La Lugubre Gondola I*

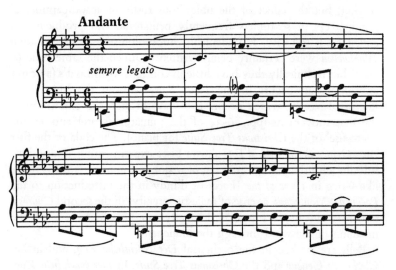

Two of the strangest water-pieces of all are the two from the last period entitled 'La Lugubre Gondola'. At the start of no 1 tonality is deliberately ill-defined as a result of the augmented triad adumbrated in the left-hand ostinato and by the whole-tone suggestion in the melodic line (Ex. 3). The dream-like haze is even more pronounced in the final section, where dismembered fragments of the theme return over a muffled tremolo of consecutive augmented triads. The vagueness and imprecision of objects mirrored in a moving water surface is reflected here and also in its companion piece (no 2). This opens with a passage of quasi-recitative which seems to consist of disconnected melodic thoughts and half-thoughts claiming no particular tonal stability. Then as the gondola begins to plough through the water a variant of Ex. 3 in 4/4 retains its augmented-triad and whole-tone flavour. At 'un poco meno lento' Liszt exploits the impressionistic effect not of unrelated common chords but of alternating major and minor triads merging into one another over an ebb and flow of left-hand arpeggio—and, later, of a dirge-like procession of first inversions in the bass (in the Wagner threnody, *Richard Wagner, Venice*, a succession of augmented triads is used in this way to lugubrious effect).

The movement of trees is the subject of Liszt's own *Forest Murmurs* (the German title is *Waldesrauschen* not *Waldweben*) and of the two pieces entitled *Aux Cyprès de la Villa d'Este*. In *Waldesrauschen* the melodic line is unashamedly of bel canto origin, clear, spacious and singing, but the effect of the ubiquitous rustle of accompanimental semiquavers in sextuplets frequently pentatonic and producing an added sixth sonority, is undeniably impressionistic. Wagner's own *Waldweben* were certainly being written at much the same time (*c.* 1863) but technically they have little in common with Liszt's (a nearer approximation occurs in the *Faust Symphony*—in the 'misterioso' nocturnal passage which occurs half-way through the exposition of the first movement (pp. 26–34 of the miniature score) and in the 'Berceuse' of the *Christmas Tree Suite* for piano). The coda of the first *Aux Cyprès de la Ville d'Este* shows Liszt experimenting impressionistically with the juxtapositioning of major and minor triads to create, like Grieg in *Peace of the Woods* or d'Indy in the introduction to the *Poème des Montagnes*, a sense of majestic serenity; in the second *Cyprès* a two-part chromatic figure is discreetly interpolated to suggest the moaning of the wind through the branches.

Bells are evoked in the orchestral *Der Nächtliche Zug*, and in *Les Cloches de Genève* and the *Christmas Tree Suite*. In *Der Nächtliche Zug*, one of Liszt's most effective orchestral compositions and inexplicably neglected by modern orchestras, the procession is heard approaching in a pizzicato passage the design of which (each beat divided into two, upper strings answering the lower) surely influenced Borodin in *In the Steppes of Central Asia*. A bell begins to sound a tenor C♯ and its reverberations are picked up by off-beat chords on harp and woodwind; later trumpets and trombones join in the chiming. *Les Cloches de Genève* is an undistinguished salon piece until the coda with its 'non-functional' use of dominant sevenths, ninths and added sixths, all separated by rests to allow the reverberations to die away. 'Carillon' from the *Christmas Tree Suite* ends with a very impressionistic cadence on a pentatonic 'discord' (Ex. 4), but most remarkable of all is 'Cloches

Ex. 4
Liszt, 'Carillon' (*Christmas Tree Suite*)

du Soir', the last piece in the same set. Here the main theme is introduced by three phrases each built round a dominant ninth on a different degree of the scale, and then the bells begin to chime in a typically Impressionist pentatonic sonority (Ex. 5), culminating in a descending

Ex. 5
Liszt, 'Evening Bells' (*Christmas Tree Suite*)

passage of alternating sevenths and ninths. Sensitively evoked in the coda is the impression of bells tingling in the distance; deep-breathed reverberations in the bass are offset by the treble tolling a clear ninth above and a muffled peal sounding hazily in the void between. Liszt makes no attempt to end on a conventional cadence: he simply allows the reverberations to hum themselves into nothingness and the point at which they pass the threshold of audibility happens to occur upon a first inversion relative minor triad. Here we have all the later Impressionist bell-pieces in embryonic form—the remoteness, the indefiniteness, the *impression floue*, the keen appreciation of the way that sounds reverberate in the atmosphere.

A passage from Mussorgsky's song-cycle *Sunless* has frequently been cited as the progenitor of Debussy's 'Nuages', but an even more probable source is Liszt's own cloud-piece entitled *Nuages Gris*—another product of the composer's last period. Here a rising and falling seven-note figure is not developed but repeated, etched against a barely perceptible bass tremolo; its progress is interrupted by a series of descending augmented triads, still over the amorphous shudder of the tremolo. The final bars leave behind their discords suspended, as it were, in mid-air. Although technically this piece has little in common with 'Nuages' there is no mistaking the similarity in mood between them; they are both Whistlerian 'studies in grey', and the improvisatory spirit of Liszt's conception and the unresolved discord on which it ends both point the way to the future. In the same way the cadence of the nocturne *En Rêve* anticipates the rapt atmosphere of many an Impressionist nocturnal evocation, and *Abschied* with its modal inflections and the almost non-functional diatonic harmony of its last bars foreshadows Debussy's improvisatory naturalism.

Equally radical departures in the direction of Impressionism can be observed in these works which, like *Nuages Gris* and *En Rêve*, belong to the last period of Liszt's creativity but unlike them are of an abstract nature or at any rate are not overtly Impressionist in conception. Many of these compositions have been discovered and disseminated only comparatively recently, since there was what has been termed a 'conspiracy of silence' surrounding them; so irresponsibly iconoclastic did they appear when they were written that they were dismissed as the worthless doodlings of an amiable old maniac and were withheld deliberately in order to safeguard the few remaining shreds and tatters of their composer's reputation. Now, however, we can see that in this music Liszt was looking so far into the future that few of his contemporaries could reasonably have been expected to keep pace with him. The seeds not only of Impressionism but also of atonality are here sown.

It seems probable that the whole-tone scale as it emerges on occasions in these works came about as a result of Liszt's lifelong fondness for the augmented triad. No doubt he chanced one day to be playing, say, an augmented triad in C, sustained it via the pedal, struck another such triad on its neighbouring tone, D, and discovered the whole-tone sonority thus produced to be by no means wholly unpleasant. The most thoroughgoing use of the whole-tone scale in Liszt's work occurs in the melodrama for voice and piano, *Der traurige Mönch*. The poem by Lenau tells of the ghost of a grief-stricken monk haunting a tower in Sweden and so affecting those who look on him that all they want to do is to go away and die. In this instance a horseman who stumbles into the tower by accident is overcome by pity for the monk but cannot bring himself to allow him to speak his trouble. So the apparition vanishes and the horseman rides quietly away to drown himself in the lake. There is no vocal part as such—the poem is declaimed throughout, now over music, now alone. The function of the whole-tone scale in the prelude is obviously to invoke the supernatural: and as the rider goes on his way in the grey of the morning, mindful only of death, he is accompanied by a variant of the opening whole-tone passage, which now is totally bared of its original rhythmic tensions and so produces an effect of drained calm.

The climax of the thirteenth and last of Liszt's symphonic poems, *From the cradle to the grave*, exploits the whole-tone sonority at the end of its second section and the recitative-like opening of the third, but a more interesting work in every respect is *Via Crucis*, the Fourteen Stations of the Cross, for soloists, chorus and organ. In Stations IV and XIII the scale is almost sounded as a chord (but for a dissident B♭), in Station XII there is a passage for organ solo which consists entirely of augmented triad-progressions, completely devoid of any tonal sense and thus anticipating the sound of a work such as 'Voiles'. Similarly in the march music in Stations II and V there is a noticeable flavour both of the augmented triad and of the whole-tone scale. Other impressionist features which occur in these late works and pull us up short are the use of chains of consecutive open fifths (*Czardas macabre*) and of chords built of superimposed fourths (*Mephisto Waltz* no 3). The rather earlier *Mephisto Waltz* no 1 even begins with a cumulative build-up of fifths, just like the opening of *La Mer*. They are not of course used impressionistically in Liszt's piece, any more than the unresolved seventh partial at the end of Chopin's 23rd Prelude; but in these cases we do at least see the foundations of an Impressionist musical terminology being laid. Chopin and Liszt sensed the wider range of expression which could so easily be brought into focus though the development of harmony and the concept of timbre *qua* timbre, and Liszt at least began to associate these innovations with the evocation of natural phenomena, a process which was ultimately to culminate in the musical Impressionist movement. But one of the first composers to employ Impressionist techniques in this way—i.e. impressionistically not *in abstracto*—on a large and fine scale was the Norwegian, Edvard Grieg.

2

GRIEG

The many positive qualities of Grieg's music have often gone un-appreciated and the innovatory nature of many of his techniques unrecognized. This is largely because he made the fatal mistake of writing a large number of short piano pieces which presented little in the way of technical difficulties, with the result that they have become the inevitable prey of teachers, examining bodies and dilettantes of every description who have systematically dulled their freshness and robbed them of much of their youthful bloom. To relish the full flavour of Grieg's inspiration and to appreciate the prophetic character of much of his musical thought we must cleanse our minds of its jaded salon associations and view it once again in the context of the incomparable Norwegian landscape, the mountains, forests and fjords which brought it to birth.

This point is significant, for it was Grieg's attempts to express in music the lyrical essence of the fatherland he loved so dearly which led him to many of the innovatory concepts of harmony and timbre in which he anticipates the Impressionists. Born in Bergen, where he lived for the first fifteen years of his life, Grieg studied at the Leipzig Conservatory where he found the weight of the Teutonic tradition oppressive and its flavour unpalatable. Only after settling in Denmark—significantly, the Danish artistic temperament has more in common with that of the French—did the seeds of the nationalist fervour implanted in him by Ole Bull find suitable soil in which to germinate. For it was in Copenhagen that Grieg met Rikhard Nordraak, a Norwegian patriot who fired him with his own enthusiasm for Norway's folk-music and fostered in him an awareness of the scenic magnificence of their native land. From then on, though he lived and worked widely in Europe, his heart and his creative spirit were with Norway, constantly grappling with the problem of finding a musical idiom to do full justice to its beauty.

This natural beauty filled him with a perpetually self-renewing sense of wonder—wonder at the skylines of pine, birch and fir, vistas of near-vertical mountainsides, vast forests of *Tapiola*-like awesomeness, stream, waterfall, mossgrown stone—and when he endeavoured to express some measure of this in his music he found the language he had been taught in Leipzig wanting. For an alternative he turned to the virtually untapped resources of his native folk-music, instinct as it was with the life-spirit of the Norwegian countryside and its peasantry. He glimpsed in the rhythmic, melodic and (potentially) harmonic un-familiarities of folk-song a whole new dimension of expressive power—the means whereby music could become a vehicle for colour and atmosphere rather than for form and logic. Grieg became in effect the first nature mystic in music. He developed the art of mood evocation, of catching the *Stimmung* of a natural scene with a few deft impression-istic touches. He learnt how to depict, not grossly, but fastidiously and subtly; his music became suggestion rather than categorical statement of fact.

The love of colour and circumstantial detail is a native characteristic; the Norwegian loves to prettify things. Bright paint abounds in villages and towns and the brightly-coloured national costume is a very vital tradition. There is an obvious parallel here (however in-cautious such generalizations may be) with the Russians, who take a similar delight in gaudy finery and decorativeness; and in fact, con-temporary developments in Russian music were taking a similar course. The Russian nationalists also (see Chapter 3) were discovering the idiosyncrasies of folk-song to be pointing the way to far-reaching reforms of the musical syntax, although with the exception of Mus-sorgsky and, to a lesser extent, of Borodin, they were more concerned with the reconditioning of melody and timbre rather than with harmony, since harmony does not form a signally vital constituent of the Russian composer's creative thought. But folk-song, governed by a set of melodic principles at some variance with the orthodox western conception of line, cannot of necessity be harmonized in accordance with western harmonic traditions, at least not without doing consider-able violence to its highly idiomatic structure. It was undoubtedly in an attempt to match in his harmony the unconventional nature of the melodic material with which he was working that Grieg helped to inaugurate the re-orientation of European harmonic thought that was to be consolidated by Debussy. This is not to say that he employed his new-found harmonic devices only when dealing with folk-song; it was simply that in his desire to eliminate conflict between conventional notions of harmony and his new-found source of melodic inspiration he arrived at a concept of harmony which laid open the new uncharted area of feeling later to be more thoroughly explored by Debussy. Grieg discovered the very valuable atmospheric and colouristic potential of a harmonic system in which there was no forbidden fruit, instinct and the ear being the sole means of discriminating between right and wrong, acceptable and unacceptable.

We thus find embedded in his impressions of the Norwegian country-side all manner of radical harmonic innovations, many of which passed into common currency after Debussy, and the dissemination of Impressionist techniques—unprepared and unresolved 'dissonances', triads embellished with added notes, concords or 'discords' moving in parallel motion, modal interpolations (of popular or ecclesiastical origin), avoidance of the leading note and conventional cadential formulae—all inducing tonal flux and ambiguity. The chains of organum-like open fifths so beloved of the Impressionists are to be found in Grieg—only in his case, together with a fondness for the drone bass, they can be attributed to the idiosyncrasies of those stringed instruments of the Norwegian dales, the Hardanger fiddle and the langleik. It is in such ways that the native characteristics of popular music-making and folk-song give an unwitting fillip to the evolution-ary processes of harmony.

It is to the small piano pieces and songs that we must look for the most striking anticipations of Impressionism in Grieg's music. For Grieg was essentially a miniaturist; he left the application of his innovations to large-scale canvases and broad designs to his spiritual heirs, Debussy and particularly Delius, on whom the 'miniature Viking's' influence was all-pervasive. Grieg's architectural powers were notably deficient; and, although his short orchestral pieces have poetry and finish and are in many cases perfectly scored, he never really aspired to complete mastery of the orchestral tone palette. Like John Ireland, one of the most distinguished of the post-Impressionists, he found in the song and short piano lyric a perfectly satisfactory outlet for his minuscule genius. That he was extraordinarily sensitive to timbre is self-evident; but lacking a proper command of the full range of structural and instrumental resources, he wisely bequeathed the investigation of these terrains to his successors.

The first palpable signs of originality appear as early as the *Humor-esques*, op 6, although even in the *Poetic Tone Pictures*, op 3, unorthodox

peasant elements are in evidence; and, predictably, the most enter-
prising harmonically of Grieg's early works are those in which he is
treating original folk-material, notably the *Norwegian Dances and
Songs*, op 17. But the decisive break with classical harmony was not
made until the late 1880s with the later batches of *Lyric Pieces*, the
Norwegian Folk-songs, op 66, and the astonishing *Slätter*, op 72. There
are impressionistic traits in songs and various orchestral pieces at
intervals, but the most consistently advanced developments in this
direction are to be found in the later *Lyric Pieces* for piano, and these
must therefore be examined in some detail.

The new pinnacle of expressiveness is first reached in the fifth book,
op 54 (1891). No 1, 'Shepherd boy', is a pastoral poem of modest
proportions; the use of the sharp fourth in the scale of G minor
gives the music a discreetly exotic flavour, and, at the climax, the
chromatic embellishment of the melody over consecutive superimposed
fifths produces the plaintive, languid effect familiar in Impressionist
evocations of pastoral solitudes. No 4 'Notturno', revels voluptuously
in sequences of parallel ninths, and the climax reverberates with dominant
thirteenths in a way which foreshadows the lovely 'Peace of the woods',
op 71, no 4. The final number in op 54, 'Bellringing', is perhaps the
most remarkable of all pieces of pre-Debussian Impressionism. It is
often compared with 'La cathédrale engloutie', although this and
other Impressionist bellpieces ('Cloches à travers les feuilles' and Ravel's
'La vallée des cloches') aim at an intermingling of bell-sonority with
other aural phenomena—with the sounds of the sea, organ and distant
chanting in 'La cathédrale', with rustling leaves in 'Cloches'. Grieg's is
a pure bell-piece; although his technique is much cruder, the total effect
is much wilder and weirder than that of its eminent French successors.[1]
Melody as such is virtually non-existent. An ostinato bass of consecutive fifths a fourth apart attracts a right-hand syncopated figure,
also of fifths a fourth apart, which rises and falls with uncanny per-
sistency. As the climax approaches, the right hand consecutives assert
their independence of the left hand more and more aggressively, and
only in the closing bars, after the languor has died away, is the chord
of C major rung with any degree of confidence; even here the dissonant fifths continue to sound faintly, as if from subterranean depths.
The pedal merges the individual sounds into a confused pattern of vibrations which quiver in the air and impinge on the ear with dreamlike
elusiveness.

In the ninth book, op 68, we meet the strangely haunting 'Evening in the mountains', which consists of a single unbroken line of melody presented first as a herdsman's unaccompanied impromptu and then in a harmonic setting. Grieg demonstrates the evocative power of these long-breathed *alfresco* spans of wind-melody with their proneness to quasi-oriental chromatic arabesque and pentatonic triplet figuration. This piece is akin to his own 'Shepherd boy' discussed above, also to the cor anglais solo at the beginning of the third act of *Tristan und Isolde*, and is the prototype of many such passages in the later Impressionists—for instance, in Delius's *Song of the High Hills* and Vaughan Williams's *Flos Campi*. The spell cast by the opening flute solo of *L'Après-midi d'un Faune* is the result of a similar technique.

The tenth and last book of the *Lyric Pieces* (op 71) contain two of the most accomplished of Grieg's Impressionist pieces. Comparing 'Summer evening' to the slow movement of the Piano Concerto, Kathleen Dale has well said that 'both works are instinct with the lucent serenity and expansiveness which characterize the Norwegian summer evening scene'. Parallel chords of the ninth (with triplet embroidery) and seventh (with scintillating celesta-like filigree work in descending fourths) well suggest a richly-glowing sunset sky, and nowhere except

Ex. 6a and 6b
Grieg, 'Peace of the Woods' (Lyric Pieces, book 10)

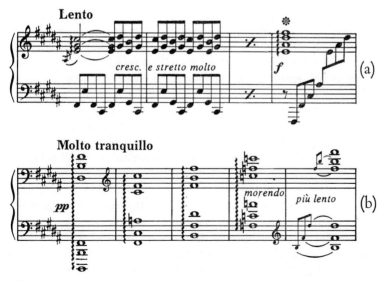

CIM

in 'Peace of the woods' does Grieg revel so unabashedly in sensuous radiance of sound. In 'Peace of the woods' one of Grieg's most beautiful creations, simple successions of common chords take on an entirely new meaning and seem instinct with the mystery of nature in her tranquillities. In Ex. 6a secondary chords of the seventh and ninth merge imperceptibly one into another in a steadily accumulative reverberation of timbre which recalls the op 54 'Notturno' and 'Bellringing'. The climactic dominant thirteenth at (*) is left suspended in the air; it is not resolved, it merely yields to an unrelated C minor chord which, in turn, is followed by a modally affiliated F major leading to a return of the original B major *cantabile* melody.[2] It is at such moments, for instance in the progression of major triads in the closing bars (Ex. 6b), that Grieg seems to lose himself in pantheistic contemplation; he discards all the regulation-ridden paraphernalia of classical harmonic procedure and enters the enchanted world of 'Nuages', 'Sirènes' or the legendary kingdom of Allemonde.

The last piano piece to be published by Grieg during his life-time, 'Mountaineer's Song' from *Moods*, op 73, is also impressionistic in character. The composer here exploits with poetic relevance the favourite Impressionist device of distance; the mountaineer's call is a simple modal melody which re-echoes back and forth canonically through a myriad different keys near and from afar until, to quote Kathleen Dale once again, 'the volume of tone gradually amassed seems to reverberate round the mountain-tops before dying away into the stillness of vast spaces'. The exotic associations of the minor scale with sharpened fourth are here called into play in a monodic interlude which separates the climax from the recapitulation.

Individual traits of Impressionism are also to be found in a number of Grieg's songs, particularly in the setting 'A swan' op 25, no 2—a sublimely calm, almost completely static piece of harmonic writing in which added-note chords are turned lovingly in hands loath to let go of them (Ex. 7). In the op 67 cycle, 'The Mountain Maid', there are more radical harmonic advances—a pronounced emphasis on the chord of the added sixth (see 'The singing' bars 1 and 2 and the recurrent F major section; 'Bilberry slopes', bars 1 and 2, and the babbling pentatonic ostinato in 'By the brook') and a very striking use of non-functional harmony in 'The singing' (parallel dominant sevenths in bars 5 and 6), in 'The Mountain Maid' (parallel thirteenths in bars 5 and 6) and in 'Love' (the impressionistically-poised ninth, unprepared and unresolved, in bars 1–2). Grieg's most unorthodox song is undoubtedly 'A bird flew

Ex. 7
Grieg, *A Swan*

screaming' from the *Five Songs* op 60, in which the hoarse cry of a gull as notated by Grieg in Hardanger fjord is reproduced over a static, non-resolving secondary seventh—a chord used freely in parallel motion in the main body of the song.

We have already noted that, in the main, Grieg was content to leave the development of orchestral Impressionism to his disciples. On the few occasions when he did turn to the orchestra he evinced the same sensitivity to beauty of timbre that he had shown in the songs and piano pieces discussed above. He wrote persuasively for strings—witness the *Holberg Suite* op 40, and the *Two Elegiac Melodies,* op 34, but more striking was his idiomatic treatment of the woodwind. He sensed a poetry latent in a soloistic conception of woodwind line and so anticipated Debussy but even more Delius, whose especial sympathy with this orchestral family is responsible more than anything else for the distinctive sound of his scoring. The lovely oboe solo which opens the second of the Symphonic Dances, op 64, is inconceivable on any other instrument, and the oboe's imitation of the piano figure which leads directly into the second subject of the first movement of the Piano Concerto glints with a silver light in a way similar to the dialogue between oboe and bassoon in the opening Allegro of *La Mer* (fig. 4, bars 1 and 2 of the Durand miniature score). A flute solo above the glacial shimmering of divided strings playing tremolo is a wearisomely familiar device today, but for the second subject of the last movement of the Concerto (the theme destined to reappear with breathtaking splendour in the coda) it is utterly appropriate. It is pure *Stimmung,* the sensation, light and colour of some natural phenomenon (perhaps the first glimmerings of sunrise over high mountain peaks) exquisitely transmuted into music.

The same is true of 'Morning mood' from the first *Peer Gynt* suite. Here the orchestral sonority, shaped and finished as by a master craftsman, is remarkably evocative of those clear but mysteriously melancholy mornings that are such features of the enchanting but all-too-fleeting Scandinavian summer. Marked 'allegretto pastorale', the pentatonic melody is at the outset divided between flute and oboe, the latter being accompanied by sustained string triads. It is difficult to explain why in this case the reedy sound of the oboe against the unruffled silkiness of the strings is so captivating, and we must simply ascribe it to a flair for timbre, in this case for orchestral timbre, which marks Grieg out as a true harbinger of Impressionism. Notice too at 5 bars after D the silvery ripple of the flutes playing in thirds with the lower line doubled by clarinet while a solo horn has the melody, and at 9 bars before F the gentle horn fanfares, sounding further and further away into the distance over trilling flutes and oboes with their herdsman's call. That Grieg was capable of such sustained beauty of orchestral sound—and this piece is perfect—makes one regret all the more that he had so little confidence in his ability as an orchestrator and wrote so little orchestral music.

---

1. Another progenitor of 'La cathédrale' is the French composer Albéric Magnard's 'Villebon' (from *Promenades* for piano) composed in 1893.

2. This passage is irresistibly reminiscent of Rilke's beautiful 'Gazelle' (in *New Poems*) when the animal pauses in flight to listen, its neck upheld:

Wie wenn beim Baden
im Wald die Badende sich unterbricht
den Waldsee im gewendeten Gesicht.

3

THE RUSSIAN NATIONALISTS

In 1880 Debussy's piano teacher at the Conservatoire, Antoine Marmontel, recommended the 18-year-old student to Tchaikovsky's patron Nadezhda von Meck, who was seeking a pianist to make up a trio with her resident violinist and cellist. The result was that for three years (1880–2) Debussy formed part of the von Meck entourage on its long summer journeys across Europe, and (in the two latter years) in Russia itself. When we remember that he was at this time entering upon the most critical, impressionable years of his early manhood it obviously becomes of paramount importance to examine the extent of his knowledge of contemporary Russian composers and their possible contribution to the formation of his style. Unfortunately we have very little concrete evidence of any such knowledge, but if we scrutinize the works of Tchaikovsky and the group of nationalist composers (Balakirev, Borodin, Cui, Mussorgsky and Rimsky-Korsakov) known as the 'Mighty Handful' in the light of the evolution of Impressionist techniques, we shall find it difficult to believe that the young Frenchman could have remained unresponsive to whatever Russian music he may have encountered for the first time at this period.

For several years previously there had been signs of a growing *entente cordiale*, musically speaking, between France and Russia. In 1878 works of Dargomyzhsky, Tchaikovsky and Rimsky-Korsakov were heard in concerts conducted by Nicholas Rubinstein in the World Exhibition, and with the upsurge of interest in these composers the *Revue et Gazette Musicale* published a long and authoritative series of articles on Russian music by César Cui, issued as *La Musique en Russie* in 1880; in the same year Bourgault-Ducoudray was illustrating his lectures on musical history at the Conservatoire with examples from *Boris Godunov* and Rimsky-Korsakov's *The Maid of Pskov*. In 1889 further interest was stimulated by the programmes of Russian music conducted by Rimsky-Korsakov at the Universal Exhibition, which included music of Glazunov, Dargomyzhsky and Liadov as well as of Tchaikovsky and the Mighty Handful. From this year dates what has been termed the Franco-Russian musical alliance, and in this same year Debussy not only became entranced by the sound of the Javanese gamelan but would also have had the chance to refresh his memory of the Russian gypsy music which he allegedly heard in Moscow cabarets. The climax of this *entente cordiale* was surely the fabulous and far-reaching success of the Diaghilev Ballet in Paris in the early years of the present century, and the influence of Impressionist technique on the epoch-making early ballet scores of Stravinsky, *Petrushka* and *The Rite of Spring*. This technical influence was by no means one-sided, however; in the works of the late nineteenth-century Russian composers are sown so many of the seeds of the coming Impressionism that Ravel's overt enthusiasm for their music is understandable. Debussy was generally reluctant to voice unqualified approbation of other composers' efforts, but there is evidence that he greatly admired Balakirev's *Tamara*, Mussorgsky's *Nursery Songs* and other representative works of the Nationalists' art.

Nevertheless, the extent of Debussy's acquaintance with these composers' music during his formative years must remain a matter of conjecture. What is beyond conjecture is the fact that during what we may for convenience's sake term his 'Russian' period the composer with whose music he was brought into assiduous contact was Tchaikovsky. Here we have the evidence of the von Meck–Tchaikovsky correspondence that, from necessity if not from choice, Debussy became thoroughly familiar with such works as the Fourth Symphony, *Romeo and Juliet*, the First Orchestral Suite ('yesterday he and I played your suite and he was delighted with the fugue and said "Among all modern fugues I have never found anything so beautiful: M. Massenet could never have equalled it"') and *Swan Lake* in their transcriptions for piano duet. Debussy's first published work was in fact a piano duet arrangement of the dances from Act III of *Swan Lake*.

Although Debussy's early *Danse Bohémienne* is mildly Tchaikovskian in flavour (Mme. von Meck in fact submitted it to Tchaikovsky for criticism and he was not unduly impressed) the direct influence of Tchaikovsky on his mature style is negligible, far less pronounced, certainly, than that of Borodin, Mussorgsky or Rimsky-Korsakov. This does not, however, alter the fact that pre-Impressionist elements are to be discovered in Tchaikovsky's own work, and it is accordingly from this angle that the relationship must be viewed. That such elements are present is indicative of a certain kinship of sensibility between Debussy and Tchaikovsky which we recognize again in the work of Scriabin who, as we shall see, was greatly affected by French Impressionism. Significant in this connection is the fact that Debussy's first setting of Verlaine—'En Sourdine' from the *Fêtes Galantes*—dates from the last summer he spent with Mme. von Meck, for, as Lockspeiser has pointed out, the nervously exacerbated sensibility of Verlaine is strikingly akin to that of Tchaikovsky, and the excruciatingly sensitive young Debussy cannot but have been intuitively aware of this. All three artists were exclusively preoccupied with their own sensations, and while the flamboyant melodramatic posturing, the big-hearted lyricism and the pre-Mahlerian passion for self-revelation so characteristic of Tchaikovsky's music may seem to stand leagues apart from the fastidiously-worked, objectively-biased and dimly-focused art of Debussy, there is the same tingling nervousness of response, the same razor-sharp acuity of perception which manifests itself in a natural sensitivity to timbre and a tendency towards quasi-*pointilliste* methods of textural patterning. This is allied to a characteristic common to both Russian and French composers—a delight in sonorous beauty for its own sake, a temptation to live intensely in the present moment without excess of concern for the morrow. We should remember that Tchaikovsky inherited French blood from his mother, and it is feasible that he acquired his mental constitution from her; certainly he came to rate the lesser French composers very much more highly than his German contemporaries and had a particular admiration for Bizet and Delibes. There is in fact a pronounced Mediterranean element in his music, reflecting partly the Italian opera idioms with which he would have become familiar in the St Petersburg of the 1860s, but also the 'civilized' qualities of this French music he admired so much—its elegance, shapeliness and grace, its sensuousness of texture, its economy of gesture. If in his own music he fell short of these ideals, he nevertheless effected through them a species of *rapprochement* between Russian nationalism and the Western European tradition which brought him ready recognition in a number of countries outside his own.

Those anticipations of Impressionism which occur in the works of Tchaikovsky may thus be attributed to certain idiosyncrasies of temperament and outlook common to French and Russian composers. As we have seen, Impressionism consisted above all else in a thorough-going revision of traditional concepts of harmony and timbre, and while harmonically speaking Tchaikovsky was no conservative (see, for example, his unabashed revelling in the voluptuous sonority of the added sixth in the introduction to the first movement of the B♭ minor Piano Concerto or the opening of the first movement of the *Manfred* Symphony, and his anticipation of Debussy's non-functional use of the major second in the opening bars of the Scherzo of the Second Symphony), his innovations in this sphere were by no means as radical as those of Grieg, Chabrier or Liszt. It is primarily in his attitude to texture and instrumentation that his originality lies; his discovery of the celesta in Paris in the summer of 1891 and his introduction of this instrument into the scores of the *Voevoda* symphonic poem and *The Nutcracker* is an obvious instance of his typically Russian delight in new scintillating sonorities,[1] but even the youthful First Symphony (*Winter Daydreams*) shows signs of an individual approach to the orchestral palette. The exquisitely euphonious quasi-tremolos for clarinets and flutes at the beginning of the first movement (Eulenburg miniature score, top of p. 7) is more than a simple accompaniment to the folk-song-like first subject on the violins; it is a colouristic device which suggests as much the glinting of the snow with a winter sun suddenly breaking through and lighting up the landscape as the jingle of troika bells. The Impressionists were fond of tremolo effects on high wood-wind and strings to suggest the shimmer of light.

The opening of the second movement ('A land of gloom, a land of mists') illustrates Tchaikovsky's predilection for the individualization of woodwind timbre; the oboe solo, as Martin Cooper has pointed out, sounds more reedy and harsh than conventionally suave, and here it calls up the voice of a marsh bird, suggesting with great economy of means the sinister emptiness of a deserted winter landscape as fog descends. In other words Tchaikovsky has an ear for the evocative properties of the oboe; he uses it to create a specific atmosphere, and thus anticipates, for example, the oboe solo at bar 13 of *Pelléas et Mélisande* ('doux et expressif') which evokes the 'sinister emptiness' of the dark forest.

Tchaikovsky approaches most nearly the true spirit of Impressionist scoring, however, in his orchestral scherzos and his ballet numbers of a scherzo-like character. The gossamer-light, airy, fluffy texture of these pieces—the ubiquitous *pizzicati*, the elfin splashes of demisemiquaver woodwind trimming, the frequent absence of any pronounced melodic element, all suggest the free play of fascinating sound-patterns over the surfaces of a structure rather than any positive dialectic probing of the structure itself. In the second movement of the *Manfred* Symphony, for example, the unabashedly 'luscious' melody of the Trio stands in marked contrast to the Scherzo itself, where melodic interest is minimal and the spraying and splashing of the waterfall is reflected in a cross-rhythmic interplay of restlessly-leaping string figures and gurgling woodwind arabesque—an early example of Impressionist water music in which melodic and rhythmic particles, as opposed to actual themes, are woven skilfully into a continuously evolving texture of light and colour. In the closing bars it is the filigree work of the two harps and violins (divided into five parts, playing *arco* and *pizzicato*) which alone gives the passage its thistledown quality.

The Impressionists' concern to pinpoint a sensation in terms of colour and texture alone stressed the need for laconicism and concentration of utterance—their objective was that music should appear directly to the senses without obtruding upon the intellect, and Debussy's piano *Préludes* develop this technique of seizing upon the salient details of a scene and fusing them deftly into a quick overall impression to a rare pitch of perfection. This is anticipated in the Scherzo of Tchaikovsky's Fourth Symphony. The composer explained that this movement:

. . . expresses no definite sensations. It consists of capricious arabesque, fleeting images that pass through the imagination when one has begun to drink a little wine . . . these disconnected images have nothing in common with reality, they are strange, wild, incoherent.

The realist touches which occur here (the balalaika orchestra, harmonicas and accordions, a distant brass band) are indistinctly focused, rapidly follow each other and intermingle freely, all caught in a typically Impressionist twilight zone in which the boundaries between dream and reality are extremely ill-defined. The instrumental colouration is highly individual: an entire section for *pizzicato* strings on their own (the balalaikas) which, incidentally, may well have been the instigator of the second movement of Debussy's String Quartet; fleet arabesque-like writing for the woodwind (the muzhiks) and brass playing *pianissimo* in detached semiquavers and producing an effect akin to that of the string *pizzicato* (the distant military band). We may see in this remarkable piece anticipation not only of Debussy's 'Sérénade Interrompue' or 'Minstrels', but also of the Whistlerian 'Scherzo-Nocturne'

of Vaughan Williams's *London* Symphony (his most Impressionist
work) which similarly features a fast-moving sequence of barely-
defined images—even including a merry company assembled outside
a public house beguiling the time with their mouth-organs just like
Tchaikovsky's accordeon-playing muzhiks. We have already noted the
curious affinity between the development of non-functional harmony
and the harmony brought about as a result of the acoustic idiosyncrasies
of instruments (see page 63). Tchaikovsky's piano piece *The Muzhik
plays the Accordion* ends on a repeated dominant seventh chord, just as
the second movement of Bartók's Concerto for Orchestra was later
to do. The *Tristan* horns and Debussy's guitars offer additional
examples.

Whatever the exact nature of his relationship with Tchaikovsky and
his reaction to his music, there is no doubt that the Russian element in
Debussy's own work, slight though it is, is more readily attributable to
members of the Mighty Handful, Balakirev, Rimsky-Korsakov,
Borodin and Mussorgsky, Cui in no way calling for consideration.
There are certainly many intimations of Impressionism in the work of
all these composers and we may seek the reasons for this in two main
factors—the greater technical freedom in which their spiritual descent
from Glinka had resulted, and their heightened susceptibility to literary
and even pictorial stimulants. Glinka's prime importance as a Russian
composer lies in his individual treatment of folk-song and his refusal to
submit it to the straitjacket of Teutonic symphonic form. Like Grieg,
he understood clearly that a national musical culture founded on folk-
music—and he was interested in Spanish as well as Russian folk-music—
needed to evolve an entirely new set of formal principles if the freshness
and spontaneity of its appeal were not to be tarnished. A work such as
Kamarinskaya illustrates the affinity between a folk-song style and
Impressionism—namely that in both disciplines a very highly developed sense of harmony and timbre is required of the composer. For a
sonata structure is the most alien environment conceivable for a folk-
tune, and virtually all that can be done with it is to submit it to
kaleidoscopic variations in harmony and texture. This is the technique
Glinka adopts in *Kamarinskaya* and in his Spanish pieces, *Jota Aragonesa*
and *Summer Night in Madrid*. Since interest could no longer be maintained dialectically in the Teutonic manner, resourcefulness in colour,
in the actual stuff of sound itself, became a matter of dire necessity;
Glinka's methods of scoring in fresh primary colours instituted a new
era in the concept of timbre, and in this respect, as in his rhythmic

originality (e.g. the 5/4 chorus in Act III of *A Life for the Tsar*) and his introduction of the whole-tone scale into *Russlan and Ludmila*, he exerted considerable sway over those later Russian composers who were to anticipate the Impressionists more directly.

Glinka was the idol of Balakirev's youth, and when the older man died in 1857 the future of Russian musical nationalism lay solely in his disciple's hands. He was fortunate to find an ardent propagandist for the course in Vladimir Stassov, a fervent believer in the greatness of the group of nationalist composers who sprang up around Balakirev and a constant source of inspiration to them in their struggles against the conservative, Germanic school of musical thought represented by the Rubinstein brothers. Stassov was a man of wide culture and considerable literary ability and he fostered a degree of cultural awareness among members of the Mighty Handful (a term he had invented) which acted as an unconscious stimulus to the development of their technique. We may see here a parallel with the growth of Impressionism as an ever-keener response to contemporary trends in art and literature and the greater readiness of composers to associate not only with each other but with literary and artistic colleagues as well.

Balakirev himself was in many respects the epitome of the Russian creative temperament in music. He inherited all Glinka's love of folksong, of instrumental colour and the associated tendency to think intensely in minuscule time-spans. The influence of Liszt and the fusion of national folk-music traits with oriental arabesque nurtured a highly-wrought, richly-ornamental style in which genuine development, dramatic argument and thematic proliferation is often eschewed in favour of a play of colour and timbre around an essentially static thematic entity. *Islamey*, for instance, is a virtuoso piano piece in the true Lisztian tradition, yet, as Wilfrid Mellers has pointed out, Balakirev's oriental folk-themes are far less dynamic than Liszt's Italianate fioriture; the themes are less important than the riot of harmonic and orchestral colour they provoke. The textures are concentratedly opulent, and if this is true of Balakirev's piano writing, his orchestral masterpiece *Tamara* stands in terms of lusciousness of sound almost unrivalled in the music of its time. Vallas records that after a performance of *Tamara* Debussy came away with the tears streaming down his cheeks, and we find at least one direct reference to it in the score of *L'Après-midi d'un Faune*—the harmonic–melodic outline from five bars after M to two bars before N in *Tamara* is clearly reproduced in the triplet-dominated middle section of *L'Après-midi* (cf. 9 bars after 7 *et seq.*). It is possible that the opening flute solo of *L'Après-midi* and other quasi-orientalisms originated in Rimsky-Korsakov's *Sheherazade* or *Antar* rather than directly in *Tamara*, but without the latter both the former are unthinkable. Moreover, whereas *Tamara* pulses with red warm blood, *Sheherezade* by comparison is an empty, though pretty shell. With the pagan voluptuousness of Balakirev's inspiration, the many exotically-flavoured melodic beauties, the richness of the orchestral tapestry woven about them, the sensual pleasure in lush romantic harmony (see especially the coda), a definitely new world of sound and colour is opened up, and at whatever period of Debussy's youthful career he first made the acquaintance of this masterpiece it cannot fail to have left a lasting impression.

Balakirev's harmonic sense, though unfailingly poetic, remained relatively conventional; yet within the bounds of those conventions he shows on occasions a remarkable feeling for atmosphere—for instance in the song 'A whisper, a timid breath, a rustle' (no 7 of the ten songs composed in 1903–4) where an almost *Pelléas*-like vocal line is accompanied by a shadowy continuum of gently-shifting harmony. This passage quite clearly belongs to the world of the *Ariettes oubliées* of which, needless to say, it was composed quite independently.

Balakirev's fearlessly unacademic outlook impressed itself most forcibly on a young naval cadet training in St Petersburg, Nicholas Rimsky-Korsakov, who, although he was later to free himself of his mentor's influence, absorbed from him an independence of spirit and an open-minded receptiveness to all forms of musical stimulation which largely conditioned his musical philosophy for life. More directly than any of the other members of the Handful, he anticipated certain aspects of Impressionism and certainly made a profound impact on Ravel, if not on the young Debussy himself. Like Grieg, he took a keen delight in sound for its own sake, in beauty of timbre; he was not interested in sustaining an elaborate symphonic argument, nor was he unduly concerned by the episodic nature of his structural designs. His aim was to titillate the senses by a sumptuously-woven tapestry of iridescent orchestral sound, dazzling as the brilliantly-hued cupolas of St Basil's Cathedral in Red Square. But unlike Grieg, whose interest in timbre was primarily harmonic, Rimsky was first and foremost a master of the orchestral palette. This is not to say he was indifferent to harmony—he availed himself freely on occasions of ninths, added sixths, the augmented triad, the whole-tone scale (generally, it is true, used melodically but also, in *The Snow Maiden*, harmonically)—but he was never a radical harmonic innovator like Grieg. His art was essentially decorative and superficial; but he was such a master of the beguiling outer appearance that time and again the inner hollowness is successfully masked. His was an intricate process of selecting, shaping, polishing, refining and civilizing his raw material to a state of superlative perfection. Many factors contributed to the formation of this intriguing musical personality—the ceremonial of the Russian Orthodox Church, Russian folksong, in later life a vein of lyrical pantheism, and, most prominent of all, an intense love of the sea and the magic garden of the East, both instilled in him during his early days as a sailor (the 'fine career' for which Debussy was originally intended and which Albert Roussel was actually to pursue). It is in connection with the two latter influences that Impressionist traces are most in evidence in Rimsky-Korsakov's work, so we shall do well to examine them in greater detail.

After passing out of the Naval College in 1862 Rimsky-Korsakov was appointed to the clipper *Almaz*, which after periods of duty in British and Russian waters was ordered across the Atlantic to the American coast. When she was recalled home in the spring of 1864 her course lay through the southern Atlantic, and here it was that the young composer had his first experience of tropical seas. These three years which he spent upon the sea were to leave an indelible mark upon his music, for he became the first composer to convey in musical terms not only the outward motion of the great waters but also their inner being, their essential spirit. Ernest Newman always felt that his orchestration took its peculiar lustre from the sapphires, creams and emeralds of the sea, and in certain cases the influence seems also to extend to his rhythmic flexibility and to the cut of his melody; and in no work is his feeling for the rhythm and ground-tone of the sea more consistently in evidence than in the opera *Sadko*. This germinated from the 1867 symphonic poem of the same title (revised on two subsequent occasions), and the composer always considered it one of his best works. (Posterity has been inclined to agree with him, voting it second only to *The Snow Maiden*.) In *Sadko* there are numerous foreshadowings of *La Mer*. The sea is omnipresent; it is a vital factor in the colour and texture of the music throughout the opera. The sea prelude, taken from the earliest form of the symphonic poem which was written soon after the *Almaz* cruise (and hence a study direct from life, in the manner of the Impressionists) captures the essence of the calm sea-swell, the breathing of the infinite ocean desert, in a way hitherto unknown in music and unparalleled until the advent of *La Mer*[2] (Ex. 8). Rimsky-

Ex. 8
Rimsky-Korsakov, *Sadko*

Korsakov acknowledges Liszt's *Ce qu'on entend sur la montagne* as his harmonic model here, thus forming a specific link between two highly individual sensibilities both veering in their different ways towards musical Impressionism. For there are anticipations of Debussian water music not only in the prelude but in all the scenes involving Volkhova, the Sea Princess and her retinue in Lake Ilmen. There are distinct echoes of the Rhinemaidens in certain of these scenes, but the trilling succession of ninths which greets the rising of the sea-nymphs from the water at the beginning of the second tableau is prophetic not only of Debussy but also of Scriabin. The semitonal progression of semi-diminished and augmented chords first heard in the sea-nymphs' opening chorus in the same scene is prophetic of the hoarse cry of the sea-surge in the introductory bars to the finale of *La Mer*. Towards the end of the fifth tableau the effect of this phrase sung wordlessly by the women's chorus offstage is especially evocative, and here and elsewhere there are clear anticipations of the 'Sirènes' from Debussy's *Nocturnes* or even the offstage chorus of sailors towards the end of Act I of *Pelléas*, distant wordless voices blown inland by the wind over a restless sea (the sea-nymphs vocalize for most of the time: Rimsky-Korsakov evidently had in mind a characteristically Impressionist combination of the sound of distant human voices with certain rhythmic and melodic patterns which are associated in his mind, and ours, with the movements of the sea). The ostinato-like figure of Ex. 8 insinuates itself into innumerable nooks and crannies throughout the score, subtly conditioning the texture and figuration and frequently holding the stage in its own right, especially when the sea is directly involved in the action; in this way Rimsky-Korsakov permeates his music with a constant stream of suggestion, implication rather than literal depiction, so that the listener is drawn inexorably into his sound-world, his perceptions become so inextricably involved with the natural pheno-menon itself that he loses all sense of artificially-contrived representation.

This is essentially Impressionism, and it is significant in this connection that most of those reminiscences of Rimsky-Korsakov in Debussy's mature work occur in his water music—'Reflets dans l'eau', *La Mer*, *L'Isle Joyeuse*. In *Sadko* there is unending diversity of water music (particularly in the sixth tableau with the orchestral passage entitled 'Procession of the wonders of the sea'), and the sea also plays a signifi-cant part in *The Tale of Tsar Saltan* and *Sheherezade*. The sea scene in the first movement of the latter work is vividly conceived and effectively reproduced in more brilliant orchestral garb in the last; but here the sea is less an entity in itself (as in *Sadko*) than a stage for the vicissitudes of Sinbad's ship with its ultimate destruction against the rock with the bronze horseman. None the less the suggestion of rolling breakers (both here and in the prelude to Act II of *Tsar Saltan*) by means of rising and falling arpeggios was compelling enough to find an echo in two early piano pieces of Debussy which bear broad signs of Russian influence—the Ballade and Danse, both dating from 1890. In either case there are passages in which wide-flung left-hand arpeggios support a sweep of right-hand melody in thirds, prophetic in their turn of the exultantly leaping approach to the climax (*en animant beaucoup*) in 'Jeux de vagues' (fig. 35 of the miniature score).

Although Debussy professed no great admiration for *Sheherezade*, finding it more reminiscent of a bazaar than of the Orient, he did approve of one of Rimsky-Korsakov's lesser-known essays in Orien-talism, *Antar* (as we have seen, he had a special affection for the parent of both works, Balakirev's *Tamara*). Rimsky's love of the East infused a certain warmth and vibrancy into his scoring. Although he wrote his orientalisms into his music with the same objectivity of approach and essential lack of emotional commitment with which he appropriated Russian folk-song and the chant of the Russian Orthodox Church, they brought a pronounced Mediterranean element into his scoring which bathes his fundamental clarity of texture and piquancy of contour in a sensuous, quasi-Debussian haze. Ex. 9a, from the beginning of the 'Allegretto vivace' in the first movement, and Ex. 9b, its modified reappearance as an accompaniment to the Arabian folk-melody in the fourth, are both reminiscent of *L'Après-midi d'un Faune*—the warm bed

Ex. 9a and 9b
Rimsky-Korsakov, *Antar*

of horns and muted strings with added-note chords and harp glissandi
bring to mind the opening bars, while the phosphorescent patter of the
flutes recalls the scherzo-like variation of the main theme (5 bars after
fig. 8 in the miniature score). Similarly the flute arabesques of this main
theme itself are of a distinctly oriental cast; theirs is precisely the dream-
like, hypnotic quality found in the music associated with the Queen of
Shemaka in *The Golden Cockerel*.

It is no accident, and highly significant, that in the work of a number
of post-Impressionists—Ravel in the first instance, Florent Schmitt and
Respighi among others—the dual influences of Rimsky-Korsakov and
Debussy are inextricably enmeshed. That in the melting-pot of other
men's music they meet and intermingle quite happily is proof of their

stylistic compatibility. Of more than passing interest is the extra-ordinary remark made by Rimsky-Korsakov after hearing *Pelléas* for the first time in Paris in May 1907: 'I will have nothing more to do with this music, lest I should unhappily develop a liking for it'. It was almost as if, having denounced in reactionary terms the 'new and incompre-hensible phase of development' on which music appeared to be enter-ing, he now found himself rejecting this new music in spite of himself, merely perhaps to prove himself as firmly entrenched in his considered opinions and tastes as befitted an elderly and much-respected Con-servatory pedagogue. For he cannot have failed to perceive the resemblance between the scene on the deserted battlefield in Act II of *The Golden Cockerel* and the dungeon scene in Act III of *Pelléas*. Note the stage-directions: 'It is night. The moon casts a reddish light on a narrow gorge . . . the mountain mists shroud everything in white . . . the dead bodies of warriors lie on the hill-side . . . as if turned to stone in the last battle . . . everything is quiet and sinister.' Compare the music of the opening bars with the corresponding moment in Act III, Scene 2 of *Pelléas*. In each case the atmosphere to be created is of a sinister, menacing calm; thick night, and the air charged with the stench of death ('sentez-vous l'odeur de mort qui monte . . . voyez-vous le gouffre, Pelléas? Pelléas?'). In each case the lower strings move slowly, quietly and uneasily through the whole-tone scale and there are piercing little whole-tone woodwind ejaculations, causing a thrill of terror not only by the actual whole-tone sound itself but also by force of contrast of rhythm and timbre. It is thus evident that the two composers hit on the same method of conveying a sense of desolation and eeriness quite independently of one another,[3] and it is a striking illustration of the extent to which Rimsky-Korsakov, perhaps un-consciously, formulated certain concepts and their associated tech-niques which were later to prove of paramount importance in the growth and development of the musical Impressionist school.

In a sense, Borodin occupies a position mid-way between Rimsky-Korsakov and Mussorgsky. To Rimsky-Korsakov he is allied through his sensitivity to timbre, though his orchestral writing on the whole is less flamboyant; on the other hand, he is more ambitious harmonically and in this respect stands closer to Mussorgsky, though their respective harmonic innovations have little in common with each other.

Just as Balakirev's love of the orient may be the result of a Tartar strain in his lineage (his physiognomy certainly suggests this), Borodin's pronounced feeling for sonority, for beauty of sound, may have to do with the oriental extraction of his paternal ancestors. This is well illustrated in the two string quartets; the vein of sensuous sweetness in the slow movements (as in the 'Rêverie' of the *Petite Suite* for piano with its added sixths) certainly has some kinship with the corresponding movements in the quartets of Debussy and Ravel. Part of this is due, in this context, to the beguiling beauty of the string writing itself; but of equal importance is the frequently oriental cast of the melody (First Quartet, second movement, the sequence of descending triplets at 'più vivo, animato ed appassionato'; Second Quartet, the main melody of the Notturno, a lovely, fragrant piece of mood-evocation) and the richness of the harmonic texture—the added sixth in the closing bars of the first movement of the First Quartet (miniature score, p. 22, line 4, bar 2 *et seq.*) or in bar 8 of the first movement of the Second Quartet; the Debussian dominant ninth, same movement, codetta (p. 5, line 3, bar 6), or the subsidiary theme of the Scherzo which relies almost exclusively on dominant ninth sonority. The rapt atmosphere of the 'Notturno' is recaptured in the famous A major Polovtsian Dance in *Prince Igor*, in which the melodic vein is of the purest oriental gold and the harmony spangled with added notes to match. The oboe solo is comparable to that in Grieg's Symphonic Dance no 2 and accounts for much of the radiant, glistening sensuousness of this music.

The two completed symphonies reproduce certain of these character-istics on a larger scale. The opening of the Allegro of no 1, however (p. 4 of the miniature score), presents a harmonic unorthodoxy not noticeable in the quartets—chords built of superimposed fourths, doubtless engendered by the preponderance of that interval in Russian folk-song;[4] in much the same way the characteristic fourths and fifths of Hungarian folk-song were later to induce Bartók and Kodály to construct quasi-Impressionist chords. (In Borodin's work a more striking instance of the process may be observed in the *Prince Igor* over-ture, in which a fanfare-like agglomeration of pentatonic fourths over a dominant pedal leads into the main Allegro.) In the First Symphony the chief Allegro subject features recurring fourths (in fact the fourth is the dominant interval of the entire work) and in the coda it appears in a slow lyrical transformation with an abundance of added-sixth sonority in the harmony, anticipating the insistence upon that chord in the ensuing Scherzo. The slow movement opens in a wholly impression-istic manner with a rising series of open fifths on lower strings and many arabesque-like interpolations in the melodic line; the music evokes the languid atmosphere of the steppes. The slow movement of the Second

Symphony is also sultry and orientally languorous, but the symphony as a whole is, from the technical point of view, more orthodox than the First, which contains rhythmic as well as harmonic irregularities and which, as far as the first movement is concerned, is notably original in form.

Similarly there are few technical eccentricities to be found in the short orchestral tone poem *In the Steppes of Central Asia*; yet in a sense this is the most impressionistic of all Borodin's works. 'Tone poem' is not a wholly appropriate designation since this is literally an 'impression', a thumbnail sketch, a piece of programme music in which detailed depiction and narrative development are eschewed in favour of establishing a mood. Technically the crux of the whole piece is the interplay between the 'Russian' and 'oriental' themes and their final symbolic union, but in purely atmospheric effects the score is not wanting—a sustained high E on violin harmonics to suggest the limitless expanse of the steppes, page after page where nothing is happening save the inexorable semitonal *pizzicato* plodding of the camels and horses as they come gradually into focus beneath the ethereal high E which is occasionally doubled at the lower octave or fifteenth by woodwind or horns, occasionally even pointed by an open fifth. However clear and well-defined the two folk-melodies may be, this high pedal E adds an element of Impressionist haze to the overall effect.

Harmonically the most advanced of Borodin's works are his songs; on the evidence of 'Le jet d'eau' it seems likely that Debussy knew at least one of them, *The Sleeping Princess*. The parallel dissonant seconds were sufficiently innovatory in the Russia of the 1870s to provoke an indignant outburst from the critic Laroche, who claimed that Borodin had introduced them in imitation of Liszt, mistaking the seconds in the latter's trills for independent intervals (which may indeed have been precisely how the idea of using the second as a consonance occurred to Borodin). Notice the dream-like atmosphere which the use of these parallel seconds creates, subtly enhanced by the distant chime of a bell (the C in the tenor); the tonic-dominant ostinato in the bass produces a hypnotic effect of its own, and all combines to present a subtle Impressionist portrait of the princess, pinioned fast in her æon-long sleep in the dark forest. With the flight of the witches and woodsprites in stanza 2 the seconds are no longer soothing and caressing but venomous and aggressive, and the bass-line strides downwards in ominous whole-tones. Another disturber of the peace—the knight who comes to the rescue in stanza 3—is accorded similar uncompromising musical treatment, and all the princess wants to do, as the final stanza reveals, is to slumber impressionistically on.

There is a similar use of dissonant seconds in *The Song of the Dark Forest*, but the hand of a master-craftsman is revealed in *The Wondrous Garden*, in which the chromatic ostinato in the accompaniment, moving constantly within the compass of minor seconds, constitutes a kind of Russian *Waldweben*, for it evokes the rustle of the leaves and the swaying of the flowers in the garden. However, quite the most luscious, harmonically speaking, of all Borodin's songs—in fact of all his compositions—is *The Queen of the Sea*, where Ex. 10 with its freely alternating added sixths and dominant ninths is already close to Delius. Notice the murmuring, undulating motion of the right hand and compare the passage as a whole with the main *Brigg Fair* interlude. In all these works of Borodin we can sense the unconscious inauguration of a process which Debussy was to develop—the subordination of the melodic impulse, the dynamic, to the demands of the sensory harmonic movement, the static.

Ex. 10
Borodin, *The Queen of the Sea*

Why is it that when I listen to your conversation and to the conversation of painters and sculptors . . . I am able to follow the pattern of your thoughts, your ideas and your aims and that I so seldom hear anything about technique? And why is it that when I listen to my musical brethren I hear hardly a live thought but mostly primitive chatter about the ABC of composition?

Debussy was not the author of this passage though he might well have been. It is an extract from a letter to Vladimir Stassov from Modeste Mussorgsky, and it highlights an important affinity between Russian and Frenchman—for Debussy, like Delius, found the company of artists and painters infinitely preferable to that of musicians. Debussy was likewise on intimate terms with many writers and thinkers, and in Mussorgsky's case the latter proved an important factor in his spiritual development. For as we saw in Debussy's case, constant contact with artists in different media of creativity encourages the growth of new ideas and the widening of perspectives and it was these writers and thinkers, far more than Dargomyzhsky, who first interested Mussorgsky in the concept of realism in music, and in consequence, like Debussy, found himself compelled to manufacture his own *materia musica* as he proceeded, finding what immediately came to hand unsuited to his purpose. When we realize that Mussorgsky, like Debussy, was acutely sensitive to intonations, to inflexions, to colour and the evocative properties of harmony and also rhythm, it comes as no surprise to learn that Mussorgsky's 'realism' was more akin to Debussy's 'realistic Impressionism' than to Strauss's 'realistic pictorialism'. It was the spirit of a scene, person or situation that Mussorgsky attempted to reproduce, not the letter; atmosphere and *ambiance*, the aura emanating from an object, not purely and simply the object itself. It was above all Mussorgsky's skill in catching overtones in this way which categorizes him as a harbinger of Impressionism. M. D. Calvorcoressi describes the discovery of striking processes of evocation and expression as 'positive realism'. Mussorgsky, no less than Debussy, evolved his new techniques by virtue of his own intuition, the idiosyncrasies of his musical nature and his profound distrust of all scholastic theories and conventions. The ear was the only judge. What sounded right was right, *pace* the sticklers for academic rectitude like Rimsky-Korsakov. And, like Debussy, Mussorgsky responded positively to the most natural, direct and unselfconscious form of musical expression—the folk-song.

All Mussorgsky's technical innovations—melodic, rhythmic and harmonic—can be traced to his absorption in Russian folk-music, to his canny perception of everything having to do with the ordinary people —not only their singing but their walking, speaking, dancing and their emotional reactions. The influence of *Boris Godunov* upon *Pelléas* has been much discussed. Although there are parts of *Pelléas* written in a conventionally lyrical operatic idiom (notably in the final love-scene between Pelléas and Mélisande) the vocal line for the most part follows closely the inflexions of the speaking voice, as in *Boris* (it is unlikely that Debussy was familiar with Dargomyzhsky's *The Stone Guest*, which in this respect anticipates *Boris*). In this way through a greater 'naturalism' and freedom from constraint Debussy was empowered to move closer to his ideal of music as an improvisation, making a non-stylized appeal direct to the emotions and to the senses. It was this directness, this unforcedness and complete naturalness which so impressed Debussy about the set of songs called *The Nursery*:

No one has given utterance to the best within us in tone more gentle or profound; he is unique and will remain so because his art is spontaneous and free from arid formulas.

Yet it is the fine song-cycle entitled *Sunless* which is constantly being quoted in connection with Debussy, since it seems likely that the open-ing of 'Nuages' was suggested by the third song in the series, 'The noisy day has sped its course'. As the poet, half-awake, half-dreaming, finds visions of long-forgotten days crowding into his mind and merging confusedly with the illusion of new hope, the accompaniment winds a figure of alternating thirds and sixths round the vocal line. The passage has an almost organum-like flavour and is certainly akin to that of *Nuages*. It is difficult to understand what Lockspeiser means when he says that to uphold this contention 'can only be put down to a peculiar insensitiveness to concepts of melody that were utterly opposed', for there is similarity here not only of technique (except that Debussy alternates his thirds and fifths and not sixths, thereby intensifying the organum-like flavour) but also of expressive intent.

In fact, *Sunless* bids fair to be reckoned Mussorgsky's most im-pressionistic work. In 'Within four walls' he uses chains of consecutive triads, tied to a pedal, to suggest the all-enveloping night seeping into the poet's tormented brain; In 'Elegy' the night dreaming in the mist, the single shining star and the distant cowbells are all found Impression-ist musical equivalents—Mussorgsky's cowbells are reminiscent of Wagner's whispering leaves—and in the final song, 'On the river', a triplet semiquaver figure in the bass mirrors the inexorably flowing current while above it some very Debussian parallel dominant sevenths create a sonorous aura of mystery. The *Nursery* songs have no such picturesque settings to provoke atmospheric effects, but the vocal line is far closer to continuous recitative, like *Boris*, and there is some interesting pre-Impressionist exploitation of the major second: in 'Nanny' for example, at the moment when the child is telling his nurse of 'the old lame king who lived with his queen in a fine castle by the sea' or in 'Dolly', a lullaby, where it is used to suggest drowsiness and haze very much in the manner of Borodin's *The Sleeping Princess*.

Debussy may also have been influenced in his conception of the

Préludes by Mussorgsky's *Pictures at an Exhibition* in that the latter, like
the former, are terse laconic impressions and include character sketches,
fantasy pictures and mysterious evocations. The moments which come
closest to Impressionism in spirit occur in 'Catacombs'—the quasi-
static chord-progressions; in 'Cum mortuis in lingua mortua'—the
subtly atmospheric, elusive harmony and the high tremolos; and in
'The Great Gate of Kiev' the splendid Impressionist peal of bells.
Notice in Ex. 11 the B♮ triads sounded against the reverberating tenor

Ex. 11
Mussorgsky, 'The Great Gate of Kiev' (*Pictures at an Exhibition*)

in bar 1, the added sixth in bar 2, the added-note chords in 3 and 4, the
very impressionistic agglomerations of fourths and fifths in bar 5 *et seq*.
That musical bell-depiction fascinated Mussorgsky as well as Debussy
can be seen also in the coronation scene in *Boris* where the bell-pealing
is founded on two alternating dominant sevenths with appropriate
figuration above.

By way of conclusion, some account must be taken of a solitary and
enigmatic figure whose music has passed almost completely into limbo

but who used to refer to both Debussy and Ravel, no less, as his 'imitators'. This was Vladimir Rebikov, who died in poverty and obscurity in 1922 after floundering for years in a quagmire of bitterness and resentment against a musical world which, he alleged, had accepted the Impressionist 'plagiarists'—Debussy and Ravel—and ignored the composer whose work they had pillaged so shamelessly, namely himself. Rebikov began by writing piano miniatures freshly influenced by Tchaikovsky and Grieg, and remained a miniaturist all his life. Much of his work in this relatively derivative field is in fact unduly neglected; in many of his short piano pieces the inevitable salon associations are effectively counterbalanced by impeccable craftsmanship, a feeling for the deftly-chiselled harmonic feature and, within its limits, a pleasing melodic facility. Certainly the ballet suite from *Mila and Nolli*, the three dances in the second 'picture' of his 'musico-psychological drama' *The Christmas Tree*, the second *Miniature Suite* for small orchestra, 'Evening landscape' from the op 31 *Silhouettes* for piano, 'In the Caucasus' from the *Tone Poems*, op 13 for piano or his ten settings of Krylov fables, are as deserving of recognition as similar compositions by Liadov.

So far so good. But in due course Rebikov became increasingly impatient with traditional notions of harmony and began to theorize greatly. His doctrines have a familiar ring: 'music is a language of feelings and feelings have neither form, no laws, nor rules'. 'Be filled to the brim with feeling and be able to express it adequately in sound.' In the compositions which followed he attempted to put his theories into practice by dealing in chords of fourths and fifths, the augmented triad and whole-tone scale, the parallel-chord technique and various other devices with which at very much the same time composers elsewhere were opening the gateway to Impressionism as a genre (i.e. the middle and late 1890s). The question of Grieg's influence naturally arises, and it is here that the inquiring student begins to be confronted with obstacles. For biographical and critical data on Rebikov are practically non–existent, even in Russia; only a small percentage of his quite considerable output is now available for study, and to arrange his compositions in any reliable chronological order is virtually impossible. Where dates are appended to the compositions here described they refer either to a date of composition as it appears at the end of a piece, or to a date of publication which one assumes approximates to the date of composition. Where neither is available one must take the opus numbers as a rough guide; by the turn of the century Rebikov had reached op 21 or thereabouts.

It seems safe to assume that Rebikov was familiar with the more radical of Grieg's compositions, but if the latter galvanized him into experimental harmonic activity he soon far exceeded their natural boundaries, and it seems probable that he found his way into the esoteric region of his late works quite independently of any western composer. Thus, to take an extreme case, in the *Three Idylls*, op 50, for piano (1914) there is a free use of tone-clusters and bitonality; in the *Dances*, op 51 (1914), there are pieces based entirely on fourths (like the *White Songs* of op 48 for piano), on parallel triads and, again, in no 4 an open bitonal confrontation. Moving considerably backward in time, the five *Melomimics* of op 15 entitled 'Dreams' are fashioned almost exclusively from the whole-tone scale (these date from the turn of the century or before) and nos 4, 5 and 6 of the *Melomimics*, op 11 all end on unresolved discords.

Meagre as this selection from his completed works may be, it nevertheless reveals clearly enough that Rebikov on his own initiative ran virtually the whole gamut of Impressionist harmonic effects. Unfortunately he proved himself rarely able to use them impressionistically. His technique was inferior to Grieg's—Grieg would never have written the descending secondary sevenths at the climax of the second of the *Autumn Flowers* (although there is nothing in the remainder of the piece which he need have been ashamed of), and what appears in the following bars to be a sequence of parallel dominant thirteenths is in fact a series of 5–1 progressions tastelessly overburdened with appoggiaturas and elliptically resolved. Similarly, for two-thirds of its length no 3 of the set is good music, but at the climax the composer must resort to parallel sevenths by which he then becomes so obsessed that the remainder of the piece consists of nothing else. The wholly negative results of this approach to Impressionist harmony can easily be demonstrated if one plays the 'Lyric piece' (no 9 of the *Tone Poems* for piano, op 13) first as the composer wrote it, liberally sprinkled with bare fourths, then with some of these fourths filled out with thirds below to become first inversions, in other words with the harmonic system so conventionalized as to win instant nineteenth-century academic approval. The latter version sounds natural and convincing, the original freakish and contrived. Compare this with the climax of 'The shepherd's pipe' (no 8 of the *Silhouettes*, op 31, for piano) in which the sustained unresolved secondary seventh at bar 12 is a natural outgrowth of the rapid scalic figurations going on above it, not an alien superposition (Ex. 12); its effect is to pick up their overtones and fuse them

Ex. 12
Rebikov, 'The Shepherd's Pipe' (*Silhouettes*)

impressionistically together. The moral of this passage is that harmony cannot be used as a substitute for melody in music which is basically melodically-conceived—in other words new wine cannot be poured into old bottles. If a piece of music is to use advanced Impressionist harmonic devices, it must be impressionistically conceived as a whole. Rebikov was a tragic example of a composer whose imagination and ambition far exceeded the limits of his positive creative talent.

1. The title of the opening movement of the Second Orchestral Suite—'Jeu de Sons'—reveals just such a penchant for this abstract juggling with sonorities, and the use of accordions in the 'Scherzo burlesque', and of harp glissandi in the 'Rêves d'enfant' show a very Debussian preoccupation with the exotic, with the colourful, with anything which transcended the crushing tedium of the Conservatory.

2. Compare the rising harp arpeggio in the closing bars (triad with added major seventh) with 'Jeux de vagues', from fig. 41 to the end.

3. Or did they? Rimsky interrupted his work on Act III of *The Golden Cockerel* to go to Paris to hear *Pelléas;* the orchestration was not completed until his return.

4. It is difficult to believe that Holst, in 'Mars' or 'Jupiter' or the Fugal Overture, was unfamiliar with this passage.

4

WAGNER IN FRANCE

After completing the *Lohengrin* prelude in 1847 Wagner seemed attacked by a prolonged fit of creative impotence. Although fragments and motifs for *The Ring* must have been forming themselves in his imagination, he found concentrated work on the project as yet impossible; he seemed to lack the ignition key necessary to set the the wheels of the cosmic cycle in motion. Although many of the *Ring* landscapes were first envisaged amid the scenic wonders of the Alps around Albisbrunn in 1851, not until September 1853 in Italy did true inspiration come his way. In a hotel in Spezia he fell into a quasi-cataleptic trance and seemed engulfed by water whose rushing sound made the tonality of E♭ major swirl in his ears. The triad was broken and reverberated with ever-increasing intensity.

This was the genesis of the *Rheingold* prelude, and, by extension, of much of the salient thematic material of the operatic cycle. Ravel once described his *Boléro* as consisting of 'orchestral tissue without music' and in a sense the same is true of this prelude, for there is no actual 'music' in the sense that Ravel was using the term, merely an E♭ major triad prolonged over some 130 bars. The attention is focused not so much upon the abstract constitution of the musical idea—which is rudimentary in the extreme—as upon the means of its expression. The interest lies rather in the changing patterns of orchestral colour and texture than in any formal dialectic, and the appeal is not so much to the intellect as to the nerves. The E♭ triad is the only raw material, the only 'music' of the entire passage; the 'tissue' consists of a carefully-calculated intensification and accumulation of timbre, a subtly-contrived interplay of rhythmic and melodic shapes which form, dissolve and merge into figures and outlines essentially similar yet seen afresh through changing colours of the orchestral spectrum.[1] The effect is of a constant process of fusion and regeneration of texture, sonority and movement, and the music emerges as something far more than an attempt to evoke the atmosphere of the bed of the Rhine with its rushing mighty waters. It is an extremely complex and subtle synthesis of mood, thought and sensation, a musical expression of the stirring of those hidden forces in our inner consciousness caused by stimulation of our outward perception.

Wagner was, in fact, the first to negotiate a stronger, deeper and more positive alliance between music and the other arts. Since music, no less than art and literature, is an attempt to give expression to the creator's personal vision of truth and springs from the same fundamental impulses of the human spirit, it is obviously desirable that the expressive potential of music, the range of ideas and emotions over which it has control, should at least be commensurate with those of poetry or painting. Wagner saw quite clearly that, in this respect, music was still at a comparatively primitive stage of development, and he set out to repair the deficiency. He aspired to the creation of a 'total' art experience. In his operas décor, poetry, mime and music are intermingled freely; the opera is not only music but also myth; and the legendary foundation of the libretti offers the widest appeal to human and also to racial feelings.

We know that the techniques of musical Impressionism were the first-fruits of this newly consummated union between music and the other arts, and we have examined the new areas of feeling to which music in due course found herself empowered to aspire in emulation of the Impressionist–Symbolist æsthetic. Since Wagner was thus ultimately responsible for adding this new dimension to the expressive orbit of music, we may not unreasonably expect to find some presentiment of Impressionist technique in his own work. We find it first, surely, in the *Rheingold* prelude discussed above, and we shall find others if we examine his innovatory treatment of those elements recognized as the chief agents of the emotional in music, the emotional versus the logical, instinct *vis-à-vis* reason—tone-colour, texture and harmony. Wagner was the first to take advantage of the remarkable wealth of colour obtainable from the orchestral families when they were intermingled freely like colours on a painter's palette. His was the same mid-nineteenth century preoccupation with colour that we may note in the paintings of Constable and Turner, the poetry of Hugo and

Swinburne, or the novels of Balzac and Dickens; and to achieve his ends Wagner required of all departments of the orchestra an unprecedented degree of virtuosity. He brought a new self-awareness to the instrumental ensemble, a new poetry. To the woodwind he imparted a silvery fleetness in ensemble, in solo playing a flair for exquisite tiny fragments of melody or long flowing lines of sustained eloquence. To the grandiloquent swagger of the brass he added a mellow-toned range of rich browns and reds, and by his multi-division of the string body he achieved a new warmth, a pliancy, an untrammelled ebb and flow of harmonic polyphony capable of a high degree of expressive intensity.

In depicting nature Wagner was thus able to attain a measure of sophisticated realism which strongly influenced the Impressionists. We have seen how his novel conception of orchestral sound permitted him to evoke the surging of waters along the river-bed in a way that had previously been impracticable; later in the first scene of *Das Rheingold* 'there breaks through the water from above a continuously brightening glow which kindles to a dazzling gleam of bright shining gold, and magical golden light streams from it through the water—the 'Rhinegold'. The play of light through water—a subject-area which, as we have seen, the Impressionists were to make peculiarly their own, and Wagner's technique is prophetic. He sounds the Rhinegold motif on the brass in the bass but above it maintains an undulating triplet movement on divided strings and woodwind, revolving harmonically round the chord of the added sixth (Ex. 13a). To suggest the 'ever-brightening glow' the triplets are broken down into nonuplets resulting in, virtually, a major triad with added sixth and ninth (Ex. 13b). This type of shimmering, quivering texture was to become a favourite atmospheric device of the Impressionists; it is found for instance in the scene with Yniold and the sheep in Act IV of Debussy's *Pelléas et Mélisande*, in Bartók's 'Floraison' (the first of the *Deux Images*) or in the opening section of Bax's *Tintagel*. The reiterated rhythmic pattern of triplets, sextolets or nonuplets suggests not so much movement as the illusion of movement[2] similar to that created by the flickering of light upon water, and in combination with the warmth of added-note harmony and the limpidity of orchestral timbre the effect is akin to that of iridescence.

Even more influential in this respect has been the celebrated passage in Act II of *Siegfried* where, into the drowsy murmur of trees deep in the sunlit forest there obtrudes a twitter of bird-song—the *Waldweben*.

Ex. 13a and 13b
Wagner, *Das Rheingold*

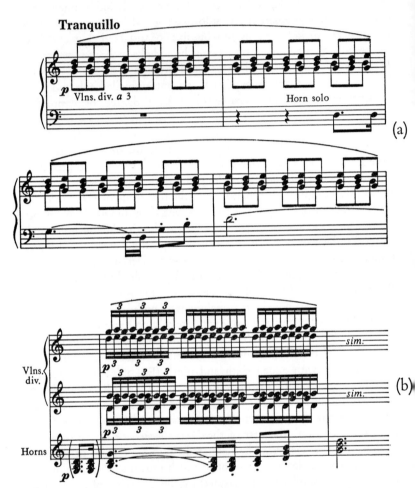

This is the first true Impressionist evocation of nature in her tranquillities. The multi-divided strings, half muted, half unmuted, whisper
and rustle over a deep tonic pedal-point of horns and double-basses,
and a fleet play of oboe and flute (later also clarinet) arabesque indicates
the presence of the woodbird (Ex. 14)—an enchanted atmosphere
recaptured in many a magical page of Debussy and Ravel. The poet

Ex. 14
Wagner, *Waldweben* (*Siegfried*)

and critic Jules Laforgue, one of the first to perceive an affinity between Wagner and Impressionism, commented after studying an exhibition of Impressionist art that the pictures seemed to be composed of 'a thousand dancing touches of colour like the "voices in the forest" of Wagner'. It was this same fleeting, intangible quality, wonderfully shaded colour combinations and differentiated light effects which Strauss perceived in Turner's paintings and compared to the *Feuerzauber* music in *Die Walküre*, consisting as it does (as he describes it) of 'an impression of seething flames flickering in a thousand tints'.

A like sensitivity to broad effects of colour and light is to be found in the final scene of *Rheingold*, and again the technical means employed —a variant of the foregoing—were to pass into the lingua franca of Impressionism. After Donner has swung his hammer, 'the clouds disperse, and a rainbow bridge stretches with dazzling radiance across the valley to the castle which now glows in the light of the setting sun' —a technicolour panorama which is evoked by Wagner through a broad span of diatonic melody in the lower regions of the orchestra, with an opalescent shimmer of added sixth arpeggios in high strings and woodwind. It is easy to see in this marvellous passage the progenitor of the dawn scene in *Daphnis et Chloé.*

Wagner was equally adept at creating a sensuous atmosphere less specific in reference. One of the main preoccupations of the Impressionists in general, and of Debussy in particular, was, as we have noted, with the world of night, sleep and dreams—the world of *Tristan und Isolde* and even more of *Parsifal*, with its dark, suggestive symbolism. The Impressionist–Symbolist world derived in the main from Baudelaire and through him from Poe, Wagner's world from Schopenhauer, Novalis and Friedrich von Schlegel; but the appeal of his music and even more of his æsthetic doctrines (his ideal of the *Gesamtkunstwerk* found a ready parallel in Baudelaire's poem 'Correspondances')[3] was powerful enough to enthrone him as the musical mascot of the Symbolist movement in French literature. The fact is that in *Tristan* Wagner's style began to change from the relatively explicit to the allusive and evocative. At the beginning of Act II, the distant re-echoing hunting-horns merge imperceptibly in Isolde's mind—and in the music—with the soft murmur of the fountains, a state of dreamy sensuous imprecision which the poet of the *Waldweben* knew well how to convey. The transition from distant horns through mellow clarinets to muted strings is beautifully effected (Ex. 15) and Wagner's is a truly impressionistic 'harmonie du soir' anticipating the rapt nocturnal musings of Nietzsche's Zarathustra in Delius's *Mass of Life*, the languidly atmospheric centre panel of Debussy's *Ibéria*, 'Cloches à travers les feuilles' or 'Les sons et les parfums tournent dans l'air du soir'. The *Tristan* horns are recalled at the end of the latter piece[4] by a short fanfare-like phrase marked 'comme une lointaine sonnerie de cors', later directed to be played 'encore plus lointain et plus retenu'.

In *Tristan* Wagner showed himself particularly sensitive to the atmospheric potency of sounds emanating from an unseen source, and the Impressionists were not slow to exploit this. The unaccompanied solo of the unseen sailor which opens Act I, the extraordinarily lugubrious piping of the shepherd in Act III, who does not appear until he has finished playing (his tune has elusive oriental or medieval overtones), anticipates the scene with Yniold and the sheep in *Pélleas*,

Ex. 15
Wagner, *Tristan und Isolde*

where her questions with reference to the animals disappearing into the gathering dusk are answered by a shepherd 'qu'on ne voit pas'. The same aura of mystery, strangeness, elusiveness, indefiniteness again surrounds the plaintive beauty of the pentatonic oboe solo in *La boîte à Joujoux* played by 'un pâtre qui n'est pas d'ici', so reminiscent of Grieg's 'Evening in the Mountains' and of the introduction to Vaughan William's *Flos Campi*. The opening scene of Act II of *Tristan* is given an added depth of mystery not only by the fact that the horns are placed off-stage, but also because the music they play is compounded of interlocking fourths and fifths producing a primitive pentatonic sonority—another example of the affinity between Impressionist harmonic innovations and harmonic effects produced naturally by the acoustic properties of certain instruments, between Impressionism and primitivism.

The glimmering, phosphorescent tones of the whole of the great Tristan–Isolde *Liebesnacht* which follows are as suggestive of the sultry warmth of the summer night and the heady fragrance of the flowers in the garden as of the lover's rapture, and the prelude to Act III is one of the most broodingly atmospheric pieces of music Wagner ever wrote. Gloom and melancholy hang like a pall over ruined Kareol and a Tristan sick unto death: the scene could almost belong to Poe's *Fall of the House of Usher* and Wagner's music could almost be evoking the oppressive, death-laden atmosphere in Mélisande's bedchamber. Gerald Abraham has shown that in his original version the composer actually experimented with the whole-tone scale here, and although he modified the passage later it still retains a curious whole-tonal flavour; the slowly upward-drifting violin thirds, finally disintegrating tonelessly in the stratosphere recall Liszt's *Nuages Gris*, which in turn anticipated Debussy's 'Nuages'. Significantly, the orchestral textures in both these sections of *Tristan* are prophetic of *Parsifal*—significantly because of all Wagner's operas the instrumentation of *Parsifal* held the greatest fascination for Debussy. The orchestration of *Jeux*, he told André Caplet, 'is required to produce an orchestral colour illuminated as from behind, of which there are such wonderful effects in *Parsifal*'; and it was again this opera which he mentioned to Stravinsky in speaking of *Petrushka*. The 'tour de passe-passe' section in *Petrushka* 'has a kind of sonorous magic . . . an orchestral infallibility which I have found only in *Parsifal*'.

The orchestral technique of *Parsifal* differs from its predecessors among Wagner's operas, and for a curiously mundane reason. Having scored *The Ring* for an orchestra of gigantic proportions, the composer found in practice that from Act II of *Die Walküre* onwards, the singers' voices too often became engulfed in a deluge of orchestral sound. To counteract this he experimented with the covered-over orchestral pit at

Bayreuth, but unfortunately found that, while the sheer volume of sound was effectively reduced by this expedient, the knife-edged clarity of the scoring was necessarily sacrificed in the process. Therefore the instrumental design of the *Parsifal* score was actually conceived in terms of the muted effect produced by the submerged orchestra. Hence, in Robert W. Gutman's words:

> . . . in *Parsifal* a tenuous, fluctuating Impressionistic light replaces the glow of *Tristan* and the hard glare so often glancing from *Meistersinger*, the final scene of *Siegfried*, and *Götterdämmerung* . . . the music hovers and evaporates like the kaleidoscopic images of Symbolist poetry. The atmosphere of the whole work is dream-like, the musical texture transparent, rare and vaporous . . . the disintegrating world for which Wagner feared is realised in vast and airy tonal vistas. The world of musical Impressionism arose from the opera's wondrous orchestral textures. *Pelléas* was to be its child, though a son who reacted against the father he so resembled.

If Wagner was thus one of the first to woo the pure sensuous beauty of orchestral sound he was also very much alive to the prodigious emotive potential of chromatic harmony and to the valuable, even indispensable, part it had to play in the weaving of a sheerly sensuous texture. We saw how in Ex. 13 the undulating figures in the treble produced chords of the added sixth and ninth respectively; in Act I of *Siegfried* Mime's distempered imagination, as he seems to sense Fafner's approach in the weird flickering and glinting of the forest, is tellingly suggested by parallel augmented triads, and in the prelude to Act II of *Tristan* the agglomerated fourths and fifths of the hunting fanfares momentarily prefigure bitonality, fourths-chords and the pentatonic scale. Wagner's modernistic tendency to overthrow the time-honoured regulations governing preparation and resolution of dissonance—in which he strikingly anticipated the Impressionists—is well illustrated by the famous opening bars of the prelude to Act 1 of *Tristan* (Ex. 16).

Ex. 16
Wagner, *Tristan und Isolde*

There is nothing new about the so-called semi-diminished chord at * in itself; what is new is that it is entirely unprepared and only seemingly resolved—its 'resolution' in fact consists of another discord, the dominant seventh, which by classical standards ought to be resolved and here, again, is not. There is sound psychological justification for the iconoclastic use of this chord: the chord itself thus isolated has all the impact of some profound emotional shock, the repercussions of which have insinuated themselves into the innermost recesses of the psyche, and the non-resolution, and subsequent repetition and non-resolution, indicate a profound mental turmoil and great spiritual tension.

In this way Wagner charged his chromatic discords with a weight of emotive association which far exceeded the scope of previous explorations in these regions, and it was obviously but a short step to Debussy's empirical use of these chords as individual points of sensation. The essentially polyphonic character of Wagner's harmony precluded the possibility of any such total emancipation in his own music; yet from *Das Rheingold* onwards (after he had become aware of certain harmonic innovations in Liszt's *Orpheus* and other symphonic poems) he freed many chords hitherto classed as dissonances from the restrictive practices of the classical era, in particular the dominant ninth. For instance, the magnificent orchestral passage in Act III of *Siegfried* which accompanies the hero's ascent of the 'Magic Mountain' is based on the 'Rhinemaidens' motif, in which an appoggiatura ninth is very prominent. The music progresses climactically from one statement of the theme to another on a higher degree of the scale, working a contrapuntal pattern of a number of pertinent motives in between; the effect is thus essentially that of a series of parallel ninth chords. With such unprecedented freedom in the use of chromatic discords, suspensions, appoggiaturas and accented passing-notes, unconditional emancipation was evidently only a matter of time.

Although the labyrinthine chromaticism of *Parsifal* looks forward to Reger and Schoenberg rather than to Debussy, the emotional intensity of *Tristan* had already left its mark on two French composers by whose music the young Debussy was not to go uninfluenced. These composers—César Franck and Emmanuel Chabrier—are key figures, in their different ways, in the astonishing cult of Wagner which persisted for some 20 years and affected not only musicians, but also important literary and philosophical personalities. The *Revue Wagnérienne* ran from 1885 to 1887 and those who collaborated in the undertaking included Villiers de l'Isle-Adam, Mallarmé and Catulle Mendès. This periodical, together with its successor, the *Revue Indépendante*, reveals how deeply Wagner's philosophy and æsthetics had penetrated French artistic thought by the time Debussy was ready to produce his first representative works; and though Wagner's purely musical influence had begun to decline before this, so saturated was the general intellectual atmosphere of the age with the Wagnerian ethos that only a musical intelligence of superhumanly independent outlook could have remained totally impervious to it. It is therefore hardly to be wondered at that the impressionistic traits in the music of Franck and Chabrier can be directly related to their susceptibility to Wagner.

Franck was never an ardent Wagnerian, and one may search in vain for any of the overt manifestations of enthusiasm so familiar in the case of his disciples d'Indy, Duparc and Chausson. However the very fact that for these three composers, as for others of their generation, Wagnerolatry should be allied to a profound love and reverence for Franck points unmistakably to some degree of spiritual and stylistic affinity between the two mentors. Broadly speaking, Franck, like Wagner, was a sensualist whose eroticism sought musical expression through chromatic harmony, and this, combined with the strong vein of emotional religiosity which manifested itself early in his career, imparts a mystico-sensual *ambiance* to the latter's work which is strikingly akin to that of *Parsifal*. How much of Wagner's work Franck knew and how well he knew it must to a great extent remain a matter of conjecture,[5] but it is significant that all his greatest works were written after 1874, when he would have had a chance to hear the *Tristan* prelude at a Pasdeloup concert. The obvious Wagnerian reminiscences in Franck's music are pre-eminently those of *Tristan*.

From the harmonic point of view the denominator common to Wagner and Franck was Liszt. We have noted that Wagner absorbed harmonic ideas from *Orpheus* and other symphonic poems into *Das Rheingold* and *Tristan*; Liszt was certainly one of the greatest influences on Franck's formative years. However in his later works the boldness of Franck's harmony outstrips Wagner's. He was one of the first to discern, implicit in the Wagnerian concept of emancipated dissonance, the parallel-chord technique; this he then applied to the chord which in Wagner's harmonic syntax approached most nearly to this process, the dominant ninth—Debussy was to accord similar treatment to even higher chromatic discords. The opening of the first movement of the

Violin Sonata offers a choice example of this pre-Debussian harmonic hedonism: the protagonist is the beautifully poised dominant ninth which takes its place at the outset as naturally and unselfconsciously as any common chord, and holds the stage for a full four bars before the solo violin takes flight. The B minor modulation at bar 6 is but a momentary change of perspective; the dominant chord returns in the next bar, and only with the modulation to A major in bar 8 is full resolution attained. Thus the dominant ninth is the pre-eminent structural entity of this passage.

The cantata–symphonic poem *Psyché* forms the most interesting compendium of Franck's pre-Impressionist harmonic techniques. The third movement, 'Les jardins d'Éros', opens with a gentle play of woodwind figuration based entirely on the pentatonic scale (Ex. 17.) It must be remembered that the appeal of the pentatonic scale in the most familiar of its five transpositions (i.e. the diatonic major scale without

Ex. 17
Franck, *Psyché*

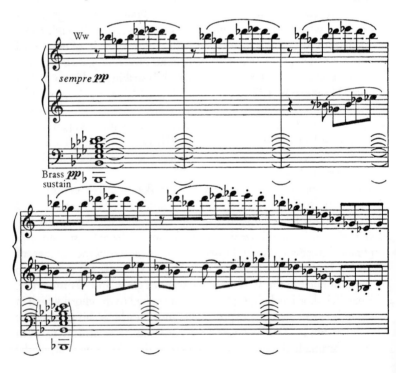

the fourth or seventh) lay largely in the fact that its constituent notes, when sounded vertically, formed the luscious sonority of major triad with added sixth and ninth; the added sixth was to become in later years one of the worst platitudes of commercial harmony, but here it is as yet devoid of such associations. This opening passage—a glitter of pentatonic figuration over static deep-breathed pentatonic chords—anticipates quite remarkably the first movement of Debussy's *Estampes* for piano, 'Pagodes'. Added-sixth harmony is again in evidence in the form of chiming horn chords accompanying the second theme and the falling fourths of the third. In a magnificent recapitulation the second theme is rhythmically developed with a striking series of parallel-ninth chords, and in the coda this same theme appears in C major, oscillating between the sixth and fifth of the scale and all but coming to rest on an unresolved added-sixth chord as, indeed, several of Debussy's works, and even more of Delius's, were later to do.

It was not only in the sphere of harmony that Franck proved himself a harbinger of Impressionism. Although his orchestration is in many cases disappointingly pedestrian and belies the vitality of his thought, the opening of his unpublished symphonic poem *Ce qu'on entend sur la montagne*[6] is, according to Norman Demuth, markedly Impressionistic in character, with a gently-moving viola theme under sustained violin harmonics—presumably anticipating 'De l'aube à midi sur la mer'. These tendencies are developed in only one of Franck's later works, but the result is a true anticipation of Debussy. The work in question is the symphonic poem *Les Éolides*. The ethereal fragility of this music is of the same cast as that of the Scherzo of the String Quartet and lies at the farthest remove from the Lisztian rhetoric of *Le Chasseur Maudit*; Franck made a remarkably successful effort to complement the spirit of the poem by Leconte de Lisle, which takes as its subject the daughters of Aeolus, god of the breezes. Franck evokes, he does not depict. To this end the strings are freely divided, sometimes into as many as eight parts, which was unheard of in the France of the 1870s; the woodwind sparkle and glitter; the use of the brass is restrained and the colouristic properties of harp and suspended cymbal (a favourite device of the Impressionists) are discreetly exploited.

The textures are thus light, airy and phosphorescent, the effect fragrant, elusive and freely sensuous. The momentary onslaught at the climax is extrovert and bracing in a manner unique in Franck's work, and surely anticipates the surging breakers of *La Mer* or the hedonistic abandon of *L'Isle Joyeuse*; this may be ascribed to the significant fact that inspiration for this work came while the composer was on holiday in Valence near Grenoble in the south of France. Here he experienced at first hand the impact of the mistral, the biting north wind which sweeps across south-east France. This cannot fail to suggest the discovery made by the Impressionist painters that working out of doors, in direct contact with nature, offered them a wealth of new inspiration. The one weakness of *Les Éolides* is its form; Franck eschews conventional development in favour of a sprawling mosaic consisting of seemingly interminable repetitions and alternations of the principal themes. Yet its very weakness is its strength, for the composer had instinctively realized that in this particular case his conception would not lend itself to symphonic manipulation in the traditional way; so he chose the only alternative available to him. He was unknowingly groping his way towards a new æsthetic of style and formal design which was to find its perfect realization some twenty years later in the *Prélude à l'Après-midi d'un Faune*.

Debussy's personal relations with Franck were not of the happiest; it is difficult to imagine an instrument more antipathetic to the Debussian sensibilities than the organ, and the time spent by the *enfant prodigue* in the organ class of the *père séraphique* at the Conservatoire was predictably unfruitful and of short duration. Amongst other irritants, Debussy was so incensed by his teacher's continual exhortations to modulate that he later referred to him as the *machine à moduler*. None the less, for Franck as a composer he had a healthy respect and spoke with particular warmth of the Symphony and the Piano Quintet. Franck's more specific influence upon Debussy can be observed in the early *Fantaisie* for piano and orchestra, in the String Quartet with its cyclic format, and above all in *La Mer*. No other work by Debussy reverts so closely to traditional methods of symphonic construction, and it is one of the finest examples of the truly creative use of cyclic motifs. Furthermore, several of the themes themselves are of an undeniably Franckian cast. The first of the cyclic motifs (oboe, p. 2 of the miniature score) pivots around its G$\sharp$ in a manner very reminiscent of Franck; the third cyclic theme (p. 29) is a majestic brass chorale, Franckian in ethos if not in design; and the second main thematic element in the finale (woodwind, p. 89) is, with its semitonal ambiguity, the most Franckian of all. Franck died in 1890, three years before *L'Après-midi*. Though he did not profess to understand the *Ariettes Oubliées* of 1888, he nevertheless described them as 'de la musique sur les pointes d'aiguilles'—which conveys, in fact, the very effect for which Debussy was striving and which indicates the nervous, *pointilliste* appeal of his textures even in those comparatively early days.

When in 1882 Renoir conversed with Wagner on the subject of 'the Impressionists in music'—seemingly the first time the term was applied to music—it is highly probably that he was thinking, if not exclusively, of Chabrier's *Pièces Pittoresques* for piano which had been published the previous year. Of all the composers who contributed to the formation of the Impressionist style in music, Chabrier was the only one to be intimately involved in the world of Impressionist art itself, and he alone, before Debussy, tended to introduce into his music effects clearly derived from the Impressionists' theories of the handling of colour and light. He was, in fact, much more closely connected than Debussy with the Impressionist painters themselves, and he not only had his portrait painted by them no fewer than three times (twice by Manet and once by Renoir) but also owned at his death one of the greatest, probably the greatest, of contemporary collections of Impressionist pictures—this at a time when such art was still imperfectly appreciated and worth but a fraction of its present value.

In his early days Chabrier had even considered making painting his career, and although in the early 1860s he was obliged to enter the Ministry of the Interior (the French Home Office) to earn a living, he lost no time in finding his way into the salons frequented by many of the poets, painters and musicians then prominent in Parisian society. He became a particular friend of Verlaine and even collaborated with him on two little *opéras-bouffes*; becoming a regular visitor to the Verlaine household he would often play piano duets with Charles de Sivry, Verlaine's brother-in-law, who was responsible for furthering the musical interests of the boy Debussy. Chabrier's innate feeling for the plastic arts made him into something of a connoisseur of painting and he instinctively appreciated the true merit of the *avant-garde* school of Impressionism which at that time was still scandalizing society and the Establishment. In 1879, on the occasion of the second Impressionist exhibition, Chabrier purchased four Manets, having in the meantime formed a close friendship with the painter (Manet actually died in Chabrier's arms, and Chabrier shortly before his own death expressed a wish to be buried beside him), and at his death his collection included eleven Manets, eight Monets, six Renoirs, two Sisleys and one Cézanne.

If his artistic sympathies thus lay with the Impressionists, his lifelong idol was the by no means incompatible figure of Wagner, and it was from a choice blend of these two influences that Chabrier evolved his advanced brand of musical Impressionism. His works may be roughly divided into two categories: those in which he openly aspires to the grand Wagnerian manner (e.g. the opera *Gwendoline* or the cantata *La Sulamite*), and those in which Wagnerian phraseology and texture is more thoroughly assimilated into the composer's own idiom, e.g. the *Bourrée Fantasque* for piano or the orchestral rhapsody *España*. Naturally the latter works are those which represent the quintessential Chabrier and which have won him the greatest esteem; they also attracted the particular attention of the younger generation in France, notably Debussy and Ravel and, even later, Poulenc, Honegger and Milhaud. Like Debussy, Chabrier responded freely to the purely sensuous phenomena of orchestral colour and harmony; both composers strove for an uninhibited naturalism in music, and for Chabrier music was a steady spontaneous expression of his own ebullient personality, untrammelled by traditional concepts of syntax or structure. Hence the waywardness and asymmetry in his melodic patterns and phrases, the irrepressible *élan* of his rhythmic structure, the fearlessly unacademic employment of unprepared and unresolved dissonances in his harmony, and the variety and brilliance of his orchestral palette.

The emotional resonance of Wagner's work appealed as much to this sensual nature as to Debussy's, and simultaneously with Franck he developed the concept of parallel harmony implicit in *Tristan*, *The Ring* and *Parsifal*; but whereas Franck in general restricted himself to stepwise progressions of the dominant ninth, the overture to the comic opera *Le Roi Malgré Lui* freely employs ninths, added sixths, and sequences of dominant sevenths approached by leap. In fact, throughout Chabrier's work there runs this vein of rich post-Wagnerian harmony, and when in a work like *España* it is allied to his highly-developed orchestral sense the result is remarkable. Chabrier was one of the finest orchestrators of his day, having painstakingly acquired his technique through copying out the full scores of works such as the *Tannhäuser* overture. The warmth, colour and vitality of Spanish folk-music captivated him as Debussy was later to be captivated, and *España* spawned a distinguished if more sophisticated progeny in the form of *Ibéria* and Ravel's *Rapsodie Espagnole*. Chabrier's work however has such immediacy of impact that the orchestral canvas suggests the explosive colour combinations of the mature Cézanne or Van Gogh rather than the muted subtleties of Monet or Pissarro: a striking instance is the sudden irruption of the noisy swaggering trombone theme into a glinting void of harps and tremolo violas at the centre of the work. More nearly akin in texture and sonority to Debussy is 'Sous-bois', the third movement of the *Suite pastorale* (in fact orchestrations of four selected numbers from the *Pièces Pittoresques* for piano). The music suggests trees murmuring in the heat of the summer sun in some part of the Provençal countryside, and is predictably reminiscent of the *Waldweben*. In this little piece a fluid interchange of melody, harmony and rhythm is merged with a play of soft orchestral colours, gently shifting and reforming beneath the persistent ostinato-like murmur of cellos and basses; the melodic line is sensitively blurred through grace-notes, rests and wide-ranging intervals, the harmony alternates intriguingly between augmented fifths and common chords, and the tiny wisps and flecks of instrumental colour unfailingly call to mind the *pointilliste* technique in painting. 'Sous-bois', as an impressionistic evocation of nature in her tranquillities, forms the bridge between the *Waldweben* and the *Prélude à l'Après-midi d'un Faune*, and its chiaroscuro-like qualities even anticipate such a later development of the same technique as Delius's *Summer Night on the River*. Chabrier's striving for novel colour effects also prompted him to write a pianistic *tour de force*, the *Bourrée Fantasque*, in which the piano emulates the colouristic properties of the full orchestra. The central section deploys a wide range of rich chromatic harmony, the whole-tone scale used melodically and harmonically, and syncopated pedal-points of major seconds—all devices which Debussy was to make peculiarly his own.[7]

Aesthetically Chabrier lacked the intense preoccupation with personal sensation so characteristic of Debussy. His was a less introspective approach, less aristocratically sybaritic, and his music is more redolent of the traditionally Gallic qualities of *bonhomie* and *désinvolture*, neither of which is predominant in the exquisitely sculpted art of Debussy; in many ways, in fact, he anticipated the post-war *Six* with their mascot Satie, who initially promulgated a rigorously anti-Impressionist doctrine.[8] Nevertheless the fact remains that Chabrier was the first to translate the Impressionist theories from visual terms of colour and light to aural, and to fuse the stylistic aims and tendencies of those adjacent provinces of the imaginative mind in a manner previously deemed impracticable. It is noteworthy that whereas Debussy was generally inconsistent in his attitude towards the composers who had most influenced him, of Chabrier he spoke unfailingly in the warmest terms. 'Chabrier, Mussorgsky, Palestrina—voilà ce que j'aime'—he is reported to have said on one occasion, and to Gustave Samazeuilh he even admitted having been influenced by *La Sulamite* when composing *La Damoiselle Élue*. There were no barriers, personal, emotional or artistic, to be broken down, and for once Debussy was able to respond warmly and wholeheartedly to a fellow-artist's work, to establish a viable relationship with it and creatively to make it his own.

1. There took place in Paris in 1893 a lecture on *The Ring* given by the pretentious literary figure Catulle Mendès, to illustrate which Debussy and the piano virtuoso Raoul Pugno accompanied extracts from the operas on two pianos. Amazingly, they began with the *Rheingold* prelude, the fortunes of which in a piano reduction can readily be imagined.

2. cf. Anthony Cross's remark ('Debussy and Bartók', *Musical Times*, February 1967) that 'with Debussy, rhythm is frequently reduced to a continual vibration . . . to permit, as it were, the realisation of timbre-effects'. It is so here.

3. In his 1933 essay 'The Sufferings and Greatness of Richard Wagner' Thomas Mann drew a parallel between the influence of Wagner on Baudelaire and that of Poe: 'Wagner and Poe . . . what an extraordinary juxtaposition! Immediately we see the works of Wagner in a new light. We see a deeper colour in his work, a world haunted by death and beauty, intoxicated by sensuous refinement.' When Tristan in his delirious ecstasy at Isolde's approach to the shores of Kareol cries that he can hear the light, Wagner echoes the concept of the interchangeability of the senses, the fluidity of scent, sound and colour impressions—that suggestive indefiniteness of vague emotive states for which Poe and his European disciples favoured music above all.

4. There is also a vague reference to them in the opening bars of 'Recueillement', no 4 of the very Wagnerian *Cinq Poèmes de Charles Baudelaire*.

5. d'Indy recalls that at one time Franck studied Wagner's works 'passionné-ment' and that he used to play the overture to *Die Meistersinger* on the piano.

6. Liszt's attention may well have been drawn to the Hugo poem through acquaintance with this piece of juvenilia.

7. The third of the *Trois Valses Romantiques* hints at the Debussy of the parallel triad technique—and the Ravel of the 'white-note' minuets.

8. There has been controversy as to whether or not the parallel ninths of Satie's 1887 *Sarabande* influenced those of Debussy in his 'Sarabande' (in *Pour le piano*) of 1896. From our point of view this is immaterial since at no time did Satie, despite his harmonic unorthodoxy, in any way embrace the Impressionist aesthetic.

PART TWO

The Post-Impressionists

5

IN FRANCE

As early as 1895, when the only major works he had published were the String Quartet and *L'Après-midi d'un Faune*, Debussy was already aware that he was destined to have a dominant influence on music of the future. 'I am working', he said to his friend Pierre Louÿs, 'on things which will only be understood by our grandchildren in the twentieth century.' He did not aspire to the position of a *chef d'école*, nor, understandably, did he look with anything but disfavour on the 'Debussyistes', those lesser luminaries of his own and the next generation who were pilfering freely from the treasure-house of harmonic and textural novelties he had built himself. His truly creative influence, like that of all great artists, was not directly on individual composers but indirectly on the whole future development of music. Nevertheless, concerned as we are here with the purely Impressionist aspects of Debussy's style rather than the *grande envergure* of his art as a whole, we must here view the question of his influence in France from a particular rather than from a general vantage-point. In France, as elsewhere, there were a number of composers who could scarcely be classified among the small fry, the Debussyistes, but who nevertheless responded keenly to Impressionism and turned certain aspects of its syntax to their own advantage, widening the scope of their individual modes of expression without falling prey to the more immediately seductive of its mannerisms. The composers discussed below differed widely in temperament, musical intelligence and artistic outlook, but all of them were alike in that the nature of their response to Impressionism was essentially creative and not merely imitative. First, however, there is the formidable question of Debussy's most distinguished contemporary, Maurice Ravel.

When Ravel late in life heard a recording of the *Prélude à l'Après-midi d'un Faune* he turned to a friend with tears in his eyes and said: 'It was when I first heard that many years ago that I realized what music was.' Ravel emerged in 1895 a complete master of his craft without, apparently, ever having had to learn anything about it; nevertheless, as the remark quoted above clearly indicates, *L'Après-midi d'un Faune* was in fact the beginning of all his music, and he later repaid his debt to Debussy when the pianistic innovations of *Jeux d'Eau* helped shape the Impressionist piano style of the *Estampes* and later works (at the time of *Jeux d'Eau* Debussy had written nothing of any great moment for the piano except the pianistically rather jejune *Pour le Piano*.)

In the early days the two composers were often confused with each other. Although today we can see the very clear distinctions between them, it is foolish to deny obvious affinities or to minimize the extent to which Ravel wrote under the aegis of Impressionism. Of this he evolved his own highly personal brand, but the initial stimulus came from Debussy, and it is for this reason that he is here codified as a 'post-Impressionist' even though his major works were being written contemporaneously with Debussy's. There were certainly many factors linking him with Debussy and the Impressionist æsthetic. He was less inhibited than Debussy in proclaiming his indebtedness to the composers whose harmonic originality he admired—Liszt, Grieg, and especially Chabrier and Satie. More overtly than Debussy he championed the cause of the Russian Nationalists—there was a deep underlying affinity between him and Rimsky-Korsakov which consisted not merely in a child-like enjoyment of lavishly exotic orchestral coloration but also in their common conception of art as, fundamentally, artifice. To Mussorgsky he paid practical tribute in the form of an orchestration of *Pictures at an Exhibition* and, in collaboration with Stravinsky, of *Khovanshchina* (Stravinsky said that he was the only musician who immediately understood *The Rite of Spring*). Balakirev and Borodin he also admired, particularly the latter's Third Symphony and *In the Steppes of Central Asia*. Spain was another centre of mutual musical attraction; Ravel's *Rapsodie Espagnole*, *L'Heure Espagnole*, *Alborado del Gracioso* and other works are among the most distinguished examples of French musical Hispanicism. Debussy and Ravel shared many literary loves: Maeterlinck, Mallarmé, Verlaine (three poets whom they both set to music) Baudelaire, Poe, de l'Isle-Adam and Oscar Wilde. All these manifold interests and influences so conditioned the æsthetic and intellectual atmosphere of the period that any musician who reacted to them as positively as Ravel could scarcely fail to find himself cultivating what was in so many respects, as we have seen, their natural musical counterpart and complement—Impressionism.

The originality of Ravel's Impressionism lay in the compromise he effected between the studied vagueness and sensuousness of Debussian Impressionism on the one hand, and the clean hard contours, pragmatism and logic of classicism on the other. His was a classically objectified art; he deliberately distanced himself from his inspiration (he preferred stylized representations of nature to nature herself, and peopled his works with animals, children, marionettes and characters from myth and fairy-tale) in order to reduce to a minimum all danger of attack upon his excessively vulnerable sensibilities. But in the soundness and creativity of his response to Debussy's concept of emancipated harmony and the reconditioning of texture he was second to none.

His first Impressionist work, *Jeux d'Eau*, was at one and the same time a sterling piece of Impressionism in its own right and a landmark in the history of piano literature. Consciously modelled on Liszt's *Les Jeux d'Eaux à la Villa d'Este* (Liszt was the most important influence on Ravel's piano style) it inaugurated a quasi-renaissance of piano music in France and elsewhere, for in it for the first time he explored realms of expression diametrically opposed to the prevailing style of the German Romantics. It was the first piece to exploit to the full the illusory, evocative properties of the instrument. According to the pianist Ricardo Viñes, Ravel here recommended the use of the pedal in the higher registers to bring out 'not the clarity of the notes, but the hazy impression ("L'impression floue") of vibrations in the air'. A gravitation towards an ideal of pianistic Impressionism is clearly implied here, and it was undoubtedly this quality which attracted Debussy to *Jeux d'Eau* and prompted him thoroughly to revise his conception of piano sonority. However, the piece also pinpoints the essential difference between the Impressionist styles of Debussy and Ravel: Debussy aims at an all-enveloping haze, Ravel retains a certain firmness of line while capturing that fluidity which is the essence of musical Impressionism. Ravel's themes are real melodies, not motivic fragments, however subtly they may be embedded in or fused with a sensuous Impressionistic accompanimental texture. All the now familiar characteristics of Impressionist water music are here assembled as such for the first time—rippling arpeggio figuration in the right hand, melodic contours etched by the left, a strong pentatonic flavour (cf. Ex. 18), much play

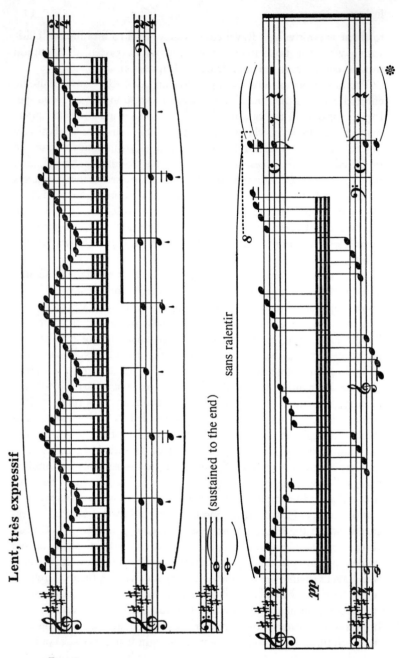

Ex. 18
Ravel, *Jeux d'Eau*

with open fourths and fifths, major seconds, ninths, elevenths and thirteenths in the harmony. Some variant of the pattern established by Ex. 18 (from the closing bars) is found in almost the entire progeny of this remarkable piece.

The three songs collectively entitled *Shéhérezade* were the first work by Ravel in which the influences of Rimsky-Korsakov and Debussy amalgamate, resulting in what might be termed the characteristic Franco-Russian Impressionist style which we shall encounter again in the music of Paul Dukas and Florent Schmitt. Tristan Klingsor's poems, nostalgic, exotically-coloured and romantically self-indulgent, lent themselves naturally to the luscious brand of hedonistic refinement, and this particular type of orchestral Impressionism was to be brought to a high pitch of virtuosity in *Daphnis et Chloé*. In the opening bars of 'Asie' a sophisticated Orientalism is given a new edge of Impressionist piquancy and nervousness (cf. the writing for strings and woodwind in bars 5–6), and elsewhere in the song the orchestra and harmony of *Antar* and *L'Après-midi d'un Faune* combine to produce many passages of sensuous, iridescent and shimmering sound. The flute arabesques in 'La flûte enchantée' look backward to *L'Après-midi* and forward to the *Daphnis et Chloé* dawn scene; and in 'L'Indifférent', the last song of the set, muted strings murmur and undulate in a way that derives ulti-mately from the *Waldweben*.

The influence of Debussy is less apparent in Ravel's next major Impressionist work, the *Miroirs* for piano. Described by the composer as 'a collection of piano pieces that mark a change in my harmonic development so profound as to put out of countenance many musicians who up to now have been the most familiar with my style', they establish what is henceforward to be the characteristically Ravelian norm of dissonance, a norm considerably more advanced than that of Debussy. Wholly typical is the first of the set, 'Noctuelles' (Moths), unmistakably Impressionistic in its nervous kaleidoscopic succession of flitting shapes and motions. Here again the impetus is basically melodic, but so evanescent and unsubstantial are the textures that the fact is barely perceptible. The second piece, 'Oiseaux tristes', evokes 'birds lost in the torpor of a dark forest during the most torrid hours of summertime' and is the most languidly atmospheric of the set with *Waldweben*-like undulating figuration and discreetly stylized bird-song. 'Une barque sur l'océan', Ravel's only piece of sea-music,[1] reverts to some extent to the manner of *Jeux d'Eau* with billowing waves of arpeggio and a descending arc of melody which attracts to itself the most prominent intervals of Impressionist harmony—the major second, open fourth and open fifth; and the opening is marked 'très doux et enveloppé de pédales'. 'La vallée des cloches', the first truly Impressionist bell-piece, is perhaps a natural development from Liszt's 'Cloches du soir' but is not as subtly contrived as Debussy's 'Cloches à travers les feuilles', undoubtedly the masterpiece of this genre. The opening of 'La vallée des cloches' is very impressionistic with tinkling consecutive fourths, harmony notes struck and sustained by pedals and overtones represented by dissonant gong-like sustained notes in the lower reaches of the keyboard; but the melodic and harmonic tissue later becomes comparatively well-defined.

We have noted Ravel's natural susceptibility to Russian and Russo-oriental music, and it was undoubtedly the exotic element in Spanish music which brought him, like Debussy, permanently under its sway. (His mother was a Basque and he was actually born in the province in the Pyrenees from which her family came). Although in his *Rapsodie Espagnole* he seemed to penetrate the Spanish folk-spirit less profoundly than Debussy in *Ibéria* (in this respect Falla's comparative lack of enthusiasm for Ravel's *espagnolerie* is significant), in this work Impressionist techniques are harnessed to the freely idiomatic treatment of popular dances in which Rimsky-Korsakov and Balakirev had specialized, the entire project thrown off with an almost Lisztian flamboyance and *désinvolture*. The most subtly evocative of all the movements is the first, the 'Prélude à la nuit', with its descending four-note ostinato pointed by dissonant seconds. Ravel's scoring here—and this in fact constitutes an essential distinction between Debussy's orchestral methods and his—is rather *pointilliste* than authentically Impressionist; he uses needle-sharp points of sonority, there is no blurring of contours, every detail tells—yet the most sensitive of one's nerve-ends respond to the whole, not to the parts.

Ravel's most celebrated piece of piano Impressionism is, like *Jeux d'Eau*, water music. *Gaspard de la Nuit* was inspired by the macabre Romanticism of three of Aloysius Bertrand's prose-poems, 'Ondine', 'Le Gibet' and 'Scarbo'. The opening lines of 'Ondine' determine the character of the musical substance:

Écoute! Écoute! C'est moi, c'est Ondine qui frôle de ces gouttes d'eau les losanges sonores de ta fenêtre illuminée par les mornes rayons de la lune: et voici, en robe de moire, la dame châtelaine qui contemple à son balcon la belle nuit étoilée et le beau lac endormi.

Chaque flot est un ondin qui nage dans le courant, chaque courant est un

sentier qui serpente vers mon palais, et mon palais est bâti fluide, au fond du
lac, dans le triangle du feu, de la terre et de l'air.

Over a shimmer of harmony in which the fifth of the major triad
alternates with the minor sixth with a quasi-tremolo effect, a magnificent
arc-like sweep of melody is brought gradually into focus, anticipating
the technique of the *Daphnis* dawn scene. This is wholly typical of
Ravel's more melodically-orientated Impressionism—the sturdy
thematic background gives consistent shape and purpose to the iridescent
wash of figuration. 'Le Gibet' broods dolefully round a syncopated
internal pedal-point which, again, controls the uneasily, incessantly
shifting harmonic textures and disciplines what might otherwise
emerge as a featureless expanse of sound.

If 'Ondine' is the *chef-d'œuvre* of Ravel's piano Impressionism, the
hushed and exalted *Daphnis et Chloé*, one of the great masterpieces of
twentieth-century music, has no rivals in the orchestral field. It is in the
richness and diversity of its scoring that part of its perennial fascination
lies. Ravel here employs fully a device which Debussy had introduced
in his 'Sirènes'—the wordless chorus, the contribution of which to the
sensuous sheen of this music should not be underrated. In the opening
scene the chorus is off-stage and evokes the luminous calm of a clear
spring afternoon in swaying fourths which evidently hail from
'Sirènes'. This choral rhythm dominates the introduction and the
'Danse religieuse', and, after swelling to a great climax, the music is
lulled by the voices, now singing *bouche fermée*, to a rapt dream-like
conclusion. In the same way they join the orchestra lost in contemplation of Daphnis and Chloë enfolded in each other's arms (after the
ungainly Dorcon has been vanquished in the dance-contest) and swathe
it in a golden aureole of sound. The nymphs' slow mysterious dance
after the brigands have abducted Chloë is markedly Impressionistic
with its subtly veiled bitonal harmony and glimmering, weirdly-muted
orchestral textures (multi-divided muted strings, often playing tremolo
and in harmonics); this dance is introduced by some shimmeringly
evocative high string tremolos to suggest the 'unreal light which
envelopes the landscape'. Not at all dissimilar is the long transitional
passage in which Pan sends his minions to intervene and save Chloë
from the rapacious brigands, with its evocative use of string and harp
glissandi and a sprightly dance-like motif for trumpets, answered by
flutes and celesta, which recalls the gambolling of the faun in the
afternoon sun, five bars after fig. 8 of *L'Après-midi*. But most impressionistic of all is the celebrated dawn scene, in which, in Wilfrid Mellers's

words, 'a cello melody of enormous span grows out of a shimmering void'. This 'shimmering void' is composed of opalescent ostinato-like woodwind figuration, writing which has no parallel in any other music, though its actual conception may well have its origin in the Rainbow Bridge music in *Rheingold* (see p. 96). Clearly articulated, these figurations suggest Pointillism; sensitively blurred—and they can be played either way—the effect is more strictly impressionistic. Piccolo (bird-song) and flute (shepherds passing in the distance) weave in their arabesques, and, when at bar 35 the wordless chorus enters with the swaying fourths of the opening, the cup is filled to overflowing.

Daphnis was Ravel's last extended essay in orchestral Impressionism. There are isolated instances in the later works in which the familiar techniques are called into play—the murky haze in which *La Valse* opens (tremolos in divided cellos and basses with fragments of a waltz motif struggling to break through on the bassoons) or the contra-bassoon rearing itself Fafner-like through a confused murmur of fourths figuration on divided double basses at the outset of the Concerto for the Left Hand. Similarly the garden scene in *L'Enfant et les Sortilèges*, with its nocturnal evocations of insects, birds and animals may for all its naivety owe something to the spirit of Impressionism. A rather different genre of Impressionism informs the songs with chamber-music accompaniment which Ravel wrote in 1913 in the wake of *Daphnis*, and which must be classed among his finest achievements— the *Trois Poèmes de Stéphane Mallarmé*. Although in fact Ravel's know-ledge of *Pierrot Lunaire* when composing these songs was limited (it appears that he had not even heard them), the vastly increased norm of harmonic dissonance and the scoring of the accompaniment for piano, string quartet, two flutes and two clarinets certainly suggest that Schoenberg's *pointilliste* masterpiece may have been lying at the back of his mind. In the first song, 'Soupir', there is a clear, firmly-sculpted melodic line but the accompaniment is markedly impressionistic; the first sixteen bars are pure pentatony, with the harmony growing out of the figuration (this returns by way of a coda) and the icily dissonant harmonic sequences which follow are evocative in intent—for the poem is an Impressionist evocation of autumn, and the music distils an appropriate atmosphere throughout. In the passage marked 'modéré-ment animé' in the second song, 'Placet futile', Ravel's approach is almost expressionistic in Schoenberg's manner and in the third, 'Surgi de la croupe et du bond', the thread of logical discourse is snapped altogether. The approach of this weird and shadowy interplay of opaquely dissonant harmonic shapes is purely nervous, notably in the final bars, where the voice sinks into subterranean night over glassily shimmering, spectral harmonies.[2]

After the première of *Pelléas* Debussy became, with a vengeance, a force to be reckoned with on the contemporary scene. No musician who prided himself on his awareness of contemporary trends in composition could afford to ignore him or belittle the significance of the changes, however dimly apprehended, which he had wrought in the very stuff of music. One wonders exactly how much self-searching and creative uncertainty these new phenomena caused the redoubtable *pontifex maximus* of the Schola Cantorum, Vincent d'Indy. On the basis of the distinction generally drawn between him and Debussy—in that the latter's perceptions and responses were primarily instinctive and sensuous, d'Indy's rational and intellectual, that whereas Debussy was an *homme de cœur*, d'Indy was an *homme de tête*—there appears to be no point of contact between them whatsoever. In many respects, however, this is a facile generalization. First, there was little personal animosity between them; as usual it was the Debussyistes and not Debussy himself who insisted on antagonizing the Schola and its irascible director (just as they were responsible for the strained relations between Debussy and Ravel), and there is no evidence that d'Indy was ever openly hostile to or destructively critical of any of Debussy's compositions; his response to *Pelléas* was by no means wholly negative, though naturally he had his reservations. Reciprocally, Debussy was very favourably impressed with d'Indy's opera *L'Étranger*, of which he heard the première in December 1903, describing it in *Monsieur Croche* as a work of 'perfect balance' and 'unforgettable beauty'. The sea music of the orchestral prelude to Act I, Vita's apostrophe to the sea in Act II, Scene 2, the *Pelléas*-like off-stage sea chorus (wordless) at the climax of the same scene, the magnificent storm scene with which the work concludes—all this may well have acted as a mental fillip to the composer who, six months later, was to start committing *La Mer* to paper. In fact—and herein perhaps lies the real secret of the Debussy-d'Indy affinity—d'Indy's uncompromisingly professional, patriarchal exterior concealed a countryman with a passionate love of nature, especially of mountain scenery. His ancestral home was at Les Faugs, high in the mountains of the Vivarais, and he would return there regularly every summer for inspiration and recreation; much of his time was taken up with drawing and sketching, since he was in fact an excellent amateur topographical artist. His love of this country is implicit in a number of early works—*La Forêt Enchantée*, a 'symphonic ballad' after Uhland, the *Poème des Montagnes*[3] and the *Tableaux de Voyage*, both for piano (the latter a set of thirteen impressions of the Black Forest and Austrian Tyrol)—and his most popular work, the *Symphonie Cévénole*, is based on a Vivarais folk-melody.

The stars in d'Indy's heaven were basically twofold—Franck and Wagner, both in their different ways harbingers of Impressionism. Given this love of nature and of Wagner, it is hardly surprising that his best work, *Jour d'Été à la Montagne*, written in 1905 (the year of *La Mer*), is Wagnerian in that nature is represented, not in any mystical or pantheistic spirit (as in *La Mer* or Delius's *Song of the High Hills*) but as an ever-changing panoramic backdrop to human activity and emotion, just like the sea in Vaughan Williams's *Sea Symphony*. The opening of the first movement, 'Aurore' (conjuring up, as Laurence Davies has said, the sharp scent of pine as it floats across the mountainous Cévennes) is unquestionably impressionistic —wide-spread octaves on muted strings occasionally rising to the fifth and then retreating; an inkling of the whole-tone scale on a solo bassoon; woodwind sextolets accompanying a chromatic figure in unison string octaves (rather Holstian); snatches of birdsong on wood-wind, strings quivering in the manner of the *Waldweben*; a sudden incandescent burst as the trumpet theme (the only truly melodic entity of the movement) bestrides the orchestra over glittering cascades of pentatonic figuration on strings and woodwind with very prominent harps and piano. It is reminiscent of 'De l'aube à midi sur la mer'; the early-morning mist obscuring the mountain peaks and the increasingly successful efforts of the sun to break through are imaginatively con-veyed and with a sure poetic feeling. Compared with *La Mer*, the thrillingly inexorable forward surge is certainly missing, and the melodic and rhythmic structure is more solid and four-square; none the less on its own terms the movement is extremely successful. So is the centre panel of the triptych, *Jour* ('Après-midi sous les pins'). The murmuring strings which accompany the very d'Indyan lyrical violin melody again look back nostalgically to Siegfried's Germany, but neither Wagner nor Debussy need have been ashamed of the beautiful Impressionist scoring of this theme on its last appearance—high string harmonics, high thrumming harps, flutes and timpani well down in their respective registers, astutely-placed horn thirds, solidifying the texture and accompanying the melody *bien chanté* on a solo trumpet (Ex. 19); the movement expires over an unresolved chord of the major

Ex. 19
D'Indy, 'Après-midi sous les pins' (*Jour d'Été à la Montagne*)

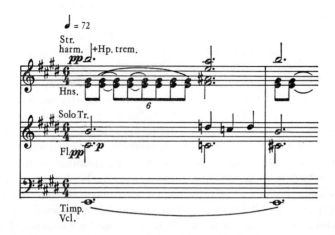

seventh, with a solo horn sounding a dreamy somnolent reminiscence of the folk-dance from the interpolated scherzo, as if from the far distance. 'Soir' brings back the opening of 'Aurore' in its coda; but before the latter, and before the expressive lyrical transformation of the opening dance-like theme, there is another passage of strikingly Impressionist sound, involving a pedal G held on violas and second violins, piano reiterating the Debussian

rhythmic figure, cymbal struck softly with a drumstick, and various instruments contributing isolated notes at intervals to form a general whole-tone impression. This employment of quasi-abstract sonorities to suggest night movement and night sound is essentially the technique of Bartók's highly individual night music.

In *Jour d'Été à la Montagne* d'Indy adopts the Impressionist manner quite instinctively and unselfconsciously. When, some twenty years later, he set out to write what on his own admission was to be an essay in Impressionism, the end-product was less satisfactory. The *Diptyque Mediterranéan* was, like the rather earlier *Poème des Rivages*, written after the composer's second marriage, to the 'chic and fluffy' Line Janson, who had managed to lure him away from his regular summer stamping-ground in the Ardèche to Agay on the Côte d'Azur, where he built her a villa. Thus in d'Indy's comparative old age his latent Mediterraneanism was brought to light. For 'light' is the subject of the *Diptyque*. 'This work', he wrote in the score, 'has no purpose other than that of noting in music two impressions of light.' In the event, however, neither movement suggests anything more than the most superficial acquaintance with Debussy's procedures. 'Soleil matinal' is squarely built on two contrasted themes (the second of them a brass chorale) and with the exception of the passage leading up to the first appearance of the latter, which is based almost entirely on the whole-tone scale, in substance the music is redolent more of Brahms than of Debussy. 'Soleil vespéral' opens more promisingly—a *forte* chord of superimposed fifths capped by glimmering string tremolos which yields to a long-drawn *diminuendo* and suggests the incandescence of the late afternoon sun gradually beginning to lose its lustre and sink in the sky. The remainder of the movement is more poetically conceived than its companion and is stronger in invention; but apart from a subtly-modified reminiscence of the whole-tone passage described above it calls for no special comment in this context.

The truly Impressionist elements in the *Poème des Rivages* are like-wise small. This suite of four sea-pieces, inspired by various parts of the Riviera coastline, is scored for a large orchestra including piano, celesta and a choir of saxophones; but even the saccharine warmth of these instruments cannot mitigate the fundamental intellectuality of d'Indy's approach. When he was able to view nature as the context of human activity and endeavour, as in *Jour d'Été à la Montagne*, he was at peace with himself, and Impressionist procedures suggested them-selves quite naturally. But the titles of the movements here—'Calme et lumière', 'La joie du bleu profond', 'Horizons verts' and 'Le mystère de l'Océan', imply a more mystical, almost pantheistic approach, for which the moralistic, basically non-sensuous d'Indy could find no satisfactory musical expression. This is not to deny the lyrical charm and architectural craftsmanship of a movement such as 'Calme et lumière'; but a fuller Impressionistic treatment is so obviously called for that we are apt to feel cheated when it is not forthcoming. The second movement, 'La Joie du bleu profond', is afire for much of the time with pentatonic figuration, but the main theme is a jovially bouncing affair in six-eight that might have come from the finale of the *Symphonie Cévénole*, and the guiding hand behind the whole conception, both structurally and texturally, is basically that of Franck. *Jour d'Été à la Montagne* remains d'Indy's Impressionist masterpiece.

In 1898 d'Indy was introduced to an ex-naval officer, nearly 30 years of age, who had decided to devote himself to music. This was Albert Roussel, fast approaching middle age when he completed his nine years of study at the Schola Cantorum. For a time his early works showed broad signs of d'Indy's influence. Soon the idiom of Debussy began to vie with this and undoubtedly helped him to a quicker and deeper understanding of his own burgeoning musical individuality in which, when fully realized, all overt traces of Impressionism are covered over. But if Roussel's Impressionist period was short-lived, it was also interesting and unusual. For although he responded freely and un-inhibitedly to natural phenomena—especially the sea—his finely-tempered intellect, which had more than a little in common with d'Indy's austere idealism, would not allow him to live, like Debussy, in a world of autonomous personal sensation. Hence the paradoxical situation that while his Impressionist music is immediate, genuine and sincerely felt, there is a palpable distance between the man and his emotional reactions to whatever natural phenomena may have in-spired him, the result being that these reactions are seen in a type of almost ironic perspective. It is this which makes for the individuality of his Impressionism.

Debussy's influence on Roussel was wholly tonic; it helped to open his eyes to the fundamentally reactionary cast of d'Indy's thought but did not induce him to ape the Impressionist mannerisms—his own personality was too individual for that. What the Impressionist aesthetic (rather than the Impressionist technique) did for Roussel was to widen the emotional range of his music, to permit him a greater degree of control over those finely-differentiated shades of perception which French composers have ever aspired to express in their work. The first work in which he attempted to reflect his love of nature was also the first to bear witness to Impressionist influence. This was the suite *Rustiques* for piano, three pieces inspired by the country round the Île de France. In the first movement, 'Danse au bord de l'eau', both the rhythmic fluidity and the evanescent quality of the melodic material suggest the movement of water and the elfin character of the dance; open fourths in the harmony add a discreetly rustic flavour. In lieu of development Roussel prefers the repetition of a melodic, rhythmic out-line through fugitive kaleidoscopic textures. Rich chromatic harmony of the conventional Impressionist variety holds no interest for Roussel, yet his harmony, like Debussy's, is purely instinctive: it is dictated by the needs of the moment and rarely pays even lip-service to scholastic tradition. The beautiful 'Promenade sentimentale en forêt' is yet another musical descendant of the *Waldweben* (with d'Indy as a possible intermediary), though its tenebrous nocturnal murmurings and susurrations, with now and again the distant cry of a bird (a bird lost in the forest, an *oiseau triste*?), are embodied in a highly complex texture of figuration given stability and direction by Roussel's peculiarly individual brand of exacerbated lyricism. This sensitive music, with its powerfully sombre evocative quality, is impressionistic in a way which bears only the most superficial of resemblances to Debussian procedures. 'Retour de fête' on the other hand, though no less poetically conceived, does end on a more familiarly impressionistic note. As the sounds of revelry die away in the distance the onlooker is left alone in a landscape suddenly vast and deserted which is evoked by the barest economy of means: dovetailed patterns of melodic fourths, fanfares from afar (an imaginative use of the whole-tone scale), a fade-out on an unresolved discord.

'Promenade sentimentale en forêt' is closely related, stylistically and conceptually, to 'Soir d'été' from the orchestral *Le Poème de la Forêt* with which it was written almost contemporaneously. This, Roussel's first symphony, is the largest of his nature evocations, a four-movement fresco inspired by the Forest of Fontainebleau, a part of France beloved by the Impressionist painters themselves and by Delius, who lived close by. It has been noted that the forest was to Roussel what the sea was to Debussy and the mountains to d'Indy (curiously enough, although Roussel had both a wide experience and lasting love of the sea he wrote no sea-music) and certainly *Le Poème de la Forêt*, *La Mer* and *Jour d'Été à la Montagne*, all written between 1904 and 1906, together constitute a French nature-triptych of imposing proportions. In the first, Debussy's influence is more clearly perceptible than in *Rustiques* and the ghosts of d'Indy are by no means completely exorcised, but even at this early stage the score can hardly be described as derivative. The prelude, 'Forêt d'hiver' (Ex. 20), is typical of Roussel's nature-poetry. The landscape is bleak and snow-bestrewn (a sustained open fifth on clarinets and bassoons) but nature in her tranquillities is never still, as the Impressionists clearly discerned (a subterranean triplet murmuring on muted violas). The next movement, 'Renouveau', is described by Martin Cooper as a typically French spring-piece, 'green, sour and gay'. Impressionist brush-strokes can be discerned, for example in the little episode at 5 bars before fig. 12 (delicate washes of colour for solo flute and two harps); when this returns in

Ex. 20
Roussel, 'Forêt d'hiver' Le Poème de la Forêt)

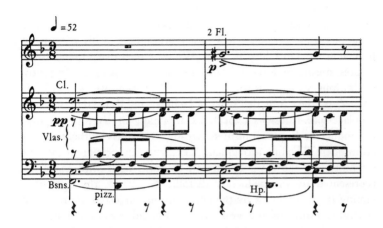

modified form at fig. 27 it leads into what is patently a reminiscence of
the *Waldweben*, no more out of place here than in the second movement
of *Rustiques*. In 'Soir d'été' long, languorous lines of melody, first on a
solo viola, then on horn answered by two flutes, rise drowsily out of a
haze of muted strings. The familiar triplet figuration soon creeps in, and
distant horncalls are answered by glinting sextolet interjections on
violins and flutes and a full-hearted d'Indyan climax is built up in the
manner of 'Promenade sentimentale en forêt'. The autumnal revelry of
'Faunes et dryades', the most quintessentially Roussellian music in the
symphony, yields ultimately, ineluctably, to the snowbound Impressionist landscape of Ex. 20; in the final bars, however, a radiant D major
is established, as if the forest were resigning itself to its long winter
vigil, consoled in the anticipation of another spring.

Something of the Impressionist spirit of 'Renouveau' is recaptured
in the symphonic sketch *Pour une fête de printemps*, an intensely
personal spring-piece, stylistically more assured than *Le Poème*; it was
in fact originally conceived as part of the B minor Symphony (no 2).
The introduction still gives off an Impressionist aroma: vague intimations of the main subject rise out of a steamily astringent haze compound of a bitonal dovetailing of the tonic chords of E♭ major and A
major, suggesting the 'slow and arduous birth of things in nature'
which Debussy had attempted to depict some forty years earlier in one

of his first tentatively Impressionist works, *Printemps* (it opens in what is fundamentally a very similar way; see p. 25).

After *Le Poème de la Forêt* Roussel's next large-scale work was the rarely-performed *Évocations*, a triptych which represents the acme of his Impressionist style. He had always been intrigued by the East, and these pieces are reminiscences of a journey he and his wife made to India and Cochin China in 1909. We have seen that Orientalism and Impressionism are closely related in music; but the Rimsky-Korsakovian stylizations which inform Dukas's *La Péri*, Schmitt's *La Tragédie de Salomé* and the exotic delicacies of Debussy and Ravel themselves, find no place here. Roussel's 'evocations' are unique in that they employ the techniques of Impressionism to create a relatively authentic oriental atmosphere. The first movement, 'Les dieux dans l'ombre des cavernes' (memories of the caves at Ellora), contrasts light with shade—light represented by the pellucidly diatonic writing of the opening and closing pages, darkness by the chromatically-inflected, more sensually rhythmic music of the god Siva in the subterranean temple. The evocative writing at the beginning and end is wholly impressionistic— a deep pedal-point of bare fifths and complex string figuration pointed by harp. As always with Roussel, a strong melodic element is ever at hand rigorously to discipline the fundamentally sensuous temper of the conception.

The second *Évocation*—of a Rajah's procession at Jaipur ('La ville rose')—is scherzo-like in character; in Basil Deane's words it suggests 'the city of Lahore, the sparkling minarets and temples, the majesty and opulence of its ceremonial, the bustle of its market-place, the hypnotic grace of its dancers'. The movement is a vividly Impressionist amalgam of colour, heat, light and movement with glittering orchestral textures and fleet-footed rhythms, exotically flavoured both by the pentatonic main theme of the opening section and by the authentic Hindu melody which announces the entry of the Rajah—the latter attracting to itself a profusion of woodwind arabesque and those trance-inducing repetitions which are so prominent a feature of both primitive and Impressionist music. The third panel of the triptych, 'Aux bords du fleuve sacré', is the most impressionistic of all; it represents a fakir on the banks of the Ganges at night and adds both chorus and solo voices to the orchestra. Calvocoressi's text provides a sequence of suitably concrete images to set alight the composer's instinct for mood-evocation; the words themselves are of no great distinction or importance and, more often than not, the voices pass imperceptibly (and typically) over into vocalise. The opening pages (from figs. 4 to 6) present a compendium of Impressionist devices—open fifths, modal oboe arabesque ('le soleil est plongé dans la mer'), and at fig. 5 characteristic woodwind triplets with syncopated trumpet fifths sounding in the distance. At fig. 9 the chorus begin their lovely wordless melismata, and a balmy shimmering atmosphere is created in which sounds, scents and colours all merge together in the type of voluptuous impressionistic haze that is more like Debussy than anything else in Roussel. The wordless chorus perhaps induces a characteristic 'Sirènes'-like sea-rhythm (7 bars after fig. 18): this helps to build the surge of choral–orchestral sound to a ravishing climax which for sensuous ecstasy almost rivals the dawn scene of *Daphnis et Chloé*.

The *Évocations* are among the most notable examples of French musical Impressionism and it is unfortunate that they have dropped almost completely out of the repertoire. By contrast the ballet *Le Festin de l'Araignée*, the last work of Roussel which calls for consideration in this context, has always been a great favourite. The prelude evoking the garden which is the scene of the action (its music returns to conclude the ballet) is an enchanting piece of impressionistic writing, with a haunting flute solo over softly murmuring strings, but the harmonic and instrumental texture of the entire score has an aerial fluidity which bespeaks a more general Impressionist influence.

We must now turn to those composers whose Impressionist work, though by no means necessarily lacking in individuality, stands in a more immediate line of descent from that of the progenitor of the movement himself, although it is a curious fact that most of them remained less emancipated than he was from the German symphonic tradition. This is particularly true of Paul Dukas, known the world over for his *Apprenti Sorcier*, a work which Martin Cooper has happily described as 'a refined and Gallic version of Richard Strauss'. There are fewer vestiges of Impressionism discernible here than in two of Dukas's less familiar scores, the opera *Ariane et Barbe-Bleue* and the dance-poem *La Péri*.

Ariane et Barbe-Bleue was the first-born son of *Pelléas et Mélisande*. After the sensation caused by Debussy's setting, Maeterlinck wrote his version of the Bluebeard legend[4] (drawing on traditional French sources, especially the legend of Gilles de Retz and Perrault's fairy-tale) with the idea of a musical setting by Dukas specifically in mind. That *Pelléas* should have a bearing upon the score is only to be expected, but the free use of accompanied recitative, the mannered insistence upon the whole-tone scale and the abundance of Debussian harmony do not rob the work of individuality. Dukas, having a more palpably Teutonic cast of musical mind, does not deal in shadowy, evanescent, dimly-defined orchestral shapes; his textures are rich and full, his structures more tangible and readily analysable. If *Ariane* is in genealogical terms *Pelléas*'s first-born, it bears an even greater number of resemblances to its grandfather, the Wagnerian music drama.

The Impressionist elements in the opening scene are easy to isolate: they recall the atmosphere of the scene in the castle vaults in Act III of *Pelléas*—consecutive open fifths, the whole-tone scale, a wordless men's chorus, muted scoring. The opening of each of the first six doors of Barbe-Bleue's domain brings in its wake a deluge of brilliantly-coloured diamonds and in each case the orchestra glories in a scintillating union between Rimsky-Korsakov and Debussy (each opening is depicted in the form of a different variation on a theme announced at the beginning, and symphonic 'development' is generally of the Russian variety, i.e. repetition with modification). More essentially Impressionist is the scene in the second act in which Ariane, having discovered the five former wives of Barbe-Bleue in a pitifully de-moralized and intimidated condition, reminds them of the beauties of the natural world which by their own lack of initiative they are deny-ing themselves. The text at this point waxes lyrical and evocative in the manner of *Pelléas*, Act III, Scene 3 (Pelléas's emergence from the gloom of the castle vaults into the fresh sea air and dazzling midday light). Sunlight, spring, wide open spaces, dawn, flowers, dew on the leaves, the sea. . . . Dukas takes his cue promptly in a radiant B major with glistening pentatonic figuration, frequent use of ninths and evocative scoring. The climax comes as Ariane in a delirium of ecstasy breaks all the windows of the 'vaste salle souterraine' and floods the scene with light; at this point are heard 'le murmure de la mer, les caresses du vent dans les arbres, le chant des oiseaux et les clochettes d'un troupeau qui passe au loin dans la campagne'. Appropriate Impressionist musical equivalents are heard in each case, welded into formal coherence by the constant interweaving of *Leitmotif*, several surviving from the jewel episode in Act I already mentioned. A peal of jubilant pentatonic bell-ringing, an idea inspired earlier by Ariane's description of thousands of light rays dancing in the hollow of the waves, brings the act to an end.

In *La Péri*, the dance poem which was the composer's last work of any consequence, the Rimsky-Korsakov–Debussy amalgam is even more concentrated. However, the superb professionalism of this music—its scoring opulent yet precisely-judged, its form flexible and subtle, its lyricism passionate yet unforced—makes it a worthy successor to Balakirev's *Tamara*, on which it is clearly modelled. Its exoticism is stylized, yet so skilfully integrated into the harmonic and colouristic framework that the listener finds himself implicitly accepting the convention and revelling in its sensuous beauty. The opening bars of this most lavish of oriental genre-pictures are typical: strings ascending in whole-tone progressions, a discreetly placed top G♯ on the celesta, a hushed horn-fanfare (notice the effect of the cunningly interpolated C♮ in bar 4). The chromatically-inflected arabesque in bars 6 and 7 weaves its way throughout the fabric of the score and contributes the requisite exotic colouring; the violin and clarinet upward-vanishing skirls in bar 8 and the *pizzicato* third in which they terminate constitute an admirable example of Pointillism. Harmonically, too, the idiom is lush with all the familiar appurtenances of Impressionism; but Dukas's individual use of parallel triads in their last inversions and his flair for soft but telling dissonance (for instance, the trumpet chord which coincides with the soft cymbal clash five bars after fig. 19 *bis*) give the score a characteristic sound of its own.

Emotionally the most committed of all Dukas's Impressionist pictures is the piano piece he wrote for *Le Tombeau de Debussy* entitled *La Plainte, au Loin, du Faune*, which contains, as is implied, an explicit allusion to the archetype of musical Impressionist compositions. The harmony is astringent, the texture spare, the pulse slow and funereal; a repeated G tolls a knell and an ostinato-like figure, rising and falling in sixths, invokes a plaintive chromatic arabesque which vaguely suggests the contours of the flute theme of *L'Après-midi* into a tragically disfigured quotation from which it eventually resolves (Ex. 21). The impression is of a deserted winter landscape with snow falling, recollections of the lay of the long-departed faun being heard through a haze of embittered nostalgia.

The combination of Debussian Impressionism and Russian exoticism noted in *La Péri* is more pronounced in the work of Florent Schmitt. Time has not dealt kindly with him; his Impressionism now sounds more derivative than Dukas's, his Orientalism more tawdry and stylized; yet his was an interesting and in several respects an original sensibility. He had a passion for broad, garish effects of orchestral colour. We find him again and again being drawn to exotic subjects and so gratifying his urge to score and harmonize in an advanced Franco-

EIM

Ex. 21
Dukas, *La Plainte, au Loin, du Faune* from *Le Tombeau de Debussy*

Russian manner: *Antoine et Cléopâtre* (incidental music for a production
of the Shakespeare play); *Salammbô* (background score for a film
version of Flaubert's novel); the *Danse des Dévadaïs*, a *scena* for orchestra
with women's voices; and *Le Palais Hanté*, an orchestral study after
Poe's *The Haunted Palace*. Best known of all is the Loie Fuller ballet
score *La Tragédie de Salomé*, a less subtle, less finely-composed work
than *La Péri*, but more immediately compelling in effect and technically more forward-looking: the use of additive rhythms in the
'Danse de l'effroi' as in the 'Orgies et danses' from the second *Antoine et
Cléopâtre* suite is well in advance of *The Rite of Spring*. Volcanic rhythmic eruption is a recurrent feature of Schmitt's work and, doubtless,
constitutes another reason for his so often turning to barbaric and exotic
legend for inspiration. The opening sequence of *Salomé*—sunset on
Herod's palace—is very typical of Schmitt's Impressionism. A melancholy cor anglais develops its sinuous arabesque over quietly pulsing
strings which later give way to swaying horn chords answered by
celesta.[5] Both harmony and orchestral texture are voluptuous and
caressive, with frequent recourse to the whole-tone scale and dominant
ninths. When this material returns at the beginning of Part II, 'Les
enchantements sur la mer', it brings in its wake reminiscences of *La Mer*
itself[6] and, subsequently, of 'Sirènes', as a solo contralto, distant and
wordless, is heard singing an authentic folk-melody from the shores
of the Dead Sea. The remainder of the distant female chorus joins in
gradually until an impassioned climax is reached.

Any number of basically Impressionist devices for evoking oriental atmosphere, generally sultry and nocturnal, can be found in Schmitt's scores. 'Nuit au palais de la Reine', from *Antoine et Cléopâtre*, presents a solo cor anglais directed to play his arabesques 'à l'aise et comme improvisant' while glassy string tremolos of minor seconds high up in the stratosphere are pointed by celesta and underpinned by a soft cymbal roll. In *Salammbô* the forbidding appearance of Hamilcar's palace, 'aussi solennel et impénétrable que le visage d'Hamilcar' is evoked first by a sullen muttering of muted strings gradually building up an Impressionist edifice of minor seconds, then by a throbbing fragment of orientally-flavoured solo cello and oboe melody piercing the dark haze of string tremolos and attracting random snatches of flute and clarinet arabesque. Also exotically-coloured is Schmitt's contribution to *Le Tombeau de Debussy*, but although, like Dukas's *Le Plainte, au Loin, du Faune*, it takes its cue from *L'Après-midi d'un Faune*, it eschews literal quotation. The first of a set of two *Mirages* (the title is significant) for piano, it is subtitled 'Tristesse de Pan' and is prefaced by a quotation from Paul Fort; 'et Pan, au fond des blés lunaires, s'accouda'. Like much of Schmitt's piano music, however, it lies awkwardly under the fingers and seems to demand an orchestral setting, which it in fact eventually received. It is a strange piece; its main melodic substance is a mildly voluptuous melody which seems to have wandered in from the love-idyll of *Sheherazade* by way of the 'Danse' from *La Péri*. Subject to devious, indistinctly-focused and harmonically acrid variation, it is brought to a turbulent fanfare-like climax (very characteristic of Schmitt) after which an impressionistic radiance seeps more and more into the music. Towards the end the textures become more elusive and fragmentary, as if to suggest that Pan, now resigned to whatever *tristesse* may be his lot, is now taking refuge, like his Mallarméan prototype, in sleep. The final bars are particuarly evocative (Ex. 22).

French composers of lesser stature than Schmitt have succumbed to the blandishments of impressionistic Orientalism. The opening movement of Jacques Ibert's orchestral suite *Escales* is an evocation of Palermo in Sicily, which, yet again, is Rimsky-Korsakov's semi-oriental *Sheherazade* joined in musical matrimony with Debussy's Arcadian faun.[7] It adds nothing of any consequence to the mixture as before, which is by no means to say that the languorous flute and oboe solos, clarinet arabesque, gently billowing string figuration and soft harp glissandi ravish the senses any the less effectively. A more subtle, if small-scale, synthesis of Impressionist and oriental elements was

Ex. 22
Schmitt, *Tristesse de Pan* from *Le Tombeau de Debussy*

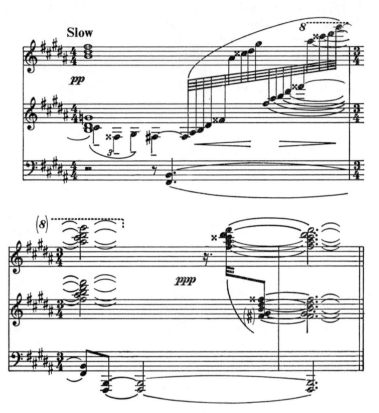

achieved by Lili Boulanger in her *Vieille Prière Bouddhique* for tenor
solo, chorus and orchestra. Certain of her earlier works had dallied
with Impressionism in a rather mannered though not wholly derivative
way—the cantata *Faust et Hélène*, *Soir sur la Plaine* (another choral-
orchestral work) and the song-cycle *Clairières dans le Ciel*, settings of
poems by Francis Jammes.

However, in the *Vieille Prière Bouddhique* all the time-honoured
Impressionist devices—modality, added-note harmony, oriental arabesque, the wordless chorus—are employed to original and beautiful effect. The work is a tripartite structure in which a 'daily prayer for
the whole universe' (in the darkly exotic Phrygian mode) is reiterated
against a constantly changing background of harmony, sonority and

texture. The mood is one of granitic impassivity temporarily relaxed in the central section in which, to a rocking harp accompaniment, the flute soars in quasi-oriental arabesque around the melodic contours of the prayer, rather like a bird suddenly let out of its cage. The Phrygian flavouring of the arabesques is quite sufficient to provide the elusively exotic aroma required. After this interlude the tenor soloist brings back the theme as if from the far distance, and the impression of illimitable desert solitudes is further enhanced by the chorus which picks up the soloist's final phrase (a minor third) and reiterates it obsessively in an undertone while soft stringchords with celesta move outwards in contrary motion, like ripples spreading on a water surface. Finally the air quivers with innumerable voices all humming in quasi-tremolo bare fifths a semitone apart. This little masterpiece deserves to be much better known and should be investigated by all those wishing for an object-lesson in the successful rehabilitation of Impressionist clichés.

The first work by Lili Boulanger to contain Impressionist elements was the cantata written for the 1913 Prix de Rome, *Faust et Hélène*. In the opening scene 'c'est le crépuscule du soir. Faust, étendu sur l'herbe, sommeille. On entend un léger bruissement de sylphes dans l'air.' The nocturnal atmosphere is evoked by rippling waves of harp around (principally) added-sixth harmony, and a fragmented melody hovering between violin and flute. The focal point of the cantata is the material-ization of Helen in response to Faust's summons, at which 'la nuit se remplit de rumeurs vagues: palpitations d'ailes, bruissement de feuilles, tintements de cloches lointaines aux sonorités alanguies, étranges'. The whirring wings, rustling leaves and distant bells provoke the expected Impressionist reaction, and it is quite possible that Lili Boulanger had heard and been inspired by an earlier quasi-Impressionist work based on the Faust legend, Roger-Ducasse's *Jardin de Marguerite*. In this 'poème symphonique avec chœurs' the com-poser imagines Faust in his old age returning to the garden where he had known and loved Marguerite. Although the chorus is fre-quently wordless, the choral writing constantly recalls Franck and Fauré rather than Debussy, and it is only in the extended orchestral intermezzo between the two parts that any truly Impressionist ele-ments shine forth. The crepuscular atmosphere to be evoked is ortho-dox enough, with 'bruissements silencieux' and 'une cloche lointaine, presqu'irréelle,' but the bell itself, sounding the seventh partial, is heard only in the coolly tranquil coda.[8] More interesting is the orchestral

Nocturne de Printemps, a later, war-time work dedicated, rather engagingly, 'à ma chère Maison des Champs'. This piece is short but concentrated; a large orchestra is employed and on several occasions is called upon for the full spectrum of sound. The texture is exceedingly complex; the woodwind parts are studded with flitting arabesque and bird calls of every description and elsewhere both string and woodwind figuration is very highly-wrought and elaborate. Little is clearly-defined either melodically or formally, and the piece as a whole leaves the impression of a beautifully fashioned fabric of sound compounded of shapes, figures and movements which come and go at random, constantly succeeded by others unmindful of their predecessors but akin to them.

If the Impressionism of Roger-Ducasse is refined and aristocratic in temper, that of Déoda de Sévérac is of the rustic, uninhibited variety. A pupil of the Schola Cantorum, Sévérac as a composer rarely left his native Languedoc, his affection for which was more intense than d'Indy's for the Cévennes. Much of his circumscribed, undisciplined yet curiously appealing output is in the form of piano suites, and the main influence upon the formation of his piano style is Chabrier's—Chabrier in whom, as in Sévérac, the bluff, good-humoured and ebullient Southerner, effervescing with Mediterranean *bonhomie* and *joie de vivre*, existed cheek by jowl with the introspective dreamer inclined to melancholy and wistfulness. It is possible, therefore, that Sévérac's Impressionism, such as it is, derives from Chabrier rather than Debussy, for in terms of both temperament and technique he was more closely akin to the jovial Auvergnat. *En Languedoc*, for example, is a set of five extended pieces depicting various aspects of Provençal life. The first, 'Vers le mas en fête', sets the scene with open fifths marked "cristallin" over a bass tremolo of a major second marked 'très flou', takes the route to the 'Mas' past a river (a whole-tone melody underneath the tremolo transferred to the right hand), pauses at a waterfall (placid triplet movement coming to rest on an unresolved augmented eleventh), finally arrives at the 'Mas en fête' and expires to the sound of the Angelus (modal melody, pentatonic harmony with a final unresolved added sixth.) The fourth movement, 'Coin de cimetière au printemps', fuses the sounds of chanting and bells in a manner reminiscent in an unsophisticated way of 'La Cathédrale engloutie', bells being suggested by pointed little interpolated crotchets with accaciaturas, not necessarily in agreement with the prevailing harmony. In the centre of the piece the 'Dies irae' is introduced, directed to be played 'doucement marqué comme des cloches lointaines' and after a passionate climax it dies away 'dans une sonorité claire et plus lointaine'. Ex. 23, from a few bars before the return of the 'tempo primo', is very

Ex. 23
Sévérac, 'Coin de cimetière au printemps' (*En Languedoc*)

Debussian with its harmony at one and the same time compounded of a ninth chord, pentatonic sonority and the open fifth; and the closing bars of the last piece, 'Le jour de la foire, au Mas', purely pentatonic, could easily have occurred in a *Prélude*, *Image* or *Estampe*.

Although *En Languedoc* is a comparatively early work—it dates from 1904—even earlier is *Le Chant de la Terre* (1901), which in its anticipation of Impressionist bell-music perhaps qualifies Sévérac as a pre- rather than a post-Impressionist. Grieg rather than Chabrier seems to have been Sévérac's model here, for his influence is clearly discernible in the 'Intermezzo' (and also in the two books of children's pieces entitled *En Vacances*.) The 'cloches au loin' at the end of the 'Épilogue' are fairly conventional consecutive fourths: in 'Les moissons' the 'cloches nuptiales' are still the familiar consecutive fourths and fifths, but they are here skilfully immersed in the melodic mainstream. The 'glas' in 'La Grêle' is similarly combined with one of the many strands of folk-song or plainsong-flavoured melody which permeate this work; but the most subtle bell-music is to be found in 'Les semailles', the best movement of the suite and the most impressionistic. A rustle of even-flowing figuration, often pentatonic or shot through with the sharpened fourth of the Lydian mode, supports a melodic line which gives direction and impulse to the forward motion without ever standing out from the encircling accompanimental web, rather blending and coalescing with it. The ostinato moves down to the lower reaches of the keyboard as the sound of the Angelus is heard from afar—a passage marked, *à la* Debussy, 'tres doux et lointain en noyant le son avec les pedales'. The introduction of the whole-tone scale at this point increases the intended haziness of effect and contributes to a fine climax, the later fifths and fourths standing out by contrast with sparkling clarity and immediacy.

The same kind of fresh, pastoral note also characterizes those few pages in the work of Arthur Honegger which can be classified as Impressionist. Although Honegger spent the greater part of his life in France he came of German–Swiss stock, and there is rivalry between the Latin and Teutonic elements in his make-up; Bach, Beethoven, Wagner and Strauss played a substantial part in the formation of his idiom, but it is significant that among his contemporaries in Les Six he had the most in common with and gathered the most strength from Darius Milhaud who was strongly influenced by Debussy. To the group aesthetic of Les Six he was but tenuously affiliated, however, and if composers such as Auric and Poulenc reacted against the 'decadent' undercurrent of Impressionism, Honegger always thought of Debussy as one of his great spiritual forebears.

His contributions to Impressionism are small but valuable. The *Pastorale d'été* was inspired by the sight of a Swiss landscape in the early hours of a summer morning and is prefaced by a quotation from Rimbaud: 'J'ai embrassé l'aube d'été' (from *Les Illuminations*). It is in a direct line of descent from Chabrier's 'Sous-bois' by way of the 'Pastorale' in Milhaud's *Protée* and resembles it closely in that an element of haze is provided by the continuous murmuring ostinato of cellos and basses. Woodwind interpose their arabesques at regular intervals (looking forward to the enchanted bird-song in the visionary final pages of the *Symphonie Liturgique*) but the melodic outlines remain clear and well-defined. So they do in the magnificent *Chant de Joie*, undoubtedly the best of Honegger's shorter orchestral works; but here in the central contrasting section the haze is more pronounced, more subtly evocative of the mists of a Swiss dawn. Semiquaver scales in interlocking fourths glide tranquilly up and down on muted strings, with harp and celesta moving in contrary motion. The result is a softly glowing sheen of sound (the naturally reverberant quality of the harp when playing in rapid figuration of this kind contributing signally to an 'impression floue') on which a flowing pastoral melody is super-imposed.

One composer remains to be considered: Charles Koechlin, a valued friend and associate of Debussy[9] who in 1926 published a biographico-critical study of him which makes illuminating reading even today. He came to know Debussy's music very well during the composer's lifetime and was responsible for 'orchestrating' *Khamma*, i.e. for filling in the finer points of detail, Debussy himself having indicated the general scheme of the scoring. As a composer, Koechlin is one of the great unknowns of French music: only a handful of his shorter piano and chamber works have been published. Like Mompou (with whom he has a certain amount in common) he was not in the least interested in disseminating his music, the result being that a vast corpus of large-scale choral and orchestral compositions lies awaiting discovery and performance. On the basis of what is available, however, we can see that, for all his formidable eminence as a pedagogue (he published theoretical works on fugue and counterpart, treatises on harmony (three volumes), orchestration (four volumes), his style is neither reactionary nor conservative. He gathered his strength not only from Debussy but also from Fauré and the music of the early Renaissance and the Middle Ages. From the latter he spontaneously evolved non-metrical rhythms, polymodal lines and polyharmonic textures. Like Mompou whose music shows similar medieval–oriental propensities, Koechlin dispenses with time-signatures—and often key-signatures—but generally retains the bar-line. In this way he conforms to the Debussian idea of musical 'development' as quasi-improvisation, and his music is even more lacking in conventional notions of 'progression' than Debussy's. This non-awareness of musical 'time' coupled with an impeccable refinement of diction and transparency of texture gives Koechlin's music a spirit of what Wilfrid Mellers has termed 'paradisal calm', a strangely remote, unreal, in fact 'timeless' quality. So it is not surprising to discover that it also has, in certain places, definite affinities with Impressionism, the more so in that his early reading of Jules Verne instilled in him a love of the night sky, ocean depths, the forest, effects of light—nature in general, in fact. Examination of two of his published piano works—the two books of *Paysages et Marines* and the suite *L'Ancienne Maison de Campagne* certainly bears this out.

Paysages et Marines are evocations of nature. We need look no further than the first, 'Sur la falaise', to find Koechlin looking out to sea and limning the blue horizons in impressionistic agglomerations of fourths and fifths (Ex. 24) which are also used at the beginning and end of *Les Bandar-Log* (the only orchestral work of his so far to have been put into circulation) to evoke the luminous calm of an early morning in the jungle. 'Sur la falaise' is Impressionism of the purest water; there is no progression or development of any sort, it is a mood picture, static and atmospheric. In 'Promenade vers la mer' there is a march-like regularity

Ex. 24
Koechlin, 'Sur la falaise' (*Paysages et Marines*)

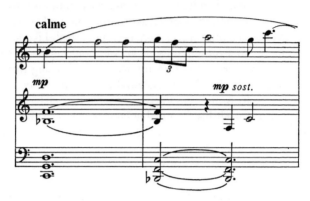

of rhythm and a steady flow of melody which urge the music forward polychordally to a fine climax. The polychords, directed to be played 'comme des souffles frais et légers', are constructed, like many of Milhaud's, from superpositions of fifths in the bass and common chords in the treble and possess that 'subtle sweetness' which the latter defined as one of their greatest virtues: Milhaud's music in fact bears many traces of Koechlin's influence whom we may perhaps regard, harmonically speaking, as a mediator between the Impressionists and Les Six.[10] Notice too the poetic effect of the sudden breath of E major melody marked 'lumineux et lointain', clashing subtly and exquisitely with the Impressionist haze of superimposed fourths and fifths, its harmonic support—perhaps a sudden tang of salt sea-air on a first glimpse of the sea in the distance.

'Le chant du chevrier' is another piece of 'pure' Impressionism, static and non-developing; over long-held chords of superimposed fifths frequently dissolving into polychords there plays a continuous stream of oriental melodic arabesque, constantly fluctuating in mode and rhythm. The result is haunting and beautiful; like the 'Poème Virgilien' it reveals a curious though understandable affinity, both technical and spiritual, with certain works of Vaughan Williams, notably the *Pastoral* Symphony and *Flos Campi*. 'Dans les grands champs' is another stylized pastoral evocation with herd-pipings in triplets over drone basses—exactly the kind of piece that Grieg might have written had he lived to develop his Impressionism to include chords of superimposed fifths, bi-modality and a greater metrical freedom.

(Another example of this particular style of Impressionist scene painting is to be found in no 8 of the *Dix Pièces Faciles*, entitled 'Des cors dans la forêt'—see the last five bars). 'Matin calme', 'Soir d'été' and 'La Chanson des pommiers en fleurs', even 'Soir d'angoisses', are all more tangibly melodic (Koechlin once said of *L'Après-midi d'un Faune*: 'Its charm is so simple, so melodic') but their evocative beauty still lies in the kaleidoscopic harmony—chords of fourths and fifths, poly-chordal sequences or Koechlin's own individual brand of chromaticism. 'Paysage d'Octobre' is more consistently polychordal, Koechlin preferring long flowing curves of such chords to the triads in root position which Debussy might have used.

L'Ancienne Maison de Campagne also contains an Impressionist autumn study, 'Promenade d'automne (no 11), in which sequences of chords, mainly added-note, are marked 'extrêmement doux et voilé' and move mechanically to an inflexible metrical pulse, throbbing with bell-like pedal-points both internal and external. Nos 8 and 9 of this suite are particularly interesting in that they illuminate the Impression-ist possibilities latent in harmony that functions consistently on two planes and indicate that Milhaud (who, as previously mentioned, stands greatly indebted to Koechlin) might well have founded a new school of Impressionism had he not become involved with aesthetic movements which encouraged the development of other aspects of his talent. For instance, in no 8, 'En ramant sur le lac', in which Koechlin makes his apologies not only to Milhaud but also to Fauré for quoting from their works, the unruffled surface of the lake is mirrored in the reiterated B major left-hand arpeggios in barcarolle rhythm; against this the right hand moves through a variety of opposing tonalities but always in this same impassively tranquil rhythm. The result is an impression-istic haze of a unique description which would not be obtained were the left-hand not to confine itself to B major: the juxtaposition of these conflicting tonalities suggests that the eye is dimly aware of other people or objects or activities in the background (the right hand), but that its attention is most immediately and consistently being caught by the vast expanse of blue (the left hand). This piece constitutes, in fact, a perfect 'impression'.

In no 9, 'Matin dans les bois' ('courses dans la jungle') hunting-horns come bounding out of a murmur of open fifths (marked 'lié et confus') and alternate with cascades of bitonal arpeggios, suggesting some other form of strenuous activity (perhaps that of the Bandar-Log) perceived or rather sensed vaguely through a thick curtain of vegetation.

Gradually the bugle-calls are lost in the distance and the music fades from the scene. The most recognizably Impressionist piece of the set is, however, no 6, 'La vieille fontaine'. Again, there is no movement here, only atmosphere. The glassily shimmering bare sevenths and ninths of the opening sound highly original and evocative in this context; having once heard this piece one could not readily mistake it for any other. The next motif is a sequence of descending dominant ninths marked 'alla Pelléas'; in his introductory note the composer explains that the water was 'pleine d'une eau profonde, cristalline et très froide. Aussi me fallut-il evoquer l'ambiance de *Pelléas et Mélisande*', and this is his way of acknowledging his debt to the masterpiece of which in his book on Debussy he showed such sensitive understanding:

In order to appreciate *Pelléas* . . . you must be moved in the face of nature to be moved afterwards by the Debussian evocations of the sea, of the sun, of the summer, of the night. You must have dreamed of fairy-tale castles to recognize the poetry of dreams on the old walls covered in ivy. You must have been under the spell of legendary times and haunted by deep forests to understand the Prologue.

Over the head of these *Pelléas*-like chords there hover desolate atonal melodic fragments, recalled in a quasi-coda in the middle of the piece as a 'cor lointain', and in the final bars reminiscences of all the motivic particles are woven together in a dream-like, wholly impressionistic web of evocative sonority. The penultimate piece, 'La veille du départ' is intended to convey the anguish of imminent departure reflected in 'la tendre lumière de cette fin d'août', in the clear blue sky with its endless processions of clouds, and the music constitutes a natural development from 'Nuages' with the same imperturbably calm, non-metric forward tread and the same uniform tints of grey. But Koechlin's 'endless processions' are polychordal and polymodal, thus infusing a greater degree of tension into the music while jealously shielding it from any taint of subjective emotion. The anguish is observed impartially, not experienced.

It is impossible to form any realistic assessment of Koechlin's true Impressionist affiliations on the basis of these few published compositions, but the titles given by *Grove's Dictionary of Music and Muscians* (fifth edition) of some of his unpublished manuscripts—the *Deux Pièces Symphoniques* ('En rêvé'; 'Au loin'), the symphonic poems *La Forêt, En Mer, la Nuit* (after Heine), *Soleil et Danse dans la Forêt, Vers la Plage Lointaine, Nocturne, Le Printemps, L'Hiver, Nuit de Juin, Midi*

en *Août*, *La course de Printemps* (after Kipling) and *Sur les Flots Lointains*,
the symphonic suite *L'Automne*—all these and many others suggest by
their very titles that, if and when the full story is told, Koechlin may
emerge as one of the most prolific and significant Impressionists of his
day.

1. This piece, together with *Alborado del gracioso*, was later orchestrated, and it
was after hearing this version that Alain-Fournier, author of *Le Grand Meaulnes* (a
novel which Ravel himself at one time considered as the basis for a musical work),
wrote to his friend the music critic, and future Stravinsky enthusiast, Jacques
Rivière that the music was both derivative of Debussy and yet lacking in the
commitment of the 'Dialogue du vent et de la Mer'. Yet the opening of Chapter
IV (Part I) of *Le Grand Meaulnes* suggests that, none the less, the experience was
not lost on him:

A une heure de l'après-midi, le lendemain, la classe du cours supérieur est claire,
au milieu du paysage gelé, comme une barque sur l'Océan.

The affinities between Debussy and Alain-Fournier have already been mentioned
(p. 31).
2. This last line in the poem may be a quotation, conscious or otherwise, from
Pelléas, Act III, Scene 1—Mélisande's 'Je vois une rose dans les ténèbres'.
3. At the beginning and end of this work, d'Indy in his evocation of the
immensities of solitude and silence experienced in the mountains, adopts a
technique very similar to that of Grieg in his impressionistic *Peace of the Woods*
discussed on p. 65—no melody, simply a sequence of common chords, not
necessarily related, wide-spread and long-held.
4. Bartok's *Bluebeard's Castle*, composed to Béla Balázs's adaptation of Maeterlinck is discussed on pp. 222–3.
5. A passage irresistibly reminiscent to English ears of Holst's 'Venus' (see
p. 159). It suggests a number of parallels between Schmitt and Holst—a love of the
East (intellectual and non-sensuous in Holst's case) and a proneness to cataclysmic
outbursts of (particularly rhythmic) violence; 'Mars' and perhaps 'Uranus', no
less than the 'Danse de l'effroi' and *The Rite*, anticipate the *ventura ira* of 1914.
6. For instance, the music from five bars before fig. 40 to fig. 42 is an almost
literal quotation from the 'Dialogue du vent et de la mer'.
7. It was Sicily also (more specifically the fountain of Arethusa near Syracuse)
which inspired the only work of Arthur Bliss with any Impressionist overtones—
Pastoral, for chorus, solo contralto, flute, strings and drums. The flute writing in
'Pan's Sarabande' and the exquisite 'Pigeon song' is clearly derived from *Syrinx*.
See also p. 216, note 2.
8. The Impressionism of Déodat de Sévérac will be discussed in its place, but it
is worth noting here that he hits on this very idea to suggest a distant chime in

'Les Muletiers devant le Christ de Llivia', the fourth movement of his otherwise non–Impressionist suite *Cerdaña*. The F major section ends on the chord

at which point, with reference to the spread E ♭/F, the composer directs 'arpégez sans hâte, en faisant resonner plus le Mi♭ que le Fa qui doit être comme une vibration de cloche'. Cf. the end of Chopin's 23rd Prelude (see p. 52) and the end of the last movement of Respighi's *Fountains of Rome* (p. 197).

9. Two other colleagues of Debussy, both composer–conductors, also inclined in their own work towards Impressionism—André Caplet in the string writing of his *Miroir de Jésus* and Désiré-Émile Inghelbrecht in his orchestral *Rapsodie de Printemps*, the fetching *chinoiserie* of his *Pour le jour de la première neige au vieux Japon* and in his *Paysages* for piano.

10. A number of Milhaud's early works are mildly Impressionistic, among them *Le Printemps* (six piano pieces), 'Le Printemps' and 'Le Pastoral' (nos 1 and 2 of the Six Chamber Symphonies), 'Pastoral' and 'Nocturne' in *Protée* (the Second Symphonic Suite), the slow movement of the 1916 Piano Sonata, the *Saudades do Brasil* and parts of *L'Homme et son Désir*.

6

IN ENGLAND

It is arguable that English music is basically Teutonic or Nordic in temperament, and as such is generally unresponsive to Latin culture. It is certainly true that the period which has become known as the 'English Musical Renaissance', inaugurated at the turn of the century by Elgar's *Dream of Gerontius*, was primarily the work not only of Elgar but also of Vaughan Williams, deriving from the world of late German Romanticism on the one hand and from English folk-song on the other. There was, however, a third stream of influence of almost equal potency, and this originated in the far more eclectic, cosmopolitan idiom of Frederick Delius who, in fact, was an Englishman by accident of birth alone. Born in Yorkshire of Prussian parents, steeped in Scandinavian lore and literature, an inveterate traveller in Norway and Germany and a one-time orange planter among Negroes in North America, he elected ultimately to make his home in France. Of all the English composers of this early period, Delius is most closely affiliated to Debussy, aesthetically and to a lesser extent stylistically; the widespread dissemination of his works in England from 1907 onwards doubtless provoked a sympathetic response to the ethos of Impressionism in many composers of a later generation. For outside France, the most substantial contribution to musical Impressionism has been made by England.

After his return from America and a period of near-profitless study in Leipzig, Delius in the late 1880s settled in the Montmartre region of Paris. Here, like Debussy, he consorted far more with *hommes de lettres* and painters than with musicians,[1] though with the exception of Gauguin (the original of whose *Nevermore* he possessed for many years) he seems to have become familiar more with Scandinavian artists than with French. The predominating influence on his early work is in fact Grieg's, whose own contribution to musical Impressionism we have already examined. To the freshness and clarity of Grieg's minia-ture Norwegian evocations (reflected for instance in the tone poem *Summer Eve*, the *Florida Suite* and the songs to Scandinavian texts) Delius wedded the technical and spiritual *grande envergure* of Wagner (of whom, and of Chopin, he was a perfervid admirer) and produced in time the vast canvases of *In a Summer Garden*, *A Song of the High Hills* and *Eventyr*.

In 1899 Delius settled permanently in Grez-sur-Loing, a tiny hamlet on the edge of the Forest of Fontainebleau, where all his best work was composed if not actually conceived. The locale is significant, for this region always seemed to possess an uncanny fascination for artists, especially for the Impressionist painters. On the other side of the forest lie Barbizon and Chailly, favourite haunts of Monet, Renoir, Sisley and Corot, one of the founders of the movement who painted a picture of the old bridge at Grez. Sisley, like Delius an Englishman in self-imposed exile, settled a little further down-river from Grez, in the old walled town of Moret-sur-Loing. Much of Delius's nature poetry seems to grow naturally from the atmosphere of this beautiful spot—especially his garden sloping down to the river, a perennially-fresh source of inspiration not only to him but to his wife, Jelka, whose artistic, as opposed to her material, influence on his life and work is apt to be underrated (she eventually abandoned her own creative endeavours in order to be able to provide more fully for her husband's welfare). Born in Belgrade of Schleswig-Holstein parents, she came to Paris to study painting and soon became familiar with the circle of painters, writers and musicians which included (in addition to Delius) Gauguin, Munch, Mucha, Strindberg and other cosmopolitan figures who had been attracted to Paris. Later she became a great friend and admirer of Rodin, who in 1901 spent two days with the Deliuses at Grez. Her own style as a painter was Impressionist, with a marked gravitation towards Pointillism, as one can clearly see if one looks at her view of the house at Grez as seen from the garden [reproduced on the record-sleeve of ASD 239F (*Requiem* and *Idyll*)]. Her paintings are studies in colour rather than form, and it is tempting to associate her fondness for light and gentle pastel shades with the cool tranquillity of much of her husband's nature-Impressionism. It is certainly true that none of Delius's works composed before he came to live at Grez with his wife show the facility for evocation which he was later to develop to such a pitch of perfection, and it is quite possible that Jelka as an artist unconsciously nurtured and shaped his own inborn sense of colour.

While there is no record of any personal intercourse between Delius and Debussy, there are many aesthetic and stylistic affinities between them. For Debussy, no experience was valid until its truth had been attested by the emotions, and his musical credo reflects this:

Music should seek to please . . . extreme complications are contrary to art. Beauty must appeal to the senses, must provide us with immediate enjoyment, must impress or insinuate itself into us without any effort on our part.

Compare this with Delius:

Music is addressed and should appeal instantly to the soul of the listener . . . never believe that one must hear music many times to appreciate it. Music is a thing of instinct rather than learning; it should never be complicated, for with complication it loses its power to move.

Thus we can see that the composers' beliefs in the nature and function of music coincided in every fundamental respect, and their affirmations of artistic faith were so similar as to be almost interchangeable. For Delius, as his amanuensis Eric Fenby tells us, 'life was completely a matter of feeling; he was contemptuous of learning and completely anti-metaphysical'. We have seen Debussy protesting vehemently against an excessively intellectual approach to music. We know that his ideal was a continuous, self-generating, quasi-improvisatory stream of beautiful sound, and that to realize this ideal he made radical departures from traditional concepts of harmony and texture. Predictably therefore we should expect to find similar characteristics in Delius's music; and we certainly do, although there are few passages in his work which could be readily mistaken for Debussy. Delius revels in the opulent sonorities of ninths, elevenths and thirteenths, chains of lush discords used in hedonistic abandon. Yet his harmonic texture is much more consistently chromatic than Debussy's, its mainspring is more self-evidently Wagnerian; moreover the invariable presence of melodic thread gives the music a continuity of argument, an essentially dynamic impulse which is fundamentally at variance with the peculiarly static quality of much of Debussy's Impressionism. (Delius once said that the only thing which mattered in music was a sense of flow.)

Like Debussy also, Delius possessed a marvellous sense of orchestral

colour and habitually conceived his music directly in terms of instrumental sonorities. The gigantic metropolitan nocturne, *Paris—The
Song of a Great City*, is the great orchestral *tour de force* of his early work,
for which the model was quite clearly the Strauss of the early tone
poems; but his powers of nature-evocation were fully revealed only
some two or three years later with *Appalachia*, a set of variations on a
Negro slave-song for orchestra with final chorus. In this impressive
work Delius enshrines memories of his early days as an orange planter
in the 'deep South' of America—days in which, alone with the immensities and wonder of nature, he first felt the creative impulse
asserting itself. On his plantation, on the banks of the St John River in
Florida, he had been awestruck by the profusion of natural growth,
by the stillness of its contained power and by its riotous colour—the
jasmine, wisteria and purple hyacinths, the grey veils of Spanish moss
hanging over the trees, the play of light through the woods, the early-
morning mist over the great river: all this imprinted itself indelibly
on his memory and cried aloud for musical depiction in an Impressionist nature poem.[2] The prelude—dawn over the waters and in the
'scented woods'—is particularly striking, with answering reverberant
horn-calls (the 'echo swelling over the mighty stream'), quivering
tremolo strings suggesting an early-morning haze, pentatonic figuration
in harps and woodwind; the upward-thrusting pentatonic triplet in
Ex. 25a is one of Delius's most readily recognizable fingerprints.
Examine too the 'misterioso lento' variation immediately preceding
the baritone soloist's first entry; as Eric Fenby has said, 'the river
heaving lazily, the mystery of the woods, the sweltering heat—one
can feel, even see their image in this music'. Echoes of Strauss linger
on in certain parts of the scoring, but both here and certainly from
A Village Romeo and Juliet onwards Delius brought an increased
refinement and a subtler sense of individuation of timbre to bear on his
palette, evidence of which may be found for instance in the climactic
central section of *Sea Drift* where the increasing tumult of the sea and
in the mind of the lone watcher on the beach is suggested by an
impressionistic merging of tiny, elusive fragments of melody, a broad
rhythmic sweep and pointed shafts of orchestral colour.

The ultimate in Delius's orchestral Impressionism is undoubtedly
the tone poem *In a Summer Garden* and an evocation on a smaller
scale, *Summer Night on the River*. Here the technique is akin to
Pointillism. In the first of these the main body of the score is composed
of innumerable tiny dots and dashes of colour, blended and juxtaposed

Ex. 25a
Delius, *Appalachia*

with a marvellous rightness and inevitability. From the opening bars, when the modal curve of the oboe melody is shattered into a thousand tiny fragments (suggesting, perhaps, a broadening of vista, the ruffling of a water surface or a momentary disturbance of the vast floral panorama) the listener is unconsciously drawn in to an all-pervasive atmosphere of summer noontide heat, a tremulous haze in which floral colours and scents, river murmurings and bird-songs seem to be inextricably interwoven. Thematic as opposed to motivic content is tenuous, though 'song' is never-ending; only in the more tranquil central section is a long-breathed arch of viola melody brought into focus beneath a delicate tracery of woodwind. Similarly in 'The march of spring' from the *North Country Sketches* a continuously dynamic impulse is generated by scintillating fragments of wood-wind and string arabesque in a texture which surges and throbs, expands and contracts with all the intensity of a living organism. In *Summer Night on the River* the orchestral forces are reduced, but in this chiaroscuro-like little piece Delius's *pointilliste* technique attains a higher-than-ever degree of visual suggestiveness; the tenuousness of the demarcation between Impressionism and realism is compellingly demonstrated. Notice, in Ex. 25b, the balance and shading of woodwind timbre, especially in the last three bars in which, 'les parfums de la nuit' and the heady accumulated languor of a hot summer's day finally compel the oarsman to take refuge in sleep; the varied and evocative string texture; and in the second bar the drowsy remnant of viola melody which has bound the shifting colours of this intimate and sensitive night-piece together.

More obviously Debussian is the opening of *Brigg Fair*, compound of flute arabesque, delicate washes of harp, and horns and muted strings producing kaleidoscopic harmony and sensitively blurring the tonality as in *L'Après-midi d'un Faune*. Debussian too is Delius's notion of the voice as an extra dimension of colour (as in the original version of Debussy's *Printemps*, 'Sirènes' and Ravel's *Daphnis et Chloé*). The tropical nocturne in Act III of *Koanga* (an early work dating from 1896) includes tenors and basses singing wordlessly from afar, thus anticipating the beautiful passage in the second picture of *Fennimore and Gerda* in which a solo tenor voice rhapsodizes wordlessly in the distance on the fjörd. In these works, as in *Appalachia, Hassan, A Mass of Life*, but most of all in *A Song of the High Hills* and the two unaccompanied choruses *To be sung of a Summer Night on the Water*, the voices are used freely for expressive and atmospheric purposes as a legitimate extension of the instrumental tone palette. The paradoxically unhuman qualities of the wordless chorus are imaginatively exploited in *A Song of the High Hills*; after enhancing the first appearance of the theme representing 'the wide far distance—the great solitude' various choral groupings, remote, wordless and unseen, interpolate their melismata at poetically relevant junctures until at the main climax the full chorus enters *a capella* and still wordless, ultimately joining the orchestra to evoke a vision of some spectacular mountain panorama which brings in its wake momentary submergence of the personality in pantheistic union with nature. Delius's Impressionism is essentially subjective; he loses himself in his dreams and visions, surrenders himself spiritually to them, whereas Debussy remains an impartial observer.

Delius loved Debussy's *L'Après-midi d'un Faune* and *Pelléas*, although he remained unimpressed by the piano music and his later work in which, he claimed, the Frenchman had degenerated into a mannerist. For Delius was essentially a reactionary, his technique a cul-de-sac; that he should have been puzzled by the forward-looking nature of his contemporary's later thought is understandable. Technically speaking,

Ex. 25b (i)
Delius, *Summer Night on the River*

Ex. 25b (ii)

Debussy had no real thoroughgoing influence upon Delius's main period of creativity (1901–12); apart from a few obvious reminiscences (the *Brigg Fair* passage referred to above, for example) stylistic similarities are more probably the result of the intuitive aesthetic affinities between the composers which we have already examined. In the period which followed Delius produced a spate of works for the most part Scandinavian in inspiration in which his style comes to show a new harmonic acerbity, a new transparency of texture and an almost Holstian clarity of outline. A correspondingly chillier, more bracing note tends to creep into the music, emotion becomes objectified in a manner more suggestive of Debussy. In fact 'Nuages' may well have been the model for 'Autumn—the wind soughs in the trees' from the *North Country Sketches*, for the orchestral texture is of a greyness *à la* Whistler, and the chains of slow-moving organum-like consecutives, broken only by the occasional intrusion of a rising-fourths motif, is reminiscent of 'the immutable aspect of the sky and the slow, solemn motion of the clouds, fading away in grey tones lightly tinged with white'. Texture rather than tune is the watchword also in the finales of the two choral works which dated from the war years— *An Arabesque* and *Requiem. An Arabesque* is a setting of a beautiful but enigmatic poem by the Impressionist J. P. Jacobsen (author of the *Songs of Gurra*) in which the blossoming and death of love (here represented by the god Pan in his darker, more sensual aspect) is set against the vividness and brevity of the Scandinavian summer. It closes with the fall of love mirrored in the desolation of a Northern winter landscape:

> Now all is past!
> In the ground all snow-bestrewn
> In the bare brown wood
> Stands a lonely thornbush,
> The black winds they scatter its leaves!
> One after another,
> One after another,
> Shedding its blood-reddened berries
> In the cold, white snow.
> Its flowing red berries in the cold, white snow—
> Knowst thou Pan?

When the voices enter with their last, lingering, long-drawn-out chromatic moan of 'Knowst thou Pan?' they are scarcely perceived as voices, rather as sounds from the circumambient air or a sigh from the snowbound earth itself. But if these bars—they have no parallel else-where in music—enshrine in Impressionist terms the essence of mid-winter, the Epilogue of the *Requiem* is vivid with the freshness of spring—chiming pentatonic chords in horns and celesta with harp arpeggios, finally a bell-like pentatonic figure on the harp, cuckoo calls on the woodwind pointed by celesta (notice the tang of the Lydian sharpened fourth), wide-spaced string chords, horns and trumpets sounding a bitonal fanfare in the distance. The simplicity and beauty of the musical substance, the freshness and lucidity of the scoring, have combined to make this passage one of Delius's most admired pieces of Impressionist nature evocation.

Delius is undoubtedly one of the greatest post-Impressionist com-posers, and his influence upon English musicians of the next generation was rivalled only by that of Vaughan Williams. There was little love lost between the two and they seemed reluctant to admit to any compatibility of outlook or temperament, yet there were affinities between them. They were both great mystics, visionaries, imbued with an insatiable love of the countryside, of nature in all her immensity and unfathomableness. Vaughan Williams's assimilation of folksong was completely natural and instinctive; as with Grieg, it was to him an essential if he were to attain to a full and vital expression of his love for his country's landscape and people. The saturated lyricism of Delius is no less a free flowering from folk-song, although far less susceptible to definition and categorization. Vaughan Williams's art has been compared to certain passages in the nature evocations of Thomas Hardy's Wessex novels; Delius's to the best of Richard Jefferies or Henry Williamson. It is arguable, however, that the basis of their musical (if not personal) *entente cordiale* is the readiness of their response in either case to the techniques of Impressionism.

In 1908, at the age of 36, Vaughan Williams went to Paris for a period of study with Ravel. Upon his return he produced the two works which established him as one of the foremost composers of the day—*On Wenlock Edge* and the *Fantasia on a Theme by Thomas Tallis*; and though he referred with his accustomed flippancy to his 'attack of French fever' and to a string quartet 'which caused a friend to say I must have been having tea with Debussy', he was no doubt perfectly well aware of the new turning his stylistic development had taken. For the Paris sojourn provided more than a mere corrective to a lumbering Teutonism. Although Debussy's music had first been heard in England in 1905, it needed a complete and unconditional surrender on Vaughan Williams's part to the musical atmosphere of Paris to prove to him that, in many respects, the paths he had been following were moving in the same direction as Debussy's own. Debussy was undoubtedly one of the liberating factors in the emergence of his mature style, and the Impressionist elements discernible in it are deeper rooted than they might at first glance appear.

In the principal works of Vaughan Williams's earlier years—the Rossetti and Stevenson settings, *In the Fen Country*, the *Norfolk Rhapsody* and *Toward the Unknown Region*—the overthrow of classical harmony and the renunciation of the major-minor hegemony in favour of modal independence, though anticipated, was by no means complete. Debussy also, as we know, rebelled against the major-minor tyranny and sought salvation in modality, the only difference being that whereas he turned to Gregorian chant, oriental pentatonicism and the whole-tone scale, Vaughan Williams relied upon English folk-song. Hitherto their paths had been moving in the same direction, though independently of one another: they converged in the sphere of harmony. For the principle of 'non-functional' harmony gains marked ascendancy in Vaughan Williams's work after 1908. Debussy's hedonistic indulgence in higher chromatic discords accorded ill, however, with an inherently Nordic austerity, and Vaughan Williams tended to confine his parallelism to common chords and their inversions; yet for all his disdain of 'succulent' harmony and the more bracing intervallic structure of his own, his textures in general are anything but ascetic. He can build the most imposing chordal edifices on a foundation of simple diatonic dissonances, elsewhere enriching his fabric with added notes or solidifying it with doublings, often to poignant effect. His own harmonic idiom would no doubt have evolved quite naturally of its own accord, irrespective of Debussy, but the process might well have been longer and, in terms of mature creative achievement, rather costlier; in the light of Debussy's precedent, however, what had heretofore been a tentative groping now asserted itself in a resolute embrace.

Given this technical affinity, it is not surprising that the atmospheric nature of much of Vaughan Williams's more contemplative music draws to some extent on Impressionist methods of evocation. We may observe these first of all in 'Bredon Hill', no 5 of the songcycle to poems by Housman, *On Wenlock Edge*. In Housman's poem the simple country tragedy is framed by the sound of the bells, which ring their subtle changes on the successive stages of the story, discreetly pointing and commenting upon it. The human interest, however, remains uppermost; the bells are never the protagonists as they are in Poe's *Bells*, where they assume a life and force of their own. Yet in Vaughan Williams's setting of Housman's poem this is exactly what does happen; it is in fact a first and foremost elaborately-wrought, impressionistic-ally-conceived sequence of bell-sonorities, not at all dissimilar to 'Cloches à travers les feuilles' of 'La vallée des cloches'. (Ravel, incident-ally, was a great admirer of *On Wenlock Edge* and even offered to play the piano part in a projected London performance.) The opening is wholly typical—chiming secondary sevenths on strings and piano with a flurried quaver figure of open fourths suggesting more energetic campanological activity, but all still sufficiently remote to leave the lovers wrapped in each others arms (Ex. 26a). A change to triple metre

Ex. 26a
Vaughan Williams, 'Bredon Hill' (*On Wenlock Edge*)

and a new melodic shape represents the summons of the church, and in the funeral procession the 'one bell only' tolls in the tenor above the clanging of hollow fourths and fifths, its reverberations reinforced by low-voiced seventh chords in the bass. A welling of semiquaver piano figuration (again the harmonic basis is the secondary seventh) suggests the humming steeples, and yet another pattern accompanies the ironic message of the bells in the final stanza. The climax comes with a frenzied outburst of fourths figuration as the young lover rails bitterly at the bells before promising them ultimate obedience.

After 'Bredon Hill' Vaughan Williams's Second Symphony, the *London*, is the work in which Impressionist techniques are most pronounced. It is particularly interesting in this connection that when in 1870, upon the outbreak of the Franco-Prussian war, Monet sought refuge in London, he found the city, especially the Thames with its mists and fogs, a new and quickening source of inspiration: so much so that he returned to the same scenes in 1899, 1901, 1903 and 1904, and produced some ninety pictures as a result, all but a few of them of the Thames at Westminster. The Impressionist painters were concerned to weld together in a visual unity the touches of colour which formed their impressions without having to arrange the elements of a scene in some contrived pattern or to impose a linear framework in conflict with their novel structural technique. The simple perspective of a river with its easily-broken boundaries provided all that was needed in the way of a backbone; the water also functioned as a uniquely strong reflector of the changing light and the colour of the inconstant sky, and the mists, smokes and fogs, as prevalent today about the wharves at Greenwich as about Westminster and the Houses of Parliament in Victorian times, caused the myriad natural colours to blend and interpenetrate in a typical Impressionist haze. The opening of Vaughan Williams's *London Symphony* is the precise equivalent in sound of Monet's *Thames and Houses of Parliament* or *Waterloo Bridge, Grey Day*. Vaughan Williams's London comes to life only gradually and haltingly from beneath a pall of river mist. This opening, as Constant Lambert pointed out to the composer, much to the latter's astonishment, is remarkably reminiscent of the opening of *La Mer*, which is also an impression of early-morning mist over water. Over a pedal-point there emerges a rising-fourths motif on violas which is verticalized in sustained violin chords. Eventually a massive chord-complex of pentatonic fourths and fifths towers above the striking of Big Ben and splits up rhythmically into particles of ever-decreasing size, heaving backwards and forwards and suggesting a surge of water (Ex. 26b)—very much in the manner of *La Mer*, in the passage culminating in the 'Modéré, sans lenteur' (p. 5 of the miniature score).

Both the slow movement and the 'Scherzo-Nocturne' have been spoken of in connection with the paintings of James McNeill Whistler, who wrote in *Ten O'Clock*:

When the evening mist clothes the riverside with poetry, as with a veil, and the poor buildings lose themselves in the dim sky, and the tall chimneys became campanili, and the warehouses are palaces in the night, and the whole city hangs in the heavens, a fairy land is before us—then Nature sings her exquisite song to the artist alone.

Although there is stylistic disparity between the Impressionists' work and Whistler's, Whistler also had been subject to the influence of Corot and Delacroix and shared with them a preoccupation with mood

Ex. 26b
Vaughan Williams, *London Symphony*

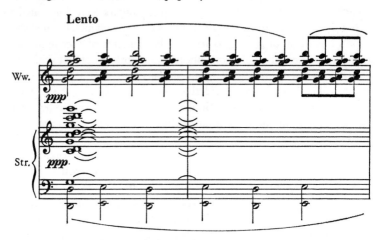

evocation. He evokes a veiled and phantom world, a pattern of delicate tones, of silhouettes, incorporeal yet purely sensuous. Only tone is positive in his work, neither form nor colour being defined, and tone rather than colour is the predominating quality in the slow movement of the *London Symphony*, music which admirably reflects the mood of the fine series of *Nocturnes*—for example *Old Battersea Bridge* or *Nocturne in Blue and Grey*. We have seen how these very nocturnes with their all-pervasive greyness were the starting point of Debussy's own grey-tinted *Nocturnes*. The technique of the third movement, the 'Scherzo-Nocturne', is more perceptibly Impressionist. People and events flurry by in a sequence consistently nebulous, fragmentary and ill-defined; this is the London of 'the unending murmuring streets, the stirring shadow, the amber-lighted gloom'. The all-pervasive element is mist; there emerges at one point a merry company outside a public house, but in the concluding bars the darkness deepens so as to blot out all traces of human activity. After the tragic Elgarian march of the finale, Impressionism reappears in the 'Epilogue' in the shape of a rippling figure washing around the rising-fourths theme of the introduction—the Thames by night. Big Ben sounds through the rising river mist (the reverberant harp once again), sounds from afar hover in the night air (augmented triads on muted horns, trumpets and cornets)—but all is ultimately enveloped once again in impenetrable obscurity.

To a certain extent an impressionistic aura encircles the *Pastoral*, Vaughan Williams's Third Symphony. This music began to germinate in the composer's mind not in the Cotswolds (to which it has often been related) but in the wastes of wartime Flanders, where he was on active service. Evening after evening at Ecoives he went with his ambulance-wagon up a steep hill at the top of which he was entranced by a Corot-type landscape in the sunset. The first movement of the *Pastoral* corresponds, as does no other English music, to the nature-Impressionism of the Debussy of 'Nuages': grey, reflective, beautiful yet passionless, almost totally—but not quite—devoid of any human involvement or incident. There is that quality of sadness which the artist will often unconsciously convey in the face of overwhelming natural beauty. Melodic contours are not blurred in the conventional Impressionist way, but symphonic argument as such is eschewed in favour of a continuous process of evolution, fusion and regeneration of tune which often takes place on several modal strata simultaneously. This absence of symphonic tension is deliberate: the sole purpose of this movement is evocation. The orchestral colours are mellow and clear-toned; a certain sameness, a uniform grey–green-ness is wooed, there are no sharp contrasts but subtle differentiations of timbre. (The light fantastic play of colours in the coda of the third movement—a thistledown classic among scherzo-codas—reflects more clearly a Ravelian piquancy.) The finale introduces a soprano soloist, who sings her beautiful wordless melisma unaccompanied, save for a barely perceptible pedal-point. The effect of this interpolated cadenza, like that of the natural trumpet in the second movement, is magical; time stands still, and it is at such moments that the power of the music to evoke huge untenanted tracts of open country approaches that of Hardy's prose in *The Return of the Native* (Egdon Heath) and *Tess of the d'Urbervilles* (Talbothays Dairy). We noted that Debussy discovered that human voices had the paradoxical property of sounding remarkably unhuman if employed wordlessly and that Delius exploited solo voices and chorus to great effect in this way in *A Song of the High Hills*. Here Vaughan Williams resorts to the same device to create, like Delius, an impression of mystic solitudes and wide open spaces.

The wordless chorus is again employed in an impressionistic manner in *Flos Campi*, a work which followed harmonically in the wake of the *Pastoral Symphony*.[4] The chorus functions more extensively here as an added colour dimension than in any other Vaughan Williams score, and forms an integral part of each of its six short movements; however their purpose here is rather to intensify the throb of earthly human passion than to introduce any non-human, purely elemental connotations, and the music is reminiscent more of *Daphnis et Chloé* than of 'Sirènes'. Most impressionistic of all is the second section: 'For lo, the winter is past, the rain is over and gone, the flowers appear on the earth, the time of the singing of birds is come, and the voice of the turtle is heard in our land.' The voices (humming or singing to vowel sounds) are so blended and interwoven with the instrumental polyphony as to produce a texture of radiantly sensuous euphony.

In the last of Vaughan Williams's works with notably impressionistic passages it is not the freshness of spring which wordless voices are called upon to evoke, but the desolate snowbound wilderness of the South Pole. In the first and last movement of the *Sinfonia Antartica* the voices have to suggest an unending soulless vacuum, and one senses in the central panel of the first movement (in which the voices are heard for the first time) and even more in the main substance of the third movement ('Landscape') that the composer found the problem of depicting vast areas of snow and ice as fascinating as did the French Impressionist painters themselves. In the former the melodic element is reduced to the absolute minimum and the emphasis is placed almost exclusively on texture and sonority—hard, glittering and transparent. Here the composer displays an almost Bartókian preoccupation with timbre—on a harmonic foundation laid by strings and muted horns all manner of filigree work on the tuned percussion creates a mosaic of sound which glows with an unearthly light. Again, the opening of 'Landscape' is, like the opening of the third movement of Bartók's *Music for Strings, Percussion and Celesta*, conceived in terms of pure sonority; the muted horn-line which merges from the bass harp glissandi, the soft drum and cymbal-rolls, the atonal interjections of the two flutes, and later from the string and xylophone note-clusters, is so benumbed, lifeless and devoid of any tonal implication as scarcely to function as melody. Later on a texture woven of woodwind, strings, soft brass, celesta, piano and glockenspiel infuses a slightly warmer spirit into the scene, as if momentarily lit up by sunlight; but the essential atmosphere remains totally objective and passionless.

It is very probable that the model for the remarkably impressionistic sequences in the *Sinfonia Antartica* was the last movement of Gustav Holst's suite *The Planets*—'Neptune'—once described by Gerald Abraham as 'perhaps the most remarkable piece of pure orchestral Impressionism ever written'. Holst's is a curious case. Early admiration for Grieg gave way eventually to a prolonged bout of Wagner worship, and he himself described his early works as 'good old Wagnerian bawling'. Then came his discovery of folk-song (but not before he had been toying at his own instigation with fourths-chords) and it is not to be wondered at that out of this heterogeneous admixture of elements—to which Stravinsky made a later contribution—something approaching the Impressionist idiom now and then took shape, if only to be dissipated immediately.

Holst's leaning towards the Orient, particularly oriental philosophy, undoubtedly has a bearing on this. His interest in mysticism and the occult had begun when he had become attracted to the philosophy of the Bhagavad Gita and had attempted to learn Sanskrit; 'Sita', the choral hymns from the *Rig Veda* and the chamber opera *Sāvitri* were the upshot of this, and an interest in oriental music is apparent in such works as the *Beni Mora* suite, *Two Eastern Pictures* for female voices and harp, or the *Japanese Suite*. A work for female chorus and orchestra, the *Hymn to Dionysius*, is important as a humble precursor of the sound world of 'Neptune'. Imogen Holst concedes that in this piece 'there is more sensuous sound than usual in Holst's music', and goes on to suggest that he may have come under the influence of one of Vaughan Williams's choruses from the *Bacchae*, written shortly after the composer's period of study with Ravel.

Shortly afterwards Holst started work on what was to prove the most popular of all his compositions and the one in which the Impressionist content is at its peak—*The Planets*. Stale and bored with repeated hearings, we are apt to underrate not only its strength of character and intrinsic beauty but also its originality. Nothing of so radical a nature existed in English music when this suite first appeared in 1917, the nearest continental equivalents being Schmitt's *Tragédie de Salomé* and Prokofiev's *Scythian Suite*. There is certainly little 'quintessential Englishness' here, except perhaps in 'Jupiter'. There are intimations of Impressionism in 'Venus', the second movement, but Holst here takes a long last lingering look at his early Wagnerian infatuation. Swaying chords for horns and woodwind with two harps, celesta and glockenspiel exploit the familiar 'lusciousness' of Impressionist harmony, and when these form the basis of the coda the texture becomes even more elaborate. The opening and closing pages of this movement have an ethereal delicacy and a transparency of colour which bring them within the Impressionist orbit, and the third movement, 'Mercury', though different, is likewise affiliated. For much of the time the interest of the music lies in the shafts and flashes of orchestral colour (with both harps and celesta very prominent, frequently used soloistically) which dart backwards and forwards in a thousand different directions at once and in daringly opposed tonalities which by their very fleetingness and insubstantiality impress themselves the more forcefully on the nerve-ends. Even when by way of a trio a fragment of melody is introduced (fig. III) it merely repeats and intensifies itself above a shifting web of harmony until a full-hearted climax is reached. In 'Saturn' flutes and harps toll a knell for the passing of youth, their augmented fourths communicating a dull ache, a quiet deadly despair which carries no intimation whatsoever of the miraculous impressionistic beauty of the coda, from fig. V. Harps chime softly in harmonics over sustained muted strings; the operative interval here is the perfect, not the augmented, fourth, and it has a consolatory quality. The sense of ecstasy grows imperceptibly as tubular bells sound in the distance over pentatonic horn and harp figurations in A minor which reach further and further upward until they come to rest on a C major triad which brings with it the radiance of the added sixth. Finally over an ineffably serene sustained secondary ninth the chimes are lost in the stillness of immeasurable distances.

This visionary quality anticipates the awe-inspiring 'Neptune'. One easily comes to the conclusion that Abraham is right and that for the acme of orchestral Impressionism an Englishman was responsible. The sound of the orchestra is of a uniform Debussian greyness ('dead tone except the clarinet after (5)', pencilled Holst in his own copy of the score), the scoring is transparent to the point of insubstantiality, the thematic content is minimal; the only reality in this limitless vista of time and space is that of sound, sound which reflects no earthly preoccupation, registers and reacts to no human emotion but simply is. Waves of quasi-incorporeal sound ebb and flow between the twin poles of E minor and G minor with ever-widening ripples of divided strings, two harps and celesta until a distant, unseen choir of women's voices is heard, so faint as to be almost a figment of the aural imagination, sustaining a high B (how much more sexless and spiritualized does a wordless women's chorus sound than a wordless men's!). These voices again are called upon to express the concept of non-humanity; not the reckless, resplendent non-humanity of mountain peaks or ocean swell, but a concept which in its implications reaches far beyond either of these. As the orchestration finally dissolves into the circumambient air the voices are left on their own, swaying backwards and forwards between the two Impressionistic chords (Ex. 27) until

Ex. 27
Holst, 'Neptune' (*The Planets*)

lost to all human perception. 'Neptune' is one of the wonders of the Impressionist world.

Holst was born in 1874. Five years later were born three composers all of whom were to become associated with Impressionism in varying degrees of intimacy—Cyril Scott, Frank Bridge and John Ireland. Of these, Scott's links are the most tenous. Although educated in Frankfurt, he showed a lively interest in French culture from an early age and wrote several overtures to Maeterlinck plays in his student days. He seems to have developed a harmonic system of emancipated discords almost simultaneously with Debussy, but even though in English musical circles before the First World War he was unhelpfully dubbed 'the English Debussy' that sensibility peculiar to musical Impressionism is to be found in his work hardly at all. As a harmonist he was original, but he failed to establish that extra elusive emotional dimension whereby Debussy was enabled to call into play whole areas of feeling which transcended the mere moment; Debussy's music is never a pleasantly superfluous aural titillation, and the vagaries of Scott's harmonic style illustrates only too clearly the dangerous course his French contemporary's development might have taken had he not been able to impose his own peculiarly personal form of spiritual discipline upon it. Many of the short piano pieces and songs by which Scott is today remembered are simple and often very beautiful, but despite many original effects their emotional range rarely exceeds that of the *Lyric Pieces* and songs by Grieg, by whom Scott was surely influenced in Frankfurt.

A similarly cosmopolitan figure was Frank Bridge, who liked Debussy exceedingly and remained, like Scott, basically impervious to both the Elgar tradition and the folk-song revival. In his later years he became much interested in German Expressionism (particularly in Berg, with whom he badly wanted his pupil Britten to study) but Impressionism, especially Impressionist harmony, exerted a great influence over the music belonging to the early part of his career. He was a great advocate of chamber music and firmly believed that this medium could attain to as great a pitch of expressive intensity as to the full symphony orchestra; yet when he turned to the orchestra he revelled in a full, rich sonority and ran the gamut of colours. He achieved a remarkable synthesis between an innate desire for firm-fibred textures with a clean, strong sound and the vagueness essential to atmospheric suggestiveness: his marked sympathy for this aspect of Impressionist aesthetics is shown by some lines from Richard Jefferies which he quotes above the score of the first of his *Two Poems* for orchestra: 'Those thoughts and feelings which are not sharply defined, but have a haze of distance and beauty about them, are always the dearest.' This piece certainly employs some typically Impressionist harmony, but such 'haze' as there is is suggested merely by the persistent if rarely self-assertive bitonal conflict between B♭ and E which remains unresolved even at the end. The scoring is sensitive, the diction refined and the texture even slightly astringent (except in the warmly lyrical central section), but if the composer perceived his thoughts and feelings 'through a haze of distance and beauty' the act of communicating them seems to have dispersed it.

In fact, Bridge's creative temperament was almost pre-Impressionist, even romantic. His piano music, much of it of exquisite beauty, is reactionary in terms of piano technique although it uses Impressionist harmony and treats of Impressionist subject-matter. The *Four Characteristic Pieces* are aptly-named, representing as they do the quintessence of Bridge's piano style; if they invoke a French spirit at all it is that of Fauré rather than Debussy, Fauré perhaps with a touch of Ravelian spice. The texture of 'Water nymphs' is freely chromatic but spare; 'Fragrance' is suggestive of Ravel with its pedal point and bitter-sweet harmony; 'Bitter–Sweet' itself is stylistically more akin to 'Water nymphs', but 'Fireflies', a fascinating piece, is almost an English counterpart of 'Noctuelles'. Bridge's texture may be smoother-shaped, his melodic lines more sustained than Ravel's in this instance, but he is as past a master of nervously exacerbated dissonance. The final bars (Ex. 28) are typical of Bridge's Impressionism. So are the *Three Poems* for piano, especially no 3, 'Sunset'; no 1, 'Solitude', shows that orientation towards a sparsely linear pattern of texture which prefigures the composer's later partiality for Berg, whereas no 2 'Ecstasy' is (perhaps intentionally) tumultuously Scriabinesque.

Bridge's larger orchestral works all call for consideration in this

Ex. 28
Bridge, 'Fireflies' (*Four Characteristic Pieces*)

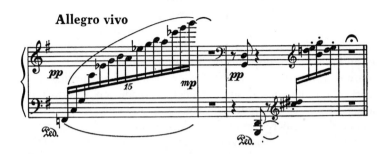

context. The suite *The Sea*, written some five years after *La Mer*, is typical of Bridge's more romantically-biased Impressionism; it is certainly no English counterpart of Debussy's masterpiece, although it comes nearer to being so than the approximately contemporaneous *Sea Symphony* of Vaughan Williams. The third movement, for example, entitled 'Moonlight', could almost be mistaken for Chausson or d'Indy with its luscious post-Wagnerian scoring, its shapely flowing curves of lyric melody and liberal indulgence in the added-sixth chord; the fourth, 'Storm', is overtly programmatic in the Straussian manner and has little of the fiercely self-consistent epic subtlety of the 'Dialogue du vent et de la mer'. On the other hand the first movement, 'Seascape', has a much more pronounced Impressionist flavour; it rejects symphonic development in favour of a continuous tide-like ebb and flow of melodic and harmonic patterns—a winged phrase of pentatonic viola melody, a repeated surge of dominant minor-ninth harmony, the tang of the augmented triad at the climax, an extraordinary passage of woodwind writing (figs. 11–12) which sounds wholly convincing in the context of a sea-scape—it is very definitely a sea sound, however elusive of definition (perhaps a momentary altercation amidst a passing flock of gulls?). The movement as a whole has that authentic sense of sea swell which bespeaks a successful piece of sea music in the tradition of *Sadko* and *La Mer*; we can almost crush the sharp shells beneath our feet. So too with the brief second movement, 'Sea foam', a kaleidoscope of buoyantly-dancing rhythmic and melodic shapes, the appeal of which is much more immediately sensuous than intellectual, however well the music stands up to formal analysis.

In terms of style the tone poem *Summer* lies somewhere between the romantic *The Sea* and the quite definitely impressionistic *Enter Spring*. In *Summer* the lines are spacious and singing, supple, but clearly and firmly drawn, although there is perhaps less concern with motivic manipulation than in *The Sea*—the whole evolves quite naturally out of the parts. *Enter Spring* is built on a large scale and though the form is roughly ABCA with a coda its shape is fluid and quite seamless; Impressionist harmony and orchestration is in evidence throughout, more consistently than in *The Sea* or *Summer*. The opening scene is markedly *pointilliste*—elusive snatches of theme on woodwind and strings, harps have whole-tone arpeggios, and only gradually does a unified theme emerge from the welded fragments. The second main section brings a deliberate aura of haze (seven bars after fig. 15) with a pentatonic harmonic and melodic substructure, distant trumpets, delicate washes of sound on harps and celesta, violas and cellos trilling, upper strings playing in harmonics. With the start of the main Andante Tranquillo bird-calls over sustained muted string-chords with harp and celesta deftly colouring the landscape evoke a pregnantly tranquil atmosphere in every way the equal of similarly rapt moments in the nature poetry of Delius or Bax (Ex. 29). The two chords here dissolving

Ex. 29
Bridge, *Enter Spring*

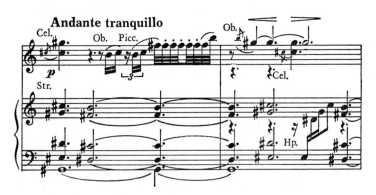

one into the other are later to form a bell-like motif in an inexorable march rhythm; in the coda they bring the work to an apotheosis of triumphant splendour with brass-calls sounding and re-echoing over the full orchestra, complete with tubular bells. This is one of the great Impressionist glorifications of spring.

John Ireland was one of the most significant exponents of musical

Impressionism in England. He confessedly wrote under the aegis of
Ravel rather than Debussy; passionate stress is contained within
precision of outline, asperity and sensuousness mingle freely in a
harmonic diction in which from time to time the ear may catch the
modal ring of English folk-song. A more searching affinity is contained
in his sympathy for the writings of Arthur Machen, whose explorations into the hinterland of the subconscious, the supernatural, the
occult and the primeval world of instincts and associations follow on
in a direct line from Poe and Maeterlinck—he has in fact been termed
'the English Maeterlinck'. Machen's musical conception of language,
as expressed in *The Hill of Dreams*, is remarkably akin to that of Poe
which, as we have seen, so conditioned the aesthetics of the nineteenth-
century French writer or musician:

Language was chiefly important for the beauty of its sounds, by its possession
of words resonant, glorious to the ear, by its capacity, when exquisitely
arranged, of suggesting wonderful and indefinable impressions, perhaps more
ravishing and farther removed from the domain of strict thought than the
impressions excited by music itself. Here lay hidden the secret of the sensuous
art of literature, it was the secret of suggestion, the art of causing delicious
sensation by the use of words.

From 1906, when Ireland chanced upon Machen's *House of Souls*,
the author's work exercised an almost uncanny influence over his own.
He once declared: 'How can the critics expect to understand my work
if they haven't read Machen?' Machen helped him to an understanding
of the sway exerted over him by places instinct with the romance of
legend, prehistory and myth, and indirectly urged him to seek expression of this romance in his music. For Ireland, Machen was the
supreme mystic, a seer in whose writing he sensed that special associa-
tive environment to which his own work aspired.
   Ireland was first and foremost a composer for the piano, and the first
work to be imbued with this characteristic atmosphere was the piano
suite *Decorations*, the supreme example of Impressionism in twentieth-
century English piano music. The score of the first movement is dated
'Fauvic, Jersey, August, 1912' (the Channel Islands were an ever-vital
source of inspiration to Ireland) and is prefixed by an evocative quotation from Arthur Symons:

I would wash the dust of the world in a soft green flood:
Here, between sea and sea, in the fairy wood,
I have found a delicate, wave-green solitude.

The lapping pentatonic *ostinato* is marked *à la* Debussy, 'in a clear, delicate sonority' and the fragmented melodic element, also pentatonic, 'as if a chime'. The entire substance of the piece grows from this elusive intermingling of sounds in the sea and air; the climax is reached as the bells reverberate in ever-increasing diminution in the right hand under glittering cascades of pentatonic arpeggios in the left, and in the coda (marked 'lontano e tranquillo') an ostinato-like murmur of fourths and fifths, as if from a depth of water, supports a rising succession of chords tapering upwards through the whole-tone scale into a silence broken only by one barely-perceptible chime at the farthest extremity of the keyboard.

The second movement of *Decorations*, 'Moonglade', is a mysterious nocturne (again prefaced by a quotation from Symons) which owes its evocative power to its subtly muted bitonality: the suggestion is of a veiled monotony of moonlight perceived in a state at mid-point between sleeping and waking. In the closing bars the pedalled intermingling of the upper partials produce an illusory effect which though quintessentially impressionistic is not paralleled by anything in the piano work of Debussy or Ravel. The third movement, the Machen-inspired 'Scarlet Ceremonies', is the most brilliant of the set, coruscating with the clear, hard quality of cut diamonds; its two fine, ringing fanfare-like themes spring from a bed of writhing pentatonic tremolos which ultimately explode into a tremendous double glissando down the keyboard, only to re-form for the least inhibited of Ireland's codas. Similarly the third movement of the piano suite *Sarnia* (inspired by the Channel Islands), the thrilling 'Song of the springtides', has a pantheistic abandon noticeably akin to that of *L'Isle Joyeuse*, and the central section presents an exultant melody over a heaving pentatonic ostinato which would not be out of place in *La Mer*. The sea forms a powerful link between Ireland and Debussy, and the 'Song of the springtides', 'The island spell', and even passages with no specified extra-musical connotations such as occur in the Andante Cantabile of the Trio no 3 in E major are impregnated with a spirit of sea-mysticism. Other impressionistic water-pieces of Ireland are *Chelsea Reach* and *Amberley Wild Brooks*, and Impressionist techniques are more or less in evidence in such pieces as *Fire of Spring*, *Equinox*, and the *Rhapsody*.

Ireland wrote comparatively little for orchestra; like Grieg, he was happiest as a writer of songs and lyrical piano pieces and possessed no special talent for orchestration. The most impressionistic of his orchestral works, *The Forgotten Rite*, is an evocation not so much of ancient pagan ritual as of its scene and setting. For the greater part of this piece the scoring is Elgarian rather than Debussian, with sweeping lyrical arches of string melody and sonorous horn counterpoint; but the true spirit of the Impressionist orchestra breaks through in the coda, with divided strings, brief but telling woodwind interjections and pellucid harp and celesta figuration. In a similar vein the *Legend* for piano and orchestra, actually dedicated to Machen, was inspired by a vision of dancing children in archaic clothing experienced by Ireland at a remote and unfrequented spot on the West Sussex Downs. The music is uncannily atmospheric, and the outer portions are charged with an intensity of tragic feeling which is only dispelled by the impressionistic central section representing the dancing children. The dance is introduced by the horn quartet playing *mezzo piano* above a pattering pentatonic ostinato, which with the pastoral simplicity of the oboe and the delicately expressive use of muted strings divisi, beautifully evokes a vision welling from the springs of psychic consciousness and filtered through a haze of memory.

The factor which determined the whole direction of Arthur Machen's inspiration was his Celtic background. He wrote of 'the woods and fields, the deep-sunken lanes, the forgotten country in the west'; a lonely boyhood in a remote Welsh parsonage left him steeped in lore and literature of the ancient Celtic world, and in this respect his musical counterpart is not so much John Ireland as another great English Impressionist, Arnold Bax.

Although Bax was born in Surrey and not 'on an island in the middle of a bog-lake in County Mayo' no composer identified himself more positively with the spirit of the Irish renaissance. In 1902 he came upon W. B. Yeats's *The Wanderings of Usheen*—Yeats who had fallen heavily under the influence of Maeterlinck the Symbolist—and, in his own words, 'the Celt within me stood revealed'. In Bax's instinctive Celticism may be found the reason for his response to the techniques of musical Impressionism. For Bax—like Yeats, like Maeterlinck, like Debussy—was essentially a dreamer. He wrote in his autobiography:

The Celt knows more clearly than the men of most races the difference between dream and reality, and deliberately chooses to follow the dream. There is certainly a tireless hunter of dreams in my own make-up. I love life. I am an appreciative inhabitant of this world, but a part of me is not of it.

Impressionism was born of Romanticism and Bax professed himself an unabashed Romantic. Gaelic poets in their restlessness and uncertainty of tenure of life and love sing of the lure of the exotic, the unreachable: the Celtic thesaurus of legend is replete with enchanted islands in the Western sea, with Hesperidean gardens, its gaiety and radiance are those of visionary other worlds, such as HyBrasil or Moy Mell. Bax on his visits to Ireland spent most of his time in the forgotten West, seeking out the most remote places on the map, lost corners of mountains, shores unvisited by tourists and by few even of the Irish themselves, especially certain islands, 'grim landscapes of stone where indigence and fever gauntly reigned. But for me all these faraway places were bathed in supernal light.'

It is thus understandable that Bax's most Impressionist scores are those in which he attempts to evoke some aspect of the Celtic twilight dream-world into whose vision he was so strangely drawn. His personal experience of Ireland impregnated his spirit with the great natural beauty not only of the Irish landscape itself but also of the sea. 'I like to fancy that on my deathbed my last vision in this life will be . . . the scene at Glencolumcille of the still, brooding, dove-grey mystery of the Atlantic at twilight; the last glow of sunset behind Glen Head in the North; and east of it the calm slope of Scraig Beefan, its glittering many-coloured surface of rock, bracken and heather, now one uniform purple glow.' It is the sea which plays the dominant role in his two Impressionist orchestral masterpieces, *Tintagel* and *The Garden of Fand*.

By the time he came to compose this music he had purged his style of obtrusively alien elements. Inevitably he had early come under the thrall of Wagner and Strauss, and a visit to the Ukraine in 1910 engendered a passing interest in Russian nationalism. Nevertheless, the true direction of his early learnings is best indicated by the fact that during the composition of *A Celtic Song-Cycle* in 1904 he had never heard Debussy's name, much less any of his music; yet after its first performance a critic wrote: 'This young man should be sedulously kept at present from further study of Debussy.' So thoroughly did Bax absorb his influences that it is impossible to gauge the extent of any stylistic debt to Debussy, Ravel or even Delius in his highly-wrought harmonic idiom, his profusion of melodic arabesque and his feeling for timbre and beauty of orchestral sound. *The Garden of Fand* represents the high-water mark of his Impressionistic style. Imbued with the spirit of sea-mysticism which we noted in certain works of John Ireland, the opening pages, seeking 'to create the atmosphere of an enchanted Atlantic completely beneath the spell of the Other World', are scored with a gossamer lightness; rippling filigree work on the woodwind, harp and celesta figuration, a rhythmic interplay of varied string sonorities all supporting a chromatically descending and ascending bass line much in the manner of the dawn scene in *Daphnis et Chloé*. There is much use of the undulating triplet figuration which we first observed in *Rheingold* suggesting the play of light upon water. Later, when Fand sings her 'song of immortal love' she might easily be beguiling the fancy of Mallarmé's faun (Ex. 30). The inhabitants of

Ex. 30
Bax, *The Garden of Fand*

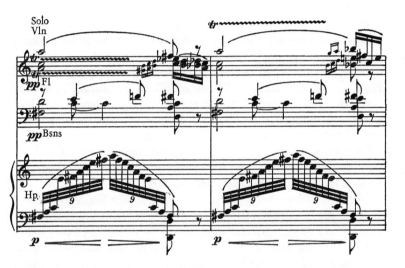

Fand's miraculous island make revelry[5] to a symphonically cumulative development in the manner of 'Jeux de vagues', although the scoring at this point has an intentional touch of uncouthness, of *diablerie* even, about it. But at the climax there is a wonderful passage marked 'full and streaming' in which a surge of high string melody over a multi-voiced swell of complex pentatonic figuration divests the imaginative mind of any shreds of earth-bound reality which may still be clinging to it and leads it to the shores of light itself. It is in such passages of visionary incandescence that Bax both fulfils and transcends his debt to Impressionism.

The sea is paramount in *Tintagel*, and though in mood, texture and sonority it bears little general resemblance to *Fand* it is unquestionably

Impressionist in conception. The programme is vague: the wide stretches of the Atlantic, seen from the castle-crowned cliff of Tintagel on a sunny but not windless summer's day, invoke memories of King Arthur, Tristram and Iseult, and other Celtic legends. The music thus progresses from purely pictorial Impressionism to a complex inter-penetration of mood, association of thought and emotion, as with the increasing turbulence of the sea deeply-ingrained racial memories stir uneasily and rise to the surface. This piece exemplifies the concern of the Impressionists to isolate the salient features of a seascape or land-scape and to present them in such a way that they will prompt an instinctive emotional reaction on the part of the onlooker and cause his subconscious mind to start functioning. In the introduction the familiar techniques set in motion the Impressionist heave and swell of the sea against which trumpet fanfares and horn-calls seem to be summoning a myriad legendary epic associations. The texture of Ex. 31 from the opening sea-music is woven of innumerable subtly-differentiated rhythmic particles lending vibrancy and life to the basically pentatonic sonority, a B major triad with a continual coming-and-going of added sixths and ninths. The middle section, which reaches its climax in a quotation from *Tristan*, is handled in a rather *pointilliste* manner, tension being engendered less by any systematic process of melodic development than by spurts and washes of orchestral sound patterns steadily increasing in frequency and intensity.

There are many other works of Bax which in their florid textures and polychrome orchestration are affiliated more or less to Impressionism:[6] *In the Faery Hills*, with the elfin fantasy of its scoring (imaginative use of a re-echoing horn and trumpet calls and solo wood-wind melismata) and the sporadic appearance of the whole-tone scale, anti-cipating in mood *The Garden of Fand*; *The Happy Forest*, fragrant and lyrical; the tempest-wracked *November Woods*, undeniably Impression-ist in the rugged brilliance of its scoring and its blisteringly fragmented textures; the rather Delian *Summer Music* with climax after rhap-sodic climax, each seemingly trying to surpass the last in exultation. At the beginning of the fine *Spring Fire*, icily coruscating wood-winds and harps maintain a basically pentatonic ostinato under which a sustained lyrical line on brass and strings heaves and swells and struggles to break through (the technique is essentially that of the dawn scene in *Daphnis*); for the rest, the work is characterized by 'the smoky blaze, the bursting, clumsy invention, the vast, stormy landscape and crippled splendour' which, as Peter J. Pirie describes it, is typical of

Ex. 31
Bax, *Tintagel*

Bax's genius at its most uncompromising. Examine also the slow movements of the third, fourth and sixth symphonies, the piano pieces

Nereid, Winter Waters—Tragic Landscape, A Hill Tune, Water Music, A Mountain Mood, The Princess' Rose Garden and *Dream in Exile* among others, *Moy Mell* and *Red Autumn* for two pianos, and, among the songs, 'The pigeons' and 'I heard a piper piping' from the *Five Irish Songs*. But although the work of reform is now well underway, many years of painstaking and sympathetic research will be necessary before we can appreciate the full stature and scope of this, in the true sense of the word, extra-ordinary man.

When the inevitable reaction against Impressionism set in, it acquired in England an increased impetus by virtue of the fact that the Romanticism ever latent in the movement had occupied a more prominent position in the work of Delius, Vaughan Williams,[7] Ireland and others than in that of their contemporaries in France. However, amidst later generations of composers there has been at least one who has shown that Impressionist soil, if tilled imaginatively, can yet yield rich and vital grain, namely Benjamin Britten. It is not without significance that the teacher to whom Britten owed the greatest debt of gratitude was Frank Bridge, for the older man evidently imbued his pupil with something of his enthusiasm for the French school. Britten has always responded keenly to Bridge's own work; before his resuscitation of *Enter Spring* he described it in a broadcast talk as 'a riot of melodic and harmonic richness, though it is thirty years since I heard it or saw the score'. The Aldeburgh Festival programmes of 1971 included *The Sea* conducted by Britten himself, and it noteworthy in this respect that in the work in which Britten's own Impressionism reaches its high water-mark—*Peter Grimes*—the sea is the undisputed protagonist. Britten feels the thrall of the sea as intensely as Debussy, and the adoption of Impressionist methods to evoke the sea at different times of the day and night—as in three of the six orchestral Interludes—doubtless suggested itself to him quite intuitively and was not consciously premeditated. The first interlude, 'Dawn', is based on three motifs: a flute theme suggesting perhaps intermittent gusts of sea-wind (notice how the accaciatura F falling on to the E lends the motif a fleeting resemblance to the D♭ major theme in the finale of *La Mer*): an arpeggio (clarinets, tremolo violas, harp with tremolo cymbal) recalling the lapping of the water, and, thirdly, a chorale-like motif which again has a slight affinity with the B♭ minor brass chorale in the last movement of *La Mer*. This, as Eric Walter White has pointed out, could well be depicting the scrunch of the shingle beneath the feet, and the false relation (G♯ against G♮ an octave lower) almost enables us to taste the salt spray on our lips. In the remainder of this evocative interlude the three motifs alternate one with another in varying degrees of intensity and a climax is reached with a great wave-like billowy surge of the chorale. The second interlude, 'Sunday Morning', depicts bell-ringing in the distance and 'Jeux de vagues' in the sunlight—almost a compendium of favourite Impressionist preoccupations. As usual Britten goes his own way: instead of conventional fourths and fifths to represent the church bells, the four horns chime in overlapping thirds, the Lydian sharpened fourth lending them an added piquancy. Notice how simply and originally Britten by this means suggests the intermingling of vibrations in the atmosphere, and how effectively the rhythmic variation of the bright, perky woodwind theme in each successive bar recalls the play of dancing sunlight on the waves. With the appearance of the melody of Ellen's first aria the music strikes a note of foreboding as deep bells and tam-tam join the assembly. The fifth interlude (the third is a descriptive storm piece, the fourth a gigantic passacaglia) is entitled 'Moonlight' and, like the sixth, is even more essentially Impressionist in that there is very little fundamental motion or development. The darkness is mirrored in the murmuring, gently heaving chords for low strings and woodwind, interspersed occasionally with a downward-glancing octave triplet on flute and harp—perhaps a momentary flicker of moonlight reflected off a wave or the gleaming wet shingle. In the inexorable surge forward to the climax and the equally inexorable surge backward the presence of the sea is sensed almost as that of a living creature. In the extraordinary sixth interlude (it has no specific title since it was not one of those extracted by the composer for separate concert performance) the all-embracing thick blanket of fog which rises up from the sea is contained in a sustained dominant seventh on muted horns *pianissimo* throughout, and through and around this impassively spectral sound weird contortions of many earlier themes stumble in, dally and fidget, and disappear just as inconclusively. This is Expressionism fused with Impressionism, since the intention is also to portray the distempered state of Grimes's mind.

The sea is by no means the only preoccupation Britten shares with Debussy. The East has long fascinated him—witness the *Songs from the Chinese*, the ballet *The Prince of the Pagodas* with its gamelan-like sonorities, and more recently and in more authentic format the church parable *Curlew River*, which is based on a Japanese *Noh* play and employs a small instrumental ensemble with quasi-oriental percussion;

the entire conception of this work, in fact, is far more eastern than
western despite the transmogrification of the original scenario. But as
far as actual Impressionism is concerned, it is the world of night, sleep
and dreams that has inspired not only some of Debussy's finest music
but also some of Britten's. In 1963 he wrote *Night Piece* for piano for the
Leeds International Competition. As might be expected, it reveals a
certain affinity with Bartók. For two-thirds of its length the music is
sustained by melody; the first section flows freely and evenly to a
rocking rhythmic motion, the second projects its supple, well-moulded
line against a murmuring sextolet figure. The third section is the
most frankly Impressionist; over a pedal of superimposed fifths the
right-hand, *senza misura*, imitates the calls of night-birds and the
churr of insects (Ex. 32). The sound of crickets is suggested also in the
evocative music for muted strings and harp which in the first act of
The Rape of Lucretia catches the atmosphere of a sultry Roman night,
with 'the sated sun falling thro' the horizon, the air sitting on [the
generals'] backs like a heavy bear': notice the skilful use of clustered
seconds in the tenor region which makes for a blurry, oppressive effect.
The appeal of the *Nocturne* for tenor solo, seven obbligato instruments

Ex. 32
Britten, *Night Piece*

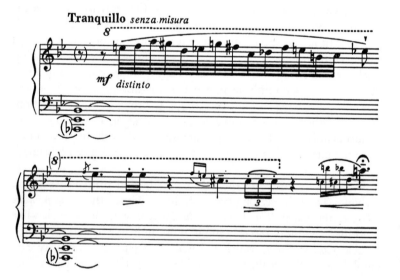

and string orchestra is more personal and intimate and it is not difficult to imagine a Debussian provenance for the Coleridge setting ('Encinctured with a twine of leaves') with its liquid harp figurations and quasi-*pointilliste* repeated minor seconds on *pizzicato* strings; or for Middleton's 'Midnight's bell goes ting, ting, ting, ting, ting'—a true piece of Impressionist night-music if ever there was one with the interesting anomaly that the bird-calls and other nocturnal sounds are entrusted not to the more usual flute or clarinet but to a virtuosic horn. The woodwinds, in fact, come into their own in an equally virtuosic Impressionist flurry in the Keats setting 'What is more gentle than a wind in summer': one is reminded of the testing woodwind figuration which begins at fig. 3 of the first movement of *Spring Symphony* and suggests, via the Impressionist introduction to *The Rite of Spring*, the gurgling sap, 'the scratching, gnawing and wiggling of birds and beasts'. The *Spring Symphony* also contains one of the most beautiful of Britten's nocturnes, the setting of Auden's poem 'Out on the lawn I lie in bed': a two-part wordless chorus, sultry, low-breathed arabesques on bass clarinet and alto flute over static, quasi-Stravinskian wind chords and various other types of woodwind figuration evoke the 'windless nights of June'. The climax of the movement, by contrast, comes with a viciously bitonal series of brass fanfares depicting the violence being done 'where Poland draws her Eastern bow' and which 'we do not care to know'; eventually the woodwind arabesque and the gentle cooing of the wordless choir return the music to the serenity with which it began.

The opera *A Midsummer Night's Dream* was perhaps the logical large-scale outcome of this preoccupation; there are strikingly original Impressionist forest-evocations to introduce Acts I and II. The scene of Act I is 'a wood-deepening twilight', and Britten conveys a remarkable sense of heavy brooding sylvan slumber by means of common chords played *tremolo* on muted strings with alternate upward-and-downward *portamenti* between them. This music recurs in the form of atmospheric interludes throughout the act and finally accompanies Tytania's distant 'Come now a roundel and a fairy song' with glockenspiel adding a scintillating touch of fairy magic. At the beginning of the next act Tytania is lying asleep in the wood. With the utmost economy of means Britten evokes both the world of her dreams and the massive tranquillity of the wood. Four chords, dependent for their effect on subtle contrasts of disposition and timbre, so ingeniously contrived that in the twinkling of an eye the listener, through an insidious wooing of his sensibilities, is transported to a realm of trance-like fantasy and unearthly beauty. This is the essence of Impressionism.

1. He did come to know Ravel and Schmitt quite well, and Messager was an admirer of his early fairy-tale opera *Irmelin*.

2. Passages from *Appalachia* (selected and adapted by Herbert Stothart) were used to complement the beauties of Charles Rosher's imaginative colour photography in Clarence Brown's highly-acclaimed film *The Yearling* (1947), a moving story of a boy growing up in the backwoods of Florida and awakening to life, love and the sorrow of parting.

3. Passages in the earlier *Sea Symphony* (e.g. 'Suckled by thee, old husky nurse' in the first movement and the evocative textures and augmented-triad colouring of the 'Scherzo—the waves') suggest a more than passing familiarity with *La Mer*.

4. Voices are used wordlessly throughout in Herbert Howells's fantasy *Sine Nomine* for soloists chorus orchestra and organ, written in 1922 before the composer had heard *Daphnis et Chloé* and before *Flos Campi*. Howells's finely-attuned lyricism and the sensuousness of his textures (and his exquisitely self-critical editorial finish) denote a temper arguably more French than English, and pieces such as the *Paradise Rondel* for orchestra work the elfin impressionistic vein of the coda to the third movement of the *Pastoral*. Moreover, Frank Howes has written intriguingly of Howells's 'impressionistic' polyphony—its vaguely imitational impulse may stem indirectly from the Tudor madrigal or Jacobean consort music, but the voice-leading is blurred, the lines indeterminate and soft-drawn, the sum-total of texture a complex seen mistily through a haze of water or light. Harmony is a result of the effortless interweaving of a myriad coloured strands, fluid, self-generating, kaleidoscopic—a sonority conceived almost in terms of a highly resonant cathedral acoustic. It is understandable that Howells's preferred media are voices, organ and strings, for these have the warmth, vibrancy and suppleness he finds essential to the achieving of his inimitable sense of flow. This is particularly true of the finest of his choral works, the *Hymnus Paradisi*, an intensely personal symphony of death and transfiguration. Howes has spoken of its 'trans-imagination of light into sound, from the dark-glowing refulgence with spurts of flame in the first section, through the blaze of glory in the "Sanctus" to the light of dawn in high summer at the end ("Holy is the true light and passing wonderful"). Long strands of counterpoint are lightly interwoven, strand is added to strand and so produces a tension that in terms of light becomes incandescence.'

5. Here again the unwitting parent of this and all such pieces may well be *L'Isle Joyeuse*.

6. The influence of Bax's chromaticism is surely to be found in the wonderful 'Awakening', the first of Eugene Goossens's *Nature Poems* for piano, which in addition to many subtleties of harmony and folk-orientated melody, has the kind of lyrical violence and powerful pantheistic sweep which is so striking a feature of *November Woods* or the Viola Sonata.

7. Impressionist influences, filtered through Delius, Vaughan Williams, Bax and Ireland, can be seen in the work of E. J. Moeran, much of whose music reflects the atmosphere of 'the mountains and seaboard of County Kerry' and 'the marshes and sand-dunes of East Norfolk'—*Stalham River* for piano, for example, or the orchestral impressions *In the Mountain Country* and *Lonely Waters*.

IN AUSTRIA AND GERMANY

Although it is scarcely true to say that the Impressionist–Symbolist movements made no impact whatsoever on German culture, as far as German music was concerned the burden of tradition rendered any whole-hearted acceptance of the constituents of French Impressionism well-nigh impossible. Yet in view of the fact that Wagner was the musical mainstay of the Symbolist movement and contributed to the formation of the Impressionist musical language, we may reasonably expect to find at least a few modest manifestations of musical Impressionism amongst composers working in Austria and Germany at the turn of the century. Those which occur are devious and erratic and in some cases barely recognizable as such; in the case of Arnold Schoenberg they arose not in emulation of contemporary trends in France but within the straitjacket of Teutonic tradition, as a natural indigenous post-Wagnerian development. Schoenberg was bitterly opposed to what he regarded as the facile eclecticism of the French, with the irresponsible readiness of their response to Romantic, Slavic and Far Eastern influences. Although he acknowledged Debussy's originality he refused to see in him the revolutionary force which we revere today, and was critical of his attitude to Wagnerian harmony—an attitude which, as we know, resulted in the use of harmonies primarily for effect of colour and for the expression of sensations and images. For Schoenberg, working within the framework of the severely dialectical Germanic tradition, this was a frivolous and reprehensibly self-indulgent approach to a precious and time-honoured musical commodity; in his own work, fourths-chords and chords derived from the whole-tone scale are not employed for purely sensuous effect but take their place quite naturally in the well-ordered scheme of expanding tonality, a scheme ever under rigorous intellectual scrutiny and control. Schoenberg's imagination may have been fired by Maeterlinck's *Pelléas* as was Debussy's, but his conception of the dungeon scene, for all its contrary-motion whole-tone chords given to flutter-tonguing woodwind, depicts the scene literally as in a Straussian symphonic poem; at the same point in Debussy's *Pelléas* the fetid, pestilential atmosphere of the vaults with their stagnant water is evoked with uncanny realism. In the one we hear a commentator objectively describing the scene; in the other we are actually present and experience the clamminess and cold terror in person. Schoenberg's *Pelléas* is certainly a magnificent piece of late romantic programme music, but it quite fails to catch the elusive poetry of Maeterlinck's original; it could be illustrating any stock melodramatic imbroglio of love, jealousy and death.

A species of Schoenbergian Impressionism is evolved, however, in the mammoth *Gurrelieder* cantata, the score with which the composer bade farewell for ever to Wagnerian Romanticism. The text was by J. P. Jacobsen, the Danish poet and novelist from whose novel *Niels Lyhne* Delius extracted the libretto for his opera *Fennimore and Gerda*, and the text for whose choral work *An Arabesque* was drawn from the same collection of poems that yielded Schoenberg the *Songs of Gurra*. Jacobsen is often referred to as an Impressionist in literature. In his work we find that paradoxical blend of dreaminess and precision—Impressionism and Realism—that we may observe in the French Impressionist painters. He started his career as a botanist (he translated Darwin into Danish) and his studies in this field—his 'professional' interest in nature—helped to condition the imagery and descriptive content of his prose and verse. Since one of his professed aims was stylistic originality and beauty, Jacobsen strove to infuse his language with his perceptions of natural phenomena—scents, colours and light —and in doing so came to embrace very nearly the stylistic tenets of Impressionism, for he was not content merely to depict but sought to evoke, to weave his impressions into the warp and woof of his writing.

The *Gurra* cycle of poems—which Schoenberg set complete—is a highly personal re-creation of the tragic story of King Valdemar and his forbidden love for the maiden Tove. Schoenberg responded superbly to all the diverse aspects of the poem, but mainly in a full-bloodedly Wagnerian manner—the rapturous 'Liebesnacht' of Valdemar and Tove in Part I and Tove's ecstatic surrender to death as a transfiguring ennobling force, the garish nightmare of the 'Wilde Jagd' of Nordic mythology in Part III. However, the most memorable music of all is that conceived in response to Jacobsen's impressionistic evocations of nature. The opening orchestral 'Abendstimmung', is miraculously beautiful and scored in a manner more reminiscent of the nature poetry of Delius than of Strauss; a soft descending trumpet call echoes and re-echoes amid the rustling of leaves and the twittering of birds—an exquisitely-woven texture of multi-divided strings, four harps, solo woodwind and glockenspiel founded harmonically on the chord of the added sixth used colouristically (despite the composer's already-quoted disapproval of such procedures). The genesis of this technique is to be found in Wagner, more specifically in the 'Rainbow Bridge' music and the *Waldweben*. But the most remarkable display of Impressionist or rather *pointilliste* technique in the *Gurrelieder*—and it forms the prototype of all similar passages in later works —occurs in the finale, 'Des Sommerwindes Wilde Jagd'. Here the poet, by a fleet succession of deftly-chosen, meticulously-annotated details, contrives to suggest all the early-morning life of the woods and fields roused to exuberant activity as the summer wind rampages on its way. Schoenberg sets this in the form of a melodrama for speaker and orchestra, and the music consists of tiny flecks and dashes of colour as if assembled from a heap of multi-hued precious stones. The textures are diffuse and fragmentary yet are made to cohere by a subtle process of motivic control, and the result is a vivid transmutation of Jacobsen's throbbing, palpitating, windswept early-morning landscape and a *tour de force* of orchestral *pointilliste* technique. A momentary lull ensues, in which the wind appears to be seeking the vanished snows of yesteryear, the lost fresh fragrance of spring; but peering aloft into the treetops it seeks consolation in a sense of the renewal of all things in nature and 'goeth on its way rejoicing' to be soothed to sleep in the splashing laughter of the lake with its pale reflected glitter of stars. The quotation of the Valdemar–Tove love-motif at this point in the orchestra, scored with a searching tenderness and heard as if through a haze of memory, subtly enhances the beauty and poignancy, and in impressionistic flute arabesque and pentatonic harp figuration sets the theme of human love and sorrow against a background of eternal nature in a manner reminiscent, both in mood and technique, of Delius (Ex. 33).

When Schoenberg applies this orchestral technique to later works such as *Pierrot Lunaire*, *Herzgewächse*, *Erwartung* and the *Five Orchestral*

Ex. 33
Schoenberg, *Gurrelieder*

Pieces they are classifiable as Impressionist or *pointilliste* only from this instrumental point of view. The textures are *pointilliste* in that they appeal to the nerves rather than to the intelligence, but their content is expressionistic—if we accept the definition of this term as having regard not to a purely visual expression of the outer world but to an expression of the artist's inner experience. (The term was coined by a German art critic in 1911 to serve as an appropriate antonym to Impressionism. The original Expressionist art group, *Die Brücken*, existed as a community from 1905–13 and Schoenberg's own paintings bear a strong likeness to their productions.) However, the strong links between the two ostensibly antagonistic aesthetic movements is typified by the fact that the Beardsleyan decadence out of which arose Debussy's *Pelléas*, Bartók's *Bluebeard*, Schmitt's *Tragédie de Salomé*—all notable Impressionist works—also sired the first important Expressionist operas: Strauss' *Salome*, Schreker's *Der ferne Klang*, Schoenberg's *Erwartung* and *Die Glückliche Hand*. None the less the very nature of Schoenberg's musical thought precludes any further bracketing of his work with Debussy's, and the same may be said for Berg and Webern despite a number of coincidental affinities and, certainly in Berg's case, a measure of direct influence.

We have now to examine the work of those composers roughly contemporary with the members of the Viennese triumvirate, but not affiliated to them. Strauss himself calls for no special consideration in this context, his symphonic poems being concerned with literal, often harshly realistic description and not with subtlety of evocation or suggestion. If Debussy, the Impressionist, paints in muted mauves and subdued greys, Strauss, the Realist, works with glaring reds and screaming yellows. There are two exceptions, both of which occur in the only symphonic poems to be inspired by nature—the first of the series, *Aus Italien*, and *Eine Alpensinfonie*, the last. The third move-ment of *Aus Italien* is a sea picture entitled 'Am Strande von Sorrent', in which a haze of sea mist is conjured up by pastel-toned chromatic figuration on *ppp* strings and woodwind—an evocative passage which interrupts the main melodic argument at one point and returns in the coda. At the beginning of the *Alpensinfonie* the emergence of the Alpine sunrise is more impressionistically handled than in *Also Sprach Zara-thustra*: a falling four-note figure gradually consolidates into an enor-mous pedal-point composed chiefly of clustered seconds over which brass intone a chorale-like motif of primeval sturdiness. *Divisi* basses begin a subdued triplet murmuring, and gradually the texture begins to brighten and fill out, flashes of light shoot across the sky (brass-calls) the figuration grows more complex and excited until a radiant A major sweeps all before it. At the very end of the work the woodwind and strings with the clustered seconds once again freeze the music into immobility, but there are several passages *en route*—the 'Wasserfall' and 'Nebel steigen auf' for instance—which may in a rather non-committal way reflect some Impressionist influence.

It was inevitable that some composers would attempt to blend the more overtly romantic elements inherent in Impressionism with the sensuous richness of the Strauss of *Don Juan*, *Heldenleben* and *Der Rosenkavalier*. Respighi is a conspicuous example, and in Austria the work of Franz Schreker is the product of just such a combination, with a generous admixture of Puccinian lyricism. Despite the basically derivative character of his music his opera *Der Ferne Klang* enjoyed considerable popularity in Germany and Austria, and the dawn-scene of Act 3, Scene 9 is a particularly celebrated piece of Teutonic Impressionism—a hushed interplay of whole-tone and chromatic elements with nightingale, thrush, finch, lark and all the others discreetly impersonated by the woodwind, dreamily at first and gradually gaining in intensity.

The liquidation of tonality as the inevitable outcome of the process of extreme chromaticism was not the monopoly of Schoenberg and his disciples. We find in Max Reger a composer whose harmony progressed further even than the labyrinthine entanglements of *Parsifal*, without however subsequently acquiring the rigorously linear orientation which would automatically render any would-be Impressionist influence null and void. Reger fed avidly on the Lutheran chorale and on Bach, but for all the choked intensity of his gargantuan polyphonic complexes he was not unresponsive to the blandishments of harmony and timbre; for this reason, when, as conductor of the Royal Orchestra at Mainigen he discovered Debussy's music in 1911 or thereabouts, he reacted favourably. The two orchestral works which followed—the *Romantic Suite* and the *Four Symphonic Poems after Böcklin*—bear some testimony to this. 'Notturno', the first movement of the *Romantic Suite*, immediately reveals a debt to Impressionism—whole-tone thirds, evocative pastoral writing for oboe and flute and, despite a continuous flow of melody, no real themes as such. Instead there is a spreading, enveloping sensuousness of harmony and orchestral texture in an attempt to capture the flavour of the rather blowzy lines from Eichendorff by which the score is prefaced. 'Im Spiel der Wellen', the second of the *Vier Tondichtungen*, is scarcely a German counterpart of 'Jeux de vagues', although in its general character and physiognomy it does bear some resemblance to Bridge's 'Sea foam', the second movement of the suite *The Sea*. The texture is light, the pace swift, the woodwind chatter and gurgle while horns bounce merrily in the tenor area, their responsibility being generally to maintain some semblance of melodic continuity. However, Reger is less important as a quasi-Impressionist than as the spiritual forebear of the man who is by far the most interesting of the German Impressionists, a composer who came nearer than any of his countrymen to understanding the essential nature of Impressionism in music—Sigfrid Karg-Elert.

Karg-Elert, the composer of the *Sixty-Six Chorale Improvisations* (the most significant work of its type since Bach) is very little known outside the notoriously circumscribed world of the organ loft. Although a prolific composer in almost every field he is remembered today solely for his organ works, although he is by no means a typical 'organists' composer' and little of his substantial output can justifiably be classified as 'organists' music'. The fact is that, having little real flair for piano or orchestral writing, he found in the organ and harmonium, with their wealth of colouristic resource, natural outlets for his hermetic, idiomatic but vital creative talent.

There are a number of interesting affinities between Karg-Elert and Delius. Both studied at Leipzig and profited there solely from the advice and encouragement of Grieg and both, like Grieg, proved natural and instinctive harmonists (Karg-Elert paid tribute to Grieg on the day of his death with an excellent little harmonium-piece entitled 'Von dem Bildnis Griegs' which quotes a motif from op 66 no 5 of *Norwegian Folk-Songs*). Karg-Elert's later enthusiasms embraced Scriabin and Debussy as well as Reger and Schoenberg, and his frankly sensual response to harmony and colour—he was far less inhibited in this respect than Reger—probably lies at the root of his unpopularity in Germany; his works are performed much more frequently in England and North America. We saw that Schoenberg valued the Wagnerian emancipation of chromatic discord chiefly for the unprecedented freedom of linear movement to which it pointed the way, and by reversing the priorities—subordinating line and form to colour—Karg-Elert is no doubt felt to have betrayed his heritage, to have contaminated the 'ethic' North with elements of the 'aesthetic' South.

Like many another creative artist of a Nordic temperament—

Wagner, Delius, Grieg, Ludwig II, Thomas Mann—Karg-Elert derived much inspiration from mountain solitudes and lakes; hence his Impressionist masterpiece, the *Seven Pastels from the Lake Constance*. The smaller Impressionist pieces—the *Six Pièces Romanesques*, certain of the *Idyllen* and the *Intarsien*, all for harmonium—tend to have the crystalline sparkle and epigrammatic terseness of Grieg's *Lyric Pieces* and reveal a similar flair for nature-evocation in miniature. The *Idyllen*, for example, contain not only the exquisite 'Sommerfaden', which evokes all the drowsy heavy warmth of a July afternoon, but an autumn piece, 'Baude im Spätherbst', atmospheric in a totally impressionistic way with its indistinctly-focused pedal-point and distant shepherd-boy's piping. In the closing bars the atonal quasi-woodwind flurries and the chord-complex of superimposed thirds recall the remarkable 'Wolken über See', another piece in the same collection in which a triple pedal-point represents the unruffled surface of the lake and an atonal melody constantly repeating itself the instability and variability of the surrounding atmosphere. As clouds begin to loom up dissonant strands of counterpoint accumulate one by one like so many leprous growths, and the climax comes in an opaquely discordant tangle of heterogeneous melodic threads. The musical language here is more akin to Schoenberg than to Debussy, but in aim and effect the piece is purely impressionistic.

The idiom of the *Pastels* is closer to that of Delius. Structurally they are more diffuse, texturally more complex, than any of the comparable harmonium works, and their harmonic language is extravagant even for this self-indulgent composer. They bear some resemblance to Percy Grainger's two *Hill-Songs* for wind band, likewise quasi-extempore impressions of mountain-country;[1] couched in a harmonic idiom hedonistically compounded of elements from Wagner, Debussy and Grieg, the scoring of Grainger's piece for wind-band alone enhances the similarity. So frighteningly involved are the registration markings that a very large, well-equipped modern organ or even an orchestral setting (here more than anywhere else Karg-Elert was obviously an orchestral composer *manqué*) seem to be required to do full justice to the music. No 1, 'The soul of the lake', catches a mood of quiet rapture at the beginning and end but lapses incongruously into rhetoric in the middle, a fault which also flaws the last piece, 'Hymn to the stars'. The nebulous effects of fourths-chords are exploited in no 2, 'Landscape in mist'; no 3, 'The legend of the mountain' has a mysteriously evocative central section with elfin bells and 'une lointaine sonnerie de cors' and in the coda parallel diatonic sevenths and whole-tone clusters are poetically contrasted. No 5, 'The sun's evensong', is in the form of a stately saraband—a glowing piece of writing but more firmly sculpted than the two by which it is flanked. 'The mirrored moon' has a deliciously cool and atmospheric opening (marked

Ex. 34
Karg-Elert, The reed-grown waters' (*Seven Pastels from Lake Constance*)

'luminoso ed argentino') and a coda in which parallel triads drift slowly upwards over an 'indeciso' clustered pedal point; the final bars sport some imaginatively-spaced whole-tone chords. 'The reed-grown waters' is the Impressionist core of the work. Mood is all-pervasive; there is little that is tangibly melodic, the textures are fragmentary and shifting, one shadowy arabesque-like shape dissolving noiselessly and effortlessly into another (Ex. 34). This little piece can stand comparison with Delius's *Summer Night on the River*, so sensitively and intricately is it worked.

1. Although harmonically (and otherwise) a great innovator and a fresh and invigorating influence on the contemporary musical scene, Grainger never really embraced the Impressionist musical aesthetic and so is not discussed in the present context.

8

IN SPAIN

The romantic lure of the Spanish scene has frequently captivated the imagination of French musicians. Bizet and Chabrier were both irresistibly attracted to Spain, and it is not surprising that Debussy and Ravel, in whose work Hispanic elements play so significant a part, should have had a warm admiration for these their predecessors. Reciprocally, the techniques of French Impressionism nurtured and helped bring to self-fulfilment a whole generation of Spanish composers who otherwise might never fully have appreciated the power of *evocación* inherent in their country's wealth of folk-music. The Spanish music of Debussy and Ravel is discussed elsewhere; it is useful here merely to recapitulate upon the connection between, on the one hand, Debussy's harmonic innovations based upon Gregorian chant and the pentatonic and whole-tone scales, and on the other the continual appearance of these modal characteristics in Spanish folk-music. There is thus an unconscious affinity of thought between the Spanish nationalists and the Impressionists, and it was natural that these two spheres of musicality should, when given the chance, converge.

We can observe this process in its early stages in the most truly representative work of Isaac Albéniz, *Iberia*. By 1893 Albéniz had all but abandoned his flamboyant, Paganini-like career as a virtuoso of the keyboard and had settled in Paris, where for the first time he enjoyed the constant companionship of musicians of learning, discernment and imagination such as Chausson, Fauré, d'Indy, Dukas and Charles Bordes; and it was in Paris, between 1906 and 1909, that he produced the twelve 'impressions' for the piano collectively entitled *Iberia*. Debussy was acquainted both with Albéniz personally and with his music, and it is possibly significant that with the exception of 'La Soirée dans Grenade' (1903) all Debussy's 'hispanizations' post-date *Iberia*. Whether or not Albéniz was aware of Debussy's music to any great extent, there are certainly a number of pieces in the series unequivocally Impressionist in the special means whereby they employ folk-material to create the essential atmosphere of the Spanish (or more specifically the Andalusian) scene. In the beautiful 'Evocation' (book 1, no 1) the whole-tone element introduced on p. 2, line 2, and fig. 80 from the coda, with its atmospheric use of the out-of-context C♮ minor chord could easily have come from a Debussy prelude; the piece ends on an unresolved added-sixth chord. Juxtapositions of unrelated common chords are also used in the spacious coda to the mighty 'Fête-Dieu à Seville' (book 1, no 3). Their peculiarly static quality reminds one vividly of 'La cathédrale engloutie'—an impression confirmed by the deep-breathed secondary seventh which underpins the distant hieratic tolling of bells.

In the second book both 'Almeria' and 'Rondeña' make use of a familiar Impressionist device—an expressive lyrical melody rising out of a murmuring background of triplet figuration. In the case of 'Almeria' the melody is a blandly diatonic 'jota', a more huskily exotic 'malagueña–rondeña' in 'Rondeña' (notice the subtle harmonic effect as the hands cross in the last two bars). Harmonically 'El Polo' (book 3) is the most advanced of Albéniz's works; he here reveals himself a master of the nervously piquant dissonance and the minor second is frequently employed in a *pointilliste*, even percussive way. In all these pieces ('Jerez' from book 4 is perhaps the supreme example) the piano texture is consistently elaborate, yet, for all its Lisztian panache, ever lucid; both in the intricacy of its ornamentation and the sumptuousness of its actual fabric it recalls the oriental tapestries of *Islamey* and *Tamara*. Of the final piece, 'Eritaña', Debussy wrote: 'Never has music achieved such colourful and diversified impressions'.

After Albéniz (who, like Sévérac might almost be considered a pre-Impressionist composer) three Spaniards, all of them trained in Paris, reacted to Impressionism in three entirely different ways. Manuel de Falla with his *Nights in the Gardens of Spain* produced something approaching a post-Impressionist masterpiece. Although he had reached a level of stylistic maturity with his two-act opera *La Vida Breve*, not until his first visit to Paris in 1907 did he come to realize the expressive possibilities of indigenous Spanish music if it were wedded to Impressionist techniques. He discovered the technical congruence between Spanish folk-music and Impressionism and only at this juncture did he arrive at a true appreciation of Albéniz's art, in whose work Impressionism began to manifest itself independently of Debussy. As J. B. Trend says of Falla in his study *Manuel de Falla and Spanish music*, 'so far he had been expressing the letter of Andalusian music; he began now to realize how Debussy had conveyed the spirit'.

The *Pièces Espagnoles*, one of the first fruits of the Paris sojourn, illustrate the truth of Trend's remark. For example, the third piece, 'Montañesa', opens with a pentatonic suggestion of distant bells, but both here and in the use of the whole-tone scale just before the return of the 'tempo primo', where these same bells are merged impressionistically with the sounds of a distant dance, there is no mere aping of mannerisms; Falla's turn of phrase is distinctly personal and the result is not a picture postcard but a genuinely Spanish Impressionist landscape. More substantial are the 'three symphonic impressions' for piano and orchestra, *Nights in the Gardens of Spain*. These blend a series of folk-derived melodic shapes into a texture where familiar Impressionist harmony (augmented triads, whole-tone chords, ninths— the climax of the first movement comes with a dominant ninth resolving on to an added sixth with sweeping waves of piano glissandi up and down the black notes) is given point and purpose by the finely-tempered blend of orchestral colours, the coolly evocative glitter of the piano and the ever-present, though rarely explicit, influence of guitar figuration. The first movement is a typically Impressionist mosaic of sensations: there is no development of the motifs, they are simply presented against an ever-changing colouristic background, although melody is prominent and there is a more flowingly lyric line than Debussy would have encouraged. The second movement, 'Distant dance', catches sounds of distant revelry borne on the night air, and fleetingly embodies them in a diaphanous instrumental fabric which, while it never alludes specifically to any one emotion, sensation, scene or memory and subordinates all to atmosphere, yet preserves a noticeable clarity of melodic outline and formal design. These qualities are always present in Falla, but in this work there is also an undercurrent of deeply-felt emotion. Impressionism enriched and solidified the inner and outer fabric of Falla's musical thought without in any way compromising his musical personality.

The same can scarcely be said of Joaquín Turina, many of whose compositions reflect an almost entirely negative Impressionist influence.

Turina studied at the Schola Cantorum under d'Indy and later received help and encouragement from Debussy and Ravel; the former much admired his well-known orchestral piece *La Procesión del Rocio*, significantly one of those works in which there are few or no traces of Impressionism. For despite the earnestness of his endeavour and the extensiveness of his output, Turina possessed no real flair for *evocación*. Such pieces as 'La noche en el campo', from his suite of Andalusian impressions for piano, *En el Cortijo*, dally persistently with all the familiar Debussian tricks-of-the-trade but with a palpable lack of inner conviction; no real mood is ever established. Turina is at his best in his mood evocations when he drops the latter-day Impressionist paraphernalia altogether, for instance in the beautiful slow movement of the *Sinfonia Sevillana* ('Por el Guadalquivir') which in terms of harmony and texture marks no real advance upon the *Waldweben*. Elsewhere his most successful works are those in which he abandons himself to a relatively uninhibited, unsophisticated treatment of the folk-dance— for instance, 'Orgia', the third of the *Danzas Fantasticas*, or the finale of the *Sinfonia Sevillana*.

A very different proposition is the work of the third of this representative trio of Spanish post-Impressionists, Federico Mompou. Although born in Catalonia and now living in Barcelona, he enjoyed a prolonged period of residence in Paris around the time of the First World War, and has continued to visit Paris regularly. An artist of rare distinction, a miniaturist (nearly all his works are collections of short pieces for the piano) among the post-Impressionists he stands almost alone in that his work evolves more from the Debussy of 'Le matin d'un jour de fête' than of *L'Après-midi d'un Faune*. In other words he writes impressionistic 'impressions', brief, pointed, often witty but never sardonic, often tender and lyrical, but always sharply and economically characterized. A piece such as 'The street, the guitarist and the old horse' from *Suburbis* brings together a heterogeneous assortment of incidents and people, presented or depicted in no logical orderly sequence but put into a broadly satisfying overall perspective through the haze by which they are distanced from us. This indeed is Impressionism as Debussy defines it in the *Préludes*.

Mompou's music aspires to the Debussian ideal of quasi-improvisation—he frequently dispenses with bar-lines, time-signatures and key-signatures, and while the composition will always have shape and ultimate logic and is rarely whimsically eccentric there is usually a certain element of unpredictability, and much of the delight in playing such works as the *Fêtes Lointaines*, *Suburbis*, *Scènes d'Enfants* or the *Paisajes* lies in the way a cannily-placed accidental will avert what threatens to be an Impressionist harmonic cliché, or a wryly-turned melodic or rhythmic detail will introduce an unobtrusive but telling element of variation. The piano writing is rarely suggestive of Debussy, more of Fauré (see for instance the lovely 'Pavillon de l'élégance', no 3 of the *Souvenirs de l'Exposition 1937*) or more frequently of the dry pragmatism of Satie—although those pieces such as the *Dialogues* which are also Satiesque in conception are less successful. However, the very title of a work such as the *Fêtes Lointaines* betrays its Impressionist inspiration. These are random impressions of festivities taking place in the distance, sounds that might well fall on the ear of a disinterested passer-by, and the chiming chords of Ex. 35 immediately suggest a

Ex. 35
Mompou, *Fêtes Lointaines I*

haze of impressionistic remoteness. After ten bars of this a jaunty fragment of dance-melody apparently dominates the scene for a further ten bars before the chimes return, but observe the alignment of melody to harmony and how the latter with the to-and-fro movement of the bass seems to merge the reverberations of bells with the rhythm of the dance (Ex. 35B). This is musical Impressionism in a nutshell. This fondness for the blurring of contours can be seen even from the freedom with which Mompou sprinkles his chords, even single notes, with ties, as in Ex. 35; and these distant bells toll with *Leitmotiv*-like persistence throughout his work even when not explicitly evoked— see for example the *Scènes d'Enfants*, no 1 ('Cries dans la rue') and no 4 ('Jeunes filles au jardin'), especially the passage marked, disarmingly, 'Chantez avec la fraîcheur de l'herbe humide'. This is allied to a strongly ritualistic element which may clearly be seen in the *Cants Magics*—

notice the bell figurations of Ex. 36 from the second piece, with its

Ex. 36
Mompou, *Cants Magics II*

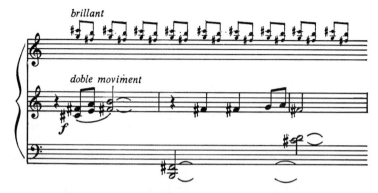

original and evocative use of fourths and fifths, and in the *Charmes*,
a set of six incantatory pieces which owe something to the mood and
content of Debussy's *Six Épigraphes Antiques*. This is merely an aspect
of the strangely unreal, remote, dream-like aura which surrounds much
of Mompou's work; Walter Starkie noted an affinity with 'the quaint,
primitive, sunlit world of the ancient miniatures of the fourteenth
or fifteenth centuries or chronicles describing the lives of Pedro the
Ceremonious or Martin the Humane among their Aragonese and
Catalan subjects'; but there is nothing precious or self-consciously
archaic about such pieces as the *Impresiones Intimas* or the *Pesebres*,
the third of which, the beautiful 'El Pastor', has a strongly modal
flavour which reminds us of the marked folkloristic element in
Mompou's music. This is most clearly observed in the ten pieces each
known as *Cancion y Danza*, but in this most elegant and fastidious of
craftsmen there is no trace of any of the more flamboyant or boisterous
forms of nationalism; folk-music inflexions are treated as a means to
an end, not as an end in themselves. Small and unpretentious as his
output is, Mompou merits a position of some eminence in the post-
Impressionist pantheon.

9

IN ITALY

Debussy's music first became widely known in Italy during the decade 1904–15. In 1907 Vincento Tommasini published an important article entitled 'Claude Debussy and Impressionism in Music' in the *Rivista Musicale Italiana*. In the following year *Pelléas et Mélisande* reached La Scala and by 1909 Italian performances of Debussy's concert works were quite common. Few composers born in the late 1870s or '80s remained unresponsive to Impressionism, and as the field is quite large it may be as well to begin with the two most internationally celebrated, Giacomo Puccini and Ottorino Respighi.

The mysteriously vague, allusive and elusive poetry of *Pelléas* seems in every way diametrically opposed to the robust, earthy, unabashedly and superabundantly lyrical idiom of a work such as *Madame Butterfly*, and certainly Debussy, in common with the majority of contemporary French composers, was inclined to regard Puccini as little more than a pretentious vulgarian. Puccini on the other hand was fascinated by Debussy's art. He was a 'musical magpie', liable to be found at any time poring over the scores of all his distinguished contemporaries, helping himself liberally to whatever he thought might conceivably embellish his own musical nest, already filled to overflowing with the gaudiest trinkets and baubles. In Debussy he found what he described as 'the soul of an artist shot through with a genuine and subtle sensibility' and borrowed freely from the Impressionist stock-in-trade with little or no attempt to conceal his borrowings. Although in Puccini's early work (*Edgar, Manon Lescaut, Tosca and La Bohème*) there are intimations of many of the devices of Impressionist harmony which were becoming common *fin-de-siècle* currency (parallel fourths and fifths, for example, in the 'Christmas song' and the introduction to Act III of *La Bohème*) Impressionist influences become truly pronounced only with *Madame Butterfly*.

In this opera Puccini realized the full potential of the novel techniques he had incorporated in his earlier work in embryonic form only. Not only is there free use of parallel chords and the whole-tone scale, but, more interestingly, his penchant for exotic subjects (cf. the later *Turandot*) lead, him naturally to the employment of oriental idioms, to pentatonic textures and thence to a rare delicacy of instrumental sonority. It is impossible not to ascribe this new lucidity and refinement in Puccini's orchestral thinking to Impressionist influence. See for instance the gamelan-like writing for woodwind and harp at fig. 8 in Act I, complete with pentatonic flute; the oriental gongs, bells, liquid harp and woodwind at fig. 62; the *pizzicato* strings and harp glissandi between fig. 74 and 76; the birdsong in seconds over string tremoli at fig. 24 of Act II; the *pizzicato* strings, reinforced solely by bassoon, at fig. 42; the fragile beauty and transparency of the scoring for wind, strings, harp and glockenspiel of Butterfly's flower song (fig. 71–82). All these and many other felicities reflect Debussy's guiding influence, for example the wordless chorus of sailors at the beginning of Act III (singing to 'oh eh!') which is clearly modelled on the closing stages of *Pelléas*, Act I; not only the technique but the emotional connotations also are similar.

Puccini's next opera, *The Girl of the Golden West*, is again notable for use of the whole-tone scale of which by this time he seems to have become inordinately fond. Again, exotic elements with their appropriate harmony are to be found in abundance, and there are a number of atmospheric effects—for instance, the finale of Act I, where Minnie's theme (the prominent intervals of which are the major seventh and ninth, added-note harmony being thereby implied) actually comes to rest on an unresolved secondary seventh reinforced by a group of distant tenors humming.

In the first two operas of the *Trittico—Il Tabarro* and *Suor Angelica—* Impressionist elements prevail. The opening of *Il Tabarro* with its parallel fourths and fifths (suggesting most effectively the sluggishly-moving waters of the Seine and reminiscent of 'La Cathédrale Engloutie') recurs somewhat later when two distant voices vocalize dreamily above and around it; at the end of this scene the sound of a tugboat is heard 'as from a very great distance'—Puccini often uses natural sounds, always with extreme discretion, to evoke a special atmosphere. Later distant church bells toll the hour, blending with parallel fourths and a drone bass to recall Debussy's submerged cathedral even more vividly. Bells are also incorporated into the opening of *Suor Angelica*, in which harp with gently dissonant seconds, celesta and strings blend with women's voices and piccolo (bird-song) to produce a bewitchingly sensuous sound.

In *Turandot* also there are striking effects of this kind. The exotic element is much more pronounced here than in *Madame Butterfly*, and the degree of stylization is correspondingly higher. Consequently Puccini unconsciously exploits the affinity between Impressionism and primitivism to produce a series of quasi-oriental mood-pictures which compensate for their lack of authenticity by their objective beauty. In Act I, the crowd's sadistically gleeful expectation of scenes of torture and execution is succeeded by a sudden hush and an invocation to the morn. A subtle synthesis of night-stillness, exotic languor and almost inarticulate nostalgia is created by the chorus (over long-held pedals) used more for the sheerly spellbinding sound of massed voices murmuring than for the sentiments to which they give expression; notice too the plaintive little splashes of exotically chromatic woodwind. Later, children's voices, accompanied by saxophones and the main chorus humming, are heard from afar singing, to a variant of Turandot's pentatonic theme, a touching little hymn to the approach of summer. There is, dramatically speaking, no good reason why these children should come into the opera at all, either here or later on before Turandot's narrative in Act II; again, it is the *sound* of their voices which justifies their presence. *Turandot* abounds in such beauties, for instance the wistful, nostalgic trio for the three ministers in Act II (beginning with Ping's 'I've a cottage in Kansou') accompanied by oscillating pentatonic fourths with a discreetly Lydian flavour.

Respighi almost alone among Italian composers has achieved world-wide recognition as a writer of orchestral music by virtue of his symphonic poems *Fountains of Rome* and *Pines of Rome*. His idiom is pleasantly, even lusciously eclectic if lacking in strong individuality; Debussy's contribution intermingles freely with that of Strauss, Rimsky-Korsakov and to a lesser extent Puccini. Harmonic and orchestral colour-effects derived from Impressionism are especially in evidence in the first movement of *Fountains of Rome* ('The fountains of the Valle Giulia at dawn') in which 'droves of cattle pass and disappear in the fresh damp mists of a Roman dawn'. Effects of mist and haze being a speciality of Impressionism, Respighi gives his woodwind a flowing pastoral melody over a running figure on the strings which later appears on harp and flute—another of the *Waldweben*'s myriad progeny. The scoring both here and in the final section, the beautiful 'Fountains of the Villa Medici at sunset' is consistently pellucid and evocative. This last movement blends intimations of a number of familiar nocturnal sounds (bells tolling, leaves rustling, birds twittering) in a characteristically Impressionist manner—intricate filigree work for two harps, celesta and woodwind, diaphanous writing for multi-divided strings, a freely sensuous use of dominant ninths—and at the end a seventh partial is left unresolved on a distant chime. Similar procedures obtain in the third section of *The Pines of Rome* ('The pines of the Janiculum'), but here the textures are less subtle and coarser-grained, and the whole conception comes nearer to Straussian literal pictorialism than to Debussian Impressionism.

Although probably the best-known of all Italian non-operatic composers (i.e. those who did not cultivate opera to the exclusion of all else) Respighi is by no means intrinsically the best; there are a number of other composers of the *generazione dell'80* as it is called in Italy who cut altogether more substantial figures and on whom Debussy made a more positive impression. Of the triumvirate comprising Gian Francesco Malipiero, Alfredo Casella and Ildebrando Pizzetti only Malipiero can be said to have undergone a definite Impressionist period. On the other hand two of the many lesser composers of this generation who came under Debussy's influence, Vincenzo Tommasini and Mario Castelnuovo-Tedesco are quite significant as Impressionists. There were many other minor Impressionist figures, such as Francesco Santoliquido, Luigi Perrachio and Vincenzo Davico, whose names are scarcely known outside Italy, but Tommasini's work deserves to reach a wider public. John C. G. Waterhouse, an authority on this period in Italian music, has described his orchestral diptych *Chiari di Luna* as one of the best examples of Italian post-Impressionism. In the first piece, a delicate piece of mood-evocation entitled 'Chiese e ruine', there are occasional echoes of Wagner and the melodic basis is strongly lyrical throughout; none the less there are frequent allusions to the whole-tone scale and the scoring is fastidious and beautiful. That Tommasini learnt much from Impressionist orchestral methods is evidenced by the second movement, 'Serenata', especially in the climactic passage in which the main theme is given out by strings against an intricately-worked background of woodwind and harp figuration. Similarly the orchestral texture of *Il Beato Regno* is 'complexe mais pas compliqué' in a way that gives more than a passing nod to Ravel.

Castelnuovo-Tedesco is not a significant composer in overall perspective but some of his early piano pieces also rank amongst the best examples of Italian post-Impressionism. His music needs to be approached with caution, since taken as a whole it reveals an extreme facility coupled (as so often) with a reluctance to apply self-critical editorial polish. Most of his best music had been written by the time he was thirty, including his most durable Impressionist piano pieces. *Cipressi* is probably his masterpiece in this genre. The cypress trees in question are those lining the road to the composer's erstwhile family home in Florence, and the slow-moving chords of the opening bars, entirely Impressionist in substance—open fifth, secondary ninth, added sixth, open fifth—set the tone of the whole piece. In marked contrast to the impassive, unyielding state of these opening bars appears the main theme, an unassuming melody of a folkish cast which, like the popular melodic elements in 'Gigues', reveals by virtue of its context and the development to which it is submitted an unsuspected strength

Ex. 37
Castelnuovo-Tedesco, *Cipressi*

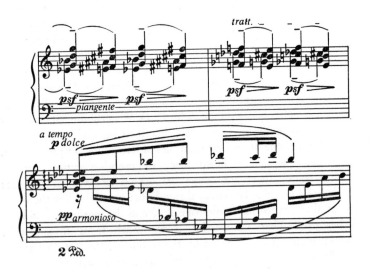

of emotional intensity—a notable characteristic of several of Castel-nuovo-Tedesco's works. Ex. 37 is typical of the indebtedness of this piece to the Impressionist lingua franca—note the open fifths, the added-note chords dissolving effortlessly one into another (the branches swaying and moaning in the wind) and the pentatonic scale, *armonioso*, letting a ray of sunlight through the shadows.

Cypress trees are also the subject of the second movement of the *Tre Poemi Campestri*, entitled 'I cipressi e le stelle'. These three pieces are more redolent of the Debussy of the *Préludes* and 'Le matin d'un jour de fête' in that they conjure up a variety of contrasted sounds and images in this case from the countryside around Usigliano di Lari—fragments of dance-music and popular song, bugle-calls from a distant barracks—all converging at once upon the musical scene and effecting in so doing some ingenious and amusing counterpoint. The opening bars of 'I cipressi e le stelle' are typical enough—slow-moving chords of superimposed fourths and fifths (the cypress trees again) and a *pianissimo* tattoo figure, marked *cristallino*, sounding in the far distance. However, the lack of any real emotional commitment in this piece, in comparison with the earlier *Cipressi*, serves rather to emphasize Castel-nuovo-Tedesco's deficiencies as an Impressionist—a tendency to long-windedness and rhetoric, even to a certain element of coarseness, which places him in terms of artistic merit at an appreciable distance from such an impeccably fastidious craftsman as Federico Mompou. 'Ritorno', for example (the first of the *Tre Poemi Campestri*) emerges as little more than a jumble of folky tunefulness and thus scarcely lives up to the implications of its designation as a 'poem'. The best movement of this suite is the third, 'Vigneti', which achieves a more ingratiatingly lyrical transmutation of its raw material. For example, the melodic interest of the opening pages centres round a folk-song and a fanfare, but these are far from being distinctly focused; apart from the fact that the right hand is maintaining a constant stream of whole-tone arpeggios (this in itself contributes an element of haze) the opening interval of the folk-tune, clearly in its original form a perfect fifth, appears here as an augmented fifth and the tune as a whole is bisected by the fanfare. But by the second time round the mist has cleared; the right-hand arpeggios are pentatonic not whole-tone, the folk-song regains its opening perfect fifth, and the fanfare bides its appointed time before bursting upon the scene. The climax of the piece (the fanfare turned into a clangorous peal of bells) yields gradually through a whole-tone cadenza to an Impressionist coda in which the air quivers

marked 'dolcissimo quasi celesta'. The closing bars (Ex. 38) are
particularly atmospheric.

Ex. 38
Castelnuovo-Tedesco, 'Vigneti' (*Tre Poemi Campestri*)

with varied reminiscences of earlier motifs heard as if through a dreamlike
haze, sprinkled with parallel descending arpeggiated first inversions,
   A companion volume to the *Tre Poemi* is the *Tre Preludi Alpestri*,
three impressions of Alpine scenery. The centre piece is a 'Vallée des
cloches' ('Campane a valle') the finale a *Waldweben* 'Il vento nel bosco'),
and like Debussy in the *Préludes* the composer places his descriptive title
at the end of each piece. Both are less derivative than their titles would
lead one to expect. The subtle chromatic inflections of 'Campane'
establish a mood of profound melancholy (in contrast to the lucid
objectivity of 'La vallée des cloches') while, given the inevitable constituents of open fourths and fifths, there is much variety of texture
and harmonic flexibility; as in *Cipressi*, the use of folk-song-like melody
in such a context heightens the emotional temperature. 'Il vento nel
bosco' is less the gentle breeze which wafts through Bax's *Happy
Forest* than the howling gale of Debussy's 'Ce qu'a vu le vent de
l'ouest'. The texture is freely chromatic with a strong whole-tone
element and in the central section a motif in parallel fifths is built to an
appassionato climax; but both here and at the main crisis of the movement ('pesante e tragico') the piano writing is conceived in terms of
Lisztian bravura. More truly Impressionist, even *pointilliste* in sonority,
is the first piece of the series, 'Il prato canto', in which from a *sotto
voce* chromatic ostinato there is born a fragment of melody which
undergoes perpetual harmonic and textural variation; in the central
contrasting section, 'subito calmo e indolente', open fifths chime softly
beneath glittering major-second figuration.

Some mention should also be made of the earlier, more miniaturist piano pieces such as the three sea-impressions, *I Naviganti*, *Alghe* and *Il raggio verde*, and especially the four *Stagioni* ('seasons'); lacking as they do something of the diffuseness of the later Impressionist works, their thought is more cogent and vital. The first of *Le stagioni* is, predictably enough, 'Inverno', and Castelnuovo-Tedesco evokes his winter landscape in very much the same way as Roussel in 'Forêt d'hiver'—a melodic line devoid of any feeling of lyrical warmth over a rocking accompaniment of open fifths. 'Primavera' is light-fingered and deftly chromatic; 'Estate' a spirited dance in open fourths and fifths; 'Autumno', a beautiful piece, has something of the nostalgic fragrance of 'La fille aux cheveux de lin', no X of the *Préludes*, with a graceful rising-and-falling ostinato over a modally-inclined melody. By way of contrast there are some desolately drooping parallel sevenths, and finally the modal melody returns harmonized in open fourths and fifths, dissolving over a long-held added sixth in the manner of the final bars of Delius's Cello Concerto or the *Songs of Sunset*.

Of the three leading composers of the *generazione dell'80* Gian Francesco Malipiero has always been the most instinctive; he has always composed primarily because he loves the sounds he makes. It is thus not surprising that he responded to Debussy, the most self-confessedly instinctive of contemporary composers in his formative years; and in fact certain of his own Impressionist works rank among the best products of the entire post-Impressionist period. He was from an early age interested in Gregorian chant and Italian folk-song (see, for instance, the delightful piano miniature *Notturno Pastorale* which features drone-basses, asymmetrical phrase-structure and a melodic line constantly flowering into arabesque) and was therefore, like Vaughan Williams, fully equipped to meet and take kindly to Debussy before even being aware of his existence; indeed, it is difficult to ascertain exactly when he did become acquainted with any of the Frenchman's work, since the very un-Debussian *Poemetti Lunari* of 1910 use non-functional harmony in a way which anticipates the Stravinsky of *The Rite of Spring* and the early polytonal works of Milhaud. The *Preludi Autunnali* of 1914 are *pointilliste* in a way reminiscent more of Scriabin than Debussy (especially the first of the set), but we may date a truly Impressionist period for Malipiero from the last few years of the First World War to the early '20s. His contribution to *Le Tombeau de Debussy* (entitled simply *A Claudio Debussy*) testifies to his admiration for the composer, based as it is almost entirely on parallel triads, so

arranged as to produce bitonal effects without relinquishing the underlying flavour of organum.

Conspicuously Impressionist among contemporary piano pieces are
the *Barlumi* and the *Poemi Asolani*. The *Barlumi* (gleams) are thumbnail
sketches, mosaic-like in construction and fragmentary in texture,
although there is a firmness and sense of purpose in the writing. The
harmonic idiom is broadly diatonic but dissonant with much use of
parallel fifths; in no 4 the whole-tone scale puts in a discreet appearance as a syncopated throbbing chord. The *Poemi Asolani* are basically
similar in constitution although the first piece, the large-scale 'Notte
dei morti', applies Impressionist techniques to a more advanced norm of
dissonance—the opening section, suggesting the approach of a distant
funeral cortège, gathers itself together from a number of sharply-
defined but essentially heterogeneous motifs, all welded together by the
opaque bell-like reverberations in the bass. The climax, with its
clashing streams of parallel triads, is reminiscent of the rough-edged,
raw-boned Impressionism of *The Rite of Spring*, and so is what is
arguably Malipiero's finest piece of Impressionism, the 'Colloquio di
campane' from the second set of *Impressioni dal Vero* (in the first set
which comprises three bird-portraits the textures are sparer, the
melodic outlines more chaste, although the refined scoring and fluid
interplay of modal and whole-tone scalic shapes do reveal a certain
debt to Debussy).

The underlying conception of 'Colloquio di campane'—the ringing
of a myriad bells and the intermingling of their vibrations in the
atmosphere—is essentially Impressionist, but this piece is no mere pale
imitation of, for example, 'Cloches à travers les feuilles'. Over a bitonal
harmonic ostinato, A♭ versus C major—the effect of the exquisitely-
clashing minor seconds is as much pleasurable as painful (Ex. 39A and
B)—a purely-diatonic C major melody (Ex. 39C) is soon counterbalanced by descending fourths in the bass suggesting A♭ (Ex. 39D)
The texture gradually becomes more complex with diminished and
augmented versions of Ex. 39C sounding simultaneously, and a boom-
ing pedal C underpinning what is by this time a splendidly heterogeneous welter of sound. After a climax a middle section introduces a
new motif which is then woven into the recapitulation, the C–A♭
antithesis having swung itself a tone higher. This exciting movement
anticipates the systematic exploitation of bell stylizations in the Terza
Sinfonia of 1945 ('Sinfonia delle campane'), although the appeal of the
latter work is not as vital or immediate as that of the 'Colloquio di

Ex. 39
Malipiero, 'Colloquio di campane' (*Impressioni dal Vero*)

campane'. No 2 of this set of *Impressioni*, 'I cipressi e il vento', breathes a
more rarified atmosphere and is Impressionism of the more self-
evidently Debussian variety.

Elements loosely derived from Impressionist sources also penetrate
other works of this period which are not specifically Impressionist in
inspiration, notably *Pause del Silenzio I* with, in its opening section,
chiming chords on celesta and widely-spaced strings and a profusion
of woodwind arabesque; even more elaborate are the melismatic
woodwind patterns in the third 'panel' over repeated added-note string
chords, this quasi-oriental exploration of ostinato and melismatic
techniques being notably indebted to Impressionism (see also the 'lento
funebre' fifth section, especially the passage marked 'un poco pesante'
which begins on p. 45 of the score). The technique of certain parts of
the *Sette Canzoni*, the second part of the operatic trilogy *L'Orfeide*,
is essentially similar, particularly the first 'panel', 'I vagabondi', the
third, 'Il Ritorno', and the fifth, 'La Serenata'. In the opera *San Francesco* the vista of unruffled Giotto-esque serenity with protracted
sequences of hugely calm, quasi-medieval triadic, diatonic chord-
formations is followed by an element of contrast provided by the
orchestral introduction to the second scene, St Francis's sermon to the
birds—an Impressionist evocation of noontide haze and bird-song.

The noticeably archaic flavour of this and many another work by Malipiero is a logical outcome both of his innate interest in folk-song and Gregorian chant and of his exposure to Debussian Impressionist techniques.

10

IN RUSSIA

Of all the composers who underwent the influence of Impressionism Scriabin is one of the most individual and controversial. Born into the generation of composers which included Rachmaninov, Glière and Medtner, with Glazunov and Tanieev looming large in the background, Scriabin ultimately showed himself to be as little in sympathy with the German symphonic tradition to which they subscribed as with any conscious display of musical nationalism. The country which attracted him the most, both musically and aesthetically, was France. From the time of his earliest published works right up to that of the First Symphony (1900) all his music bore the unmistakable mark of Chopin: pre-eminently salon miniatures, nicely fashioned for the piano (Scriabin, like Debussy, was a superb pianist and was said to have phenomenal powers of pedal control) but already marked by a heavily sensual undertone which presages the ecstatic voluptuary of late years —the man whose ambition it was to redeem the world through art, in fact through a combination of all the arts. For Scriabin—and here we see the first glimmerings of an affinity not only with Wagner but also with Debussy—was never content to be exclusively a musician; as far as he was concerned, the concept of 'pure' music was devoid of meaning. His ambition was, by breaking down the barriers which separated music from her sister arts, ultimately to raise himself and a select group of initiates into realms of transcendental bliss. This astonishing feat of megalomaniac fantasy was intended to assume tangible form as a 'mystery' to be performed in a hemispherical temple in India (mirrored in a lake so as to produce a sphere, the perfect form), in which music, poetry, dancing, colours and scents would combine to produce in the participants a supreme final ecstasy, the supreme final realization, in the form of a religious rite, of Baudelaire's theory of *correspondances*.

These febrile imaginings first began to marshal themselves in Scriabin's brain at the turn of the century, and they reflect the intellectual ferment of Russia at that time and its preoccupation with the mystical and the occult. It is here that the influence of French Symbolism begins to assume importance. Russian literature has always responded creatively to influences from abroad; Tolstoy was inspired to write *War and Peace* by Stendhal's *Chartreuse de Parme*, Dostoevsky found the form of his novels in Dickens, and Russian poets have often begun by imitating French and English models (La Fontaine influenced Krylov and Byron, Pushkin and Lermontov). The first poetic impulse at the end of the nineteenth century came from France, from the Symbolists: Balmont, Bryusov, Sologub and Blok were the leaders of the new movement, and it was doubtless in the first flush of enthusiasm for their ideas that Scriabin first began to respond to Wagner. Be that as it may, a stylistic combination of Chopin, Wagner and Liszt (with whom he had a pronounced spiritual affinity) begins to produce results which, particularly in the Second and Third Symphonies, invariably invoke the shade of that earlier arch-apostle of erotic mysticism in music, César Franck; it is doubtful whether Scriabin was ever influenced directly by Franck, nor is it easy to say when he first became familiar with Debussy's music.[1] The kinship with Debussy is many-sided—an utter dependence on personal sensations, an exacerbated nervous sensibility, an admiration for Chopin and Wagner, an urge to synthesize all forms of artistic creativity, an almost scientifically precise approach to the further emancipation of harmony.

So continuous was the process of Scriabin's evolution that it is difficult to segment it in any wholly satisfactory way, but we can date the beginnings of a systematic quest for new harmony approximately from the year of the Fourth Piano Sonata (1904). The opening of this work and many others of the period—the *Divine Poem*, the *Three Pieces*, op 45, the Prelude, op 37, no 3—demonstrate Scriabin's predilection for conventionally 'lush' harmony, chiefly ninths, elevenths, thirteenths and the whole-tone flavoured 'French sixth'; but he is still using them like Wagner, as dissonances in appoggiatura form which resolve eventually on to concords. The 'Étude', op 49, no 1, shows a greater reluctance to resolve its discords, and its textural constitution

—the whole piece consists of quick-breathed triplets with the third quaver missing in each case—anticipates the increasing fragmentation of later years. Both the 'Poème ailé' and the 'Danse languide' from op 51 are essentially similar, and in this case the titles also are prophetic of later works; but the decisive break with classical harmony is made with the magnificent Fifth Piano Sonata, op 53 and the orchestral *Poem of Ecstasy*.

In these works not only are the higher chromatic discords treated as concords and left unresolved, but the 'Promethean' or 'mystic' chord which was to dominate the production of Scriabin's final period begins to appear with some frequency (it had been adumbrated in several places previously, notably in the 'Poème', op 32, no 1, in the second and seventh bars). This chord consists of nothing more *recherché* than six notes from the harmonic series arranged in fourths, perfect, augmented and diminished, and the composer's obsession with its distinctive sound led him to derive many of the foundation-chords for his later works from it in one form or another (experimentation with chords of the fourth was being indulged in extensively at that time). The *Poem of Ecstasy* reveals, in addition to this new-found freedom of harmonic speech, a true appreciation of the glories of the Impressionist orchestra. The scoring of the *Rêverie*, the Piano Concerto, the First Symphony and most of the Second is competent but routine —with the exception of the opening and closing bars of the latter's slow movement, where the protagonists are a variety of pre-Messaienic birds (a harbinger of the dawn-scene in *Daphnis et Chloé*). There is a reminiscence of this in the second movement ('Voluptés') of the *Divine Poem*, beginning on p. 202 of the Belaiev miniature score and lasting till p. 228, well past the main climax. Again the textures become fine-spun and ethereal, activity gives place to a dream-like wonder; the woodwind twitter with bird-song, strings trill in quiet rapture, a solo violin muses ecstatically, the glockenspiel lets fall its tiny iridescent pearls of sound, the harp woos and caresses. But in the *Poem of Ecstasy* Scriabin attains even greater mastery of the wealth of evocative and colouristic resource to be drawn from the Impressionist tone-palette. The texture woven is glowing and vibrant with ecstasy. We here find in profusion the tremors and swoons and the little cries of anguished voluptuousness which had appeared as early as the Fourth Sonata, and, likewise, the fragmentation of melody, tremolos, sudden winged phrases, ecstatic trills and extravagant expression marks in French ('avec une volupté de plus en plus ecstatique', 'charmé', 'avec une noble et joyeuse émotion') all of which are characteristic of his mature manner.

Scriabin's last orchestral work, and the one which represents the logical and inevitable outcome of these tendencies gathering momentum in the *Divine Poem*, the Fifth Sonata and the *Poem of Ecstasy*, is *Prometheus—The Poem of Fire*. It is typical of this advanced specimen of the Impressionist–Pointillist genre—for by this time Scriabin's textures have become so fragmented that they must be described as Pointillist rather than Impressionist—that its subject is one which reaches far back into the mainsprings of human consciousness, for Prometheus was one of the 'sons of the flame of wisdom' of ancient Greek mythology, by virtue of whose divine spark humanity first passed to self-consciousness and creative intelligence. So we are transported to the world of the low E♮ of the Rhine or of the high bassoon solo which inaugurates *The Rite of Spring*; and in fact these three compositions—*The Rhinegold* prelude, *Prometheus* and *The Rite of Spring*—form an imposing triptych of primordial evocations of nature, each classifiable as Impressionist but each as unlike the other as it could be.

The very full orchestral complement of *Prometheus* includes solo piano, two harps, celesta, tubular bells and organ, and towards the end a wordless chorus joins the ensemble; but it is unique in its demand for a 'colour-keyboard' (termed *luce*), a part for which is precisely notated in the score. This keyboard is intended to flood the entire concert hall with a 'symphony of colours' during the performance, the sequence of colour combinations being determined by the sequence of the harmonies. The part is written (on an ordinary stave with treble clef) in two voices, to which a third is added from time to time. The upper of the two is identical with the root of the sound-centres produced by transpositions of the 'Promethean' chord; so that although the bass of the opening chord is G, its root is A, and A consequently appears on the upper line of the *luce* part. The lower part consists of long-held notes resembling pedal-points which the composer probably intended to form a generalized colour-scheme serving as an overall background to the individual colour-changes which depend on the shift of the harmonies. In such a way does Scriabin attempt to put Baudelaire's theory of *correspondances* into practice, to achieve a 'counterpoint' of the senses.

Prometheus shows Scriabin clinging as tenaciously to the structural framework of a sonata first movement as in any of the late sonatas, but, as in these works, the stuff of the music is splintered and diffuse as never before, the textures *pointilliste* in complexion; the result has a

Debussian improvisatory quality, for although the flow of thematic particles is under scrupulous intellectual control, the first appeal of all such music is to the nerves, and the nerves respond not to form but to content. The opening displays a canny feeling for evocative orchestral writing—the mystic chord *sul tasto* on the strings marked 'brumeux'; muted horns calling from out the abyss with the theme of primordial chaos answered by a swelling fourths-chord on trumpet with tam-tam marking the climax. The music then progresses through exposition, development and recapitulation with pointed dynamic contrasts, varied juxtapositions of the principal motifs and brief sharply-etched permutations, all caught within a gigantic web of multi-hued orchestral sound; melodic continuity is entirely subordinated to the demands of pure colour. The music thus moves on a constant level of tension with the harmonic and colouristic substance in a constant state of flux. Even the vowel-sounds to which the chorus sing after their extremely beautiful first entry, two bars after fig. 47, are meticulously specified and the transitions carefully graded, all in the interests of a greater intensity of colour-variation, a surer incandescence. The main climax is a blaze of trilling strings and woodwind, downward-shooting harp glissandi and tolling bells, the apotheosis of white light in music; at fig. 61, 'dans un vertige', the music hurls itself deliriously forward to a final F♯ major chord which sounds strangely inconclusive, just as if the creator had travelled to the outermost reaches of psychic consciousness only to be met by an impassable barrier—like Poe in the *Narrative of Arthur Gordon Pym* he can write no more because he knows no more.

Of the single piano pieces which succeed *Prometheus* the most closely related to it in mood and technique is *Vers la Flamme*. Motivic content in this piece is even more tenuous, the only motif as such consisting of a minor second in iambic rhythm; around this reiterated interval a harmonic tissue, emerging like *Prometheus* from a misty motionless void, evolves itself continuously and with ever-increasing complexity until an orgasmic climax is reached in which the interest lies solely in the granite-like blocks of added-note chords, hammered out as if in preparation for some cosmogonic edifice. In this work, and in the beautiful *Poème-Nocturne*, op 61, the harmony is still self-indulgent and almost late-romantic in verve; but the last four piano sonatas pursue a more untoward line of experimentation, leading into ever more rarefied regions and culminating in the extraordinary *Five Preludes*, op 74, which are close in spirit to Schoenberg's *Three Piano Pieces*, op 11,

just as there are moments in *Prometheus* very reminiscent of the orchestra of *Erwartung*—and the technique of the *pointilliste* painters is
just as surely suggested. In the last two sonatas fragmentation of line
is here taken as far as it can possibly go without resulting in total disintegration; there is constant irregularity of rhythmic ratio between
the hands (another contributory factor) and the piano writing itself
is more aerated and diffuse, more fleeting and insubstantial than
before. The substance of the music consists mainly of motivic mole-
cules, mere sounds in the air, which as they crowd together and disperse form the most exquisite patterns (like Chladni's plate) but patterns
which bear little resemblance to anything hitherto conceived by musical
man. Examine Ex. 40 from the Tenth Sonata and notice how the

Ex. 40
Scriabin, Tenth Sonata

interest lies, not in any attempt at linear continuity but in the actual
sound of the tremolos and trills themselves, their quality as *timbre*,
their efficacy as a musical Impressionist translation of shimmering
heat or light.

For all the revolutionary nature of his theories and the forward-
looking aspects of his technique, Scriabin has remained a rather
solitary and enigmatic figure in twentieth-century music.[2] Yet his
influence on the most important of the Russian Impressionists, Stravinsky, was far from negligible, however unwilling the latter may have

been to admit the fact. Stravinsky indignantly repudiated the suggestion that Scriabin could have in any way affected his musical thought during his formative years, claiming that 'one is only influenced by what one loves, and I could never love a bar of his bombastic music'. Yet the opening pages of *The Firebird* emphatically belie this declaration, and it was undoubtedly Scriabin's affinities with the aesthetics and techniques of French Impressionism which led to certain elements of his style insinuating themselves into the as yet un-crystallized idiom of his younger compatriot.

Stravinsky's lifelong Francophilia is too well-known to need much elaboration; it is yet another instance of that intuitive affinity between the Slav and Latin temperaments which we saw manifested earlier between Tchaikovsky and the Russian nationalists on the one hand, and the French Impressionists on the other. In Stravinsky's case whatever debt to the Nationalists the Impressionists may have incurred is repaid in full, and with interest to boot. His first experiences of Debussy's music proved unforgettable:

Siloti's performances of the *Nocturnes* and of *L'Après-midi d'un Faune* were among the major events of my early years. *L'Après-midi d'un Faune* was played amidst hoots, whistles and laughter, but the effect of that lovely flute solo, of the long silence, of the harp arpeggios and the horns, especially after all the post-Wagnerian noise, was not destroyed thereby.

French influences are especially marked in Stravinsky's juvenilia—*Faune et Bergère*, the Verlaine songs, the *Scherzo Fantastique* and the orchestral fantasy *Fireworks*, which gives more than a passing nod in the direction of Dukas' *L'Apprenti Sorcier*. It was *Fireworks*, with its glitter and profusion of orchestral colour and the seductive *élan* of its harmonic and melodic writing, which so impressed Diaghilev as to prompt him to invite Stravinsky to work for his Russian Ballet. After orchestrating some pieces by Chopin and Grieg, Stravinsky was invited to undertake the composition of *The Firebird*.

The predominant influence on *The Firebird* is that of Rimsky-Korsakov, and the Impressionist elements in the score may well stem not so much from Scriabin and Debussy as from Rimsky-Korsakov himself, whose flair for evocative sonority and sensuousness of texture in no small measure anticipated the Impressionist movement. The Impressionist mood is most marked in the opening scene, the depiction of Kastchei's enchanted garden, where the famous string glissando in harmonics (which, as Stravinsky describes it, 'the bass chord touches off like a Catherine Wheel') is one of the most evocative sounds in music. The Firebird's appearance and her first dance are clearly affected by the tremulous palpitating expressiveness of Scriabin. The Firebird herself is designed to be a living embodiment of coruscating light and colour, and, appropriately, Stravinsky's scoring is very reminiscent of *The Poem of Ecstasy*. Harmonically the idiom contrasts an extreme chromatic licence (the Firebird's supplication to Prince Ivan, her lullaby after the 'Infernal Dance') with an added-note diatonicism which carries the Debussian innovations of *Pour le Piano* a stage further. The score as a whole represents the ultimate of Slavonic nationalist Romanticism heavily tinctured with Impressionism—garish, iridescent, voluptuously oriental, so luxuriously appointed, in fact, that without wholesale disintegration of the thought-fabric further development along similar lines would have proved impossible.

In the reaction which followed—the result of which was the two masterpieces, *Petrushka* and *The Rite of Spring*—Impressionist influences, though more perfectly assimilated, have lost none of their potency. *Petrushka* was the first of his works to win whole-hearted approbation from Debussy himself whose keen olfactory sense had, in *The Firebird*, detected the smell of maggots in the offing. But writing on *Petrushka* to his friend Robert Godet, he praises Stravinsky's 'instinctive genius for colour and rhythm' and his ability to think directly in terms of the orchestra,[3] and later he singled out the 'tour de passe-passe' section for special praise, much to Stravinsky's gratification. It would be easy to assume that the scoring of *Petrushka*, with all its forthrightness and trenchancy, was conceived as a corrective to the languor and nebulousness of Impressionism. But Constant Lambert pointed out long ago that however greatly the essential fabric of Stravinsky's textures in *Petrushka* and *The Rite* may differ from Debussy's, Stravinsky uses sound in exactly the same way as his French contemporary. His appeal is to the musical nerves rather than to the musical reason, and his use of colour is no less impressionistic for being barbaric rather than hypersophisticated in temper.

The first and fourth tableaux of *Petrushka* (the 'Shrove-tide Fair' scenes) clearly illustrate this ambivalence. The heterogeneous assembly which here crowds the stage—organ-grinders, coach-men, wet-nurses, masqueraders, peasants with performing bears and so on—scarcely seems to lend itself to depiction in the Impressionist vernacular, designed for the evocation of languid summer nights, sunlight on water or distant bells heard through a rustle of leaves. Yet we have noted the tendency to Impressionist realism in certain works of Tchaikovsky (the Scherzo of the Fourth Symphony, the Second Orchestral Suite) and, taking his cue from his spiritual forebear, Stravinsky with the full panoply of Impressionist harmonic and orchestral technique here brings this phenomenon to a rare pitch of perfection.[4] Musically speaking, the protagonist of these tableaux (the fourth is to all intents and purposes an elaboration and intensification of the first) is the ever-present background noise of hurdy-gurdies and accordions, and it is this which furnishes Stravinsky with his harmonic substructure—alternating chords built of agglomerations of thirds. These are heard in their simplest form four bars before the end in the scene of Petrushka's death, but in the fair scenes themselves they become dissolved with a free use of tremolo in a rich warm Wagnerian blend of woodwind, string, horn and often trumpet sonority against which these melodic elements which are present in the form of folk-tunes can stand out starkly. The irregular time-signatures, the constant superposition and juxtaposition of varied rhythmic patterns, the trance-inducing *ostinati*, the spreading ripples of figuration—all contribute to the formation of a shifting web of iridescent sound which readily impresses itself on the listener's nervous susceptibilities.

The same is true of the epoch-making *Rite of Spring*, wittily described by Debussy as 'primitive with every modern convenience'. The subtle relationship between empirical primitivism and a sophisticated nervous Impressionism becomes here apparent as never before.

Craft: What did you love most in Russia?
Stravinsky: The violent Russian spring that seemed to begin in an hour and was like the whole earth cracking. That was the most wonderful event of every year of my childhood.

We noted that one of the first works of Debussy to be censured for its 'Impressionism' was the Botticelli-inspired *Printemps*, and the idea of spring and re-birth threads its way through his work like a *Leitmotif*; the *Rondes de Printemps* are in their way as violently ritualized a concept as *Le Sacre du Printemps*. Stravinsky's response, like Debussy's, is analogous to that of Wagner who in the *Rheingold* prelude similarly seeks musical expression of a fundamental truth, of a primeval facet of human consciousness, and to that of Scriabin who evokes at the beginning of *Prometheus* an abyss of primordial chaos. The bed of the Rhine is synonymous with the beginning of all things—'im Anfang war der Rhein', as Thomas Mann expressed it in one of his essays on Wagner—

and the beginning of all things is the ritual of spring. Wagner, Debussy, Stravinsky and Scriabin all had recourse in varying degrees to the language of Impressionism to articulate in music this most fundamental of all impulses. The ever-expanding E♭ triad of the *Rheingold* prelude is pure sonority just like the statically passionless pentatonic aggregates in the *Rondes* or the non-melodic, non-harmonic stamping polychords of the 'Harbingers of Spring'. The appeal of all such moments is essentially to the nerves.

Debussy's direct influence on *The Rite* is most immediately apparent in the preludes to either part. The introduction to Part 1 is intended to represent, as Stravinsky himself said, 'the awakening of nature, the scratching, gnawing and wiggling of birds and beasts' and a complex tissue is built up from the accumulation and intensification of a number of subtly-differentiated melodic and rhythmic shapes rather than actual motifs: colour is all-important, the scoring for wind-band (the strings, playing for the most part *pizzicato* or in harmonics, merely point or give unobtrusive support to the wind lines) strikes an appropriately acrid, almost physically painful, note. The opening of Part 2 is more overtly Debussian; the textures are more lush, the lines less sharply etched, and the gently oscillating polychords dissolve effortlessly into each other in a typically Impressionist nocturnal evocation. The time-signatures are constantly changing, and what melodic or tonal discipline there is is enforced by deep pedal-points and a fragment of pentatonic folk-melody high on violin harmonics. Otherwise all is a vague, tenuous fluidity, so Impressionistic as to be in this instance, as Lambert remarked, almost 'plus royaliste que le roi'.

Traces of Debussy are also distinguishable in the opera *The Nightingale*, the *Three Japanese Lyrics* for soprano and piano and the cantata *The King of the Stars*. *The Nightingale* reveals a delight in musical *chinoiserie* comparable to that of Debussy in *Pagodes*. The first act dates from 1909, the second and third were not completed until 1914 (i.e. after *The Rite of Spring*) and there is thus a certain stylistic disparity in the work; Impressionist influences are thus naturally more pronounced in the first act, better integrated in the remainder. The introduction to the first act with its monotonous quaver movement recalls the opening of 'Nuages' and hence Mussorgsky's 'The noisy day has sped its course' (in which both may have originated). The optional humming passage for chorus at fig. 5 is reminiscent of the wordless chorus in 'Sirènes', and the basically pentatonic pastoral fluting which accompanies the Fisherman's song (at figs. 8, 13 and 48) is typical of the evocative orientally-flavoured arabesque-like style of writing which evolved naturally during the Impressionist period from Debussy out of Rimsky-Korsakov. In Acts 2 and 3 (composed after *The Rite*) the pentatonic scale is used with gleeful delight in all its more specifically barbarous connotations. In the 'Chinese March', for instance, the colour scheme is basically Impressionist and totally reliant on oriental penta-tonicism; but the intricacy of the cross-rhythmic patterns within the constantly changing metric sequence, and the complexity of the harmonic structure built upon all manner of different permutations and combinations of the five notes, again demonstrates the affinity between 'empirical primitivism and a sophisticated nervous Im-pressionism' which we noted in connection with *The Rite of Spring*.

The King of the Stars was written immediately after and briefly during *The Rite*, and was dedicated to Debussy. The text was by the Symbolist poet Constantin Balmont, and Stravinsky revealed some measure of sympathy with the Symbolist aesthetic when he declared that, despite the obscurity of the text as poetry and mysticism, 'its words are good and words were what I needed, not meanings'. The men's voices blend and coalesce with the huge orchestra as a legitimate extension of the instrumental tone-palette, the score is lacking in any noticeable melodic or rhythmic impetus, and the effect is therefore of a slow-moving spectrum of harmony and colour. It is the spirit rather than the letter of Debussy which informs this music, notwithstanding the obvious reminiscence at fig. 11 with the

♪♩.

rhythm in the strings and a fragment of plaintive oboe arabesque.

Nevertheless *The Rite* remains the acme of Russian musical Impres-sionism; its identity grows quite naturally out of the aesthetic of the preceding generation and represents the Impressionist concept of sound for sound's sake pushed to its logical and uttermost conclusion. No other Russian composer responded so positively to Debussy; those Impressionist elements in the work of Prokofiev (in the early sym-phonic sketch *Autumn*, for instance, or the third movement, 'Night', of the *Scythian Suite* with its long haunting lines of pentatonic wood-wind solos and its liquid plashings of harp, celesta and piano figuration) are probably derived from Stravinsky or Scriabin rather than from Debussy directly—Prokofiev needed many years to recover from the impact of *The Rite*, and there was in his creative temperament also that paradoxical blend of primitivism and sophistication which had generated it. Small wonder that when Craft asked Stravinsky to name the composer to whom he owed the most, Stravinsky replied: 'the musicians of my generation and I myself owe the most to Debussy'.[4]

1. There is an interesting link between Debussy and Scriabin in the person of Boris Pasternak, author of *Doctor Zhivago*. Pasternak's father Leonid was a portrait-painter very much influenced by the Impressionists, and the short stories and lyric poems of Pasternak *fils* also reflect this influence, as do many of the wonderful evocative passages in *Zhivago*, for instance:

High winter came with its grinding frosts. Torn, seemingly disconnected sounds and shapes rose out of the icy mist, stood still, moved and vanished. The sun was not the sun to which the earth was used, it was a changeling. Its crimson ball hung in the forest and from it, stiffly and slowly as in a dream or in a fairy-tale, amber–yellow rays of light as thick as honey spread and, catching in the trees, froze to them in mid-air.

The point in this connection is that as a boy Pasternak was completely enthralled by Scriabin and for years studied music in the hope of gaining a reputation as a composer. Doubtless the Impressionist elements in Scriabin's music constituted one of its chief attractions.

2. In two cases only—Karol Szymanowski and William Baines—did the seeds of Scriabin's Impressionism fall upon fruitful ground. Many of Szymanowski's works composed during the period 1914–20 are Impressionist in constitution, notably *Masques* and *Métopes* for piano, *Mythes* for violin and piano (which includes the wonderful 'Fontaine d'Aréthuse') and the Third Symphony ('Le Chant de la Nuit'). Baines, who died in his native Yorkshire in 1922 at 23, wrote some clear-textured, sensitively-wrought impressionist miniatures for piano impregnated with a pantheistic spirit which transcends the superficially pictorial—*Silverpoint*, *Twilight Pieces*, *Tides*, *A Last Sheaf* and *Pictures of Light* embrace the most successful.

3. Debussy actually consulted Stravinsky over some problems of orchestration in *Jeux*.

4. Some reference must here be made to the work of the Russian naturalized American composer Dimitri Tiomkin, a one-time concert pianist (he gave the first European performance of the Gershwin F major Concerto) who has spent most of his life composing for films. His best scores frequently show impressionistic traces of a vaguely Franco-Russian cast, although they hold very little brief for the familiar concoction normally implied by the term. The central section of his best work, *Rhapsody of Steel*, is an Impressionist metropolitan evocation which might almost be subtitled 'A Russian in New York'; other scores powerful in Impressionist feeling include *Lost Horizon*, *The Old Man and the*

Sea and above all *Search for Paradise* (especially the haunting evocative beauty
of the Hunza Valley and Indus River sequences, and the rare feeling for atmospheric orchestral sonority they reveal). He also adapted music by Debussy for
David O. Selznick's Impressionist fantasy, *Portrait of Jennie.*

I I

IN HUNGARY

We have seen how Debussy, though never a self-confessed folklorist or ethnomusicologist, proved keenly susceptible to folk-influences, particularly Russian, Spanish and oriental, and that the fascination of these musics for him lay in their entirely unwestern melodic and (by implication) harmonic characteristics. These characteristics—modality, pentatonicism, even the occasional occurrence of the whole-tone scale —in due course permeated Debussy's own style, and similarly Vaughan Williams's early immersion in folk-music sharpened his receptivity to Impressionism when he eventually came into contact with it. The circumstances of Bela Bartók's early career were much the same. Growing up in Hungary when the Austro-Hungarian empire was at the zenith of its fortunes, he entered the Budapest Royal Academy of Music at a time when it was completely under the spell of German Romanticism. For a while he responded keenly to the early tone-poems of Strauss, particularly to *Also Sprach Zarathustra*, which seems to have haunted him over a number of years (the sledge-hammer organ triads of 'Sunrise,' for example, reappear to overwhelming effect in *Bluebeard's Castle* as Bluebeard flings wide the fifth of his seven doors to reveal, in a burst of dazzling sunlight, the farthermost reaches of his domains). However, this influence was soon counteracted by a growing interest in Hungarian folk-music; his first folk-song expedition was made in 1905, his first collection of arrangements published in 1906, and the Second Orchestral Suite (1905–7) was his first deliberate attempt at synthesizing authentic Hungarian folk-elements with the orthodox musical language as he had inherited it.

But yet another factor was decisively to influence the course of his future development. In 1907 his fellow folklorist and composer Zoltán Kodály returned from Paris bringing with him a quantity of Debussy's music which he persuaded Bartók to examine; and he was instantly captivated. He went on to make a careful study of the French composer's work, and we need not be surprised to learn that he found in it

pentatonic phrases similar to those contained in our peasant music, and which I was sure could be attributed to the influence of folk-music from Eastern Europe, very likely from Russia . . . it seems therefore that in our age modern music has developed along similar lines in countries geographically remote from each other. It has become rejuvenated through the influence of a kind of peasant music that has remained untouched by the musical development of the last centuries. My work . . . from opus 4 onward tried to convey something of the development just described.

Up to this point Bartók's allegiance to tradition had been orientated towards Germany rather than France, but French Impressionism now came to exert a potent influence over the evolution of his musical thought. A certain amount of harmonic influence was inevitable, but we must remember that his harmonic idiom was already being signally conditioned by folk-song: 'the strange turnings of melodies in our East European peasant music showed us new ways of harmonisation . . . the frequent use of the interval of the fourth in our old melodies suggested to us the use of chords of the fourth . . . what we heard in succession we tried to build up in a simultaneous chord' (cf. p. 21).

It was mainly in terms of orchestral texture and concepts of timbre that Impressionism left its most indelible imprint on Bartók's style, and this we can see for the first time in no 1 of *Deux Images* entitled 'Floraison'. It is therefore an evocation of spring, but as such has very little in common with *The Rite of Spring* or even with 'Rondes de Spring', always excepting the 'dream-interlude' (see p. 39). This tranquilly beautiful movement in fact distils a unique atmosphere; despite the obvious origin of a number of harmonic and orchestral devices every page bears witness to the strength of the composer's personality and as a piece of post-Impressionism it is one of the most original of all. There is a curious quality of stillness about it, a stillness of movement barely perceptible yet quietly, insistently growth-inducing. It is instinct with an unseen yet vibrant force, pure nature-Impressionism, pantheistic and mystical in conception. The music begins underground with a softly ubiquitous rustle of lower strings, the changing time-signatures instilling a sense of contained power as the ageless

ritual of rebirth begins again. A germinal motif, bearing the unmistakable imprint of Hungarian folk-song, refashions and adapts itself
constantly to the fluidity of its rhythmic context, and two bars after fig.
1 the glittering sensuousness of the writing for flutes and bisbigliando
harps anticipates the *Daphnis* dawn-scene. An element of contrast
is provided by the horn-theme at fig. 6 (again strongly influenced by folk-music), and on the basis of these two motifs the music
ebbs and flows in sympathetic vibration with the tensions and relaxa-
tions of nature, the birthpangs of the awakening earth. But this is
not the violent Russian spring, 'like the whole earth cracking open';
the miracle in this Hungarian landscape happens gradually, and the
music does convey a sense of quiet ecstasy and awe. The coda is the
most impressionistic music Bartok ever wrote. The whole orchestra
shimmers—notice the blend of string sonorities (first violins and first
basses *sul ponticello*, second violins, violas and cellos with whole-
tone tremolos), whole-tone harp glissandi, free melismata for the flute,
and tubular bells to add a final touch of mystery and remoteness
(Ex. 41).

Very similar in constitution is the first of the *Four Orchestral Pieces*,
op 12. The opening is characteristic: through a dense mist of sustained
strings (muted), harp glissandi and spread piano chords a horn melody
emerges which proliferates desultorily against an impressionistic
orchestral backcloth, in which all the notably Debussian features of
'Floraison' recur with the exception of the whole-tone scale. Again
there is that peculiarly static, dream-like quality which somehow
suggests the familiar techniques of cinematic Impressionism—vase-
lined lenses, colour filters and slow-motion. For bars on end melodic
movement virtually comes to a standstill, focusing the attention
exclusively on the beauties of harmony and timbre—the eight bars
between fig. 6 and 7 are a case in point.

This preoccupation with effects of timbre remained with Bartók
long after he had withdrawn from the immediate Impressionist orbit.
In the opening of the third movement of the *Music for Strings, Percussion and celesta*, the primary elements of music are totally subordinated to the exploration of instrumental colour. Less radical
departures from the Impressionist norm can be observed, for instance,
in the slow movement of the Second Piano Concerto, which opens
with a series of slowly oscillating muted string chords built of superimposed fifths, devoid of rhythmic or melodic definition and suggesting interstellar space; in the orchestration of 'Melody' in the

Ex. 41
Bartók, 'Floraison' (*Deux Images*)

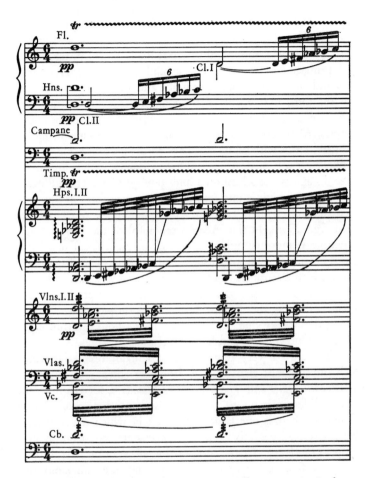

Hungarian Sketches which dissolves in a typically Impressionist haze of
sustained tremolo strings, woodwind arabesque, trills and tremolos
and upward-shooting harp glissandi; in the rapt, ethereal quality of
the passage which temporarily stems the flow of the third dance in the
Dance Suite (4 bars after fig. 29); in the fourth dance of the same work, a
nocturne which conjures up the occasional reminder of 'Les parfums
de la nuit'.

The most original application of Impressionist techniques in Bartók's work is to that strange, intensely personal empire of nocturnal sound known simply as his 'night-music'. In his piano works this is embodied in the 'Night music' from the suite *Out of Doors*, for with the exception of a unison line of folk-song-like melody introduced for the sake of contrast, this piece is pure sonority. There is no melody as such but a kaleidoscopic, though always essentially uniform, texture composed primarily of tone-clusters, in and out of which crepuscular noises and movements dart fleetingly and intangibly. In orchestral terms the third movement of the Concerto for Orchestra ('Elegy') and the second movement of the Third Piano Concerto are both fine examples. After nine introductory bars of slow-moving string music the 'Elegy' opens with wispy streaks of chromatic arabesque on clarinet and flute over sustained strings and harp glissandi, each being answered by the distant cry of a bird on a high-pitched oboe. This glimmering sheen of atmospheric sound returns in intensified form in the coda, in which all three clarinets, two flutes, piccolo and oboe are employed in similar figurations. In the 'Adagio religioso' of the Piano Concerto the texture is more complex: over a glassy tremolo of divisi violins various birds may be distinguished, among them the Baltimore oriole (piano) which Bartók had notated during a stay in Asheville, North Carolina in 1944. In bar 72 first and second violins produce a cluster-ostinato, offsetting the little pentatonic cries on piccolo and oboe and evoking the background of night with its rustlings, murmurings and frightened scurryings to and fro of nocturnal creatures.

While there are very few of Bartók's major orchestral scores in which Impressionist elements are altogether absent—various parts of *The Wooden Prince* and *The Miraculous Mandarin*, for example, testify in their different ways to the composer's awareness of Debussian techniques—there is one large-scale work in which the Impressionist substance is so all-pervasive as to require separate consideration, namely the opera *Bluebeard's Castle*, composed in 1911. Both the style of vocal writing—a free recitative closely following the inflexions of the Hungarian language, so much so that much of its characteristic atmosphere is dissipated in translation—and the shadowy orchestral continuum with its constantly shifting dark-hued tone-colours are noticeably indebted to *Pelléas*, but Bartók reserves some of his most imaginative Impressionist orchestral effects for Judith's opening of Bluebeard's third, fourth and sixth doors. The third reveals the treasure chamber, and three trumpets have somehow to sustain a D major triad in root position for 65 bars to represent the beam of light which illuminates the

hoard. This is the harmonic breakwater, as it were; against the fragmented melodic patterns woven around it by solo instruments and
voice, tremolo high strings and flutter-tonguing flutes shimmer,
tremolo harps glitter, ripples of celesta advance and recede. Nor is the
orchestral sound substantially different when the fourth door opens
on to Bluebeard's flower garden with its plethora of colours and scents.
Again the harps play tremolo (or more accurately *bisbigliando*),
flutes flutter-tongue, the celesta arpeggiates; but the harmony (sustained by *naturale* strings) is an open fifth on this occasion and the
melodic movement is a quasi-canon between solo voice and solo horn
which features the Scotch-snap rhythm, so characteristic both of folk-

music (especially Scottish and Hungarian) and of Debussy.

It is the opening of the sixth door and Judith's discovery of the lake
of tears which inspires Bartók's most original piece of Impressionist
orchestral writing. He interprets the sight of this smooth, sinister
expanse of silver-coloured lifeless water, as if sleeping in an unearthly
calm, in terms of Judith's reaction to it, which is one of numbed
horror—and as she gazes a cloud passes over the chamber, rendering
it mysteriously darker. Accordingly the orchestra approximates to a
series of shudders—a repeated *crescendo–diminuendo* lasting only two
beats of a 4/4 bar, on second, third and fourth flutes (flutter-tonguing)
divided strings (tremolo) the most evanescent of arpeggios on first
flute, first clarinet and celesta, up-and-down harp glissandi, soft rolls
on timpani and tam-tam. This is pure Impressionism—no melody, no
movement, simply sonority, a direct appeal to the nerves—and to
English ears it may prove reminiscent of Holst's 'Neptune', likewise a
vast featureless non-human void. A measure of its success as Impressionism, as a direct appeal to the nerves, is the near impossibility of
analysing the sound by ear; obviously the more intentionally nebulous
and insubstantial an orchestral effect, the more concerned it is to leave
an 'impression', the more difficult should it prove to specify its exact
nature without the aid of a score.

We saw that Bartók first became acquainted with Debussy's music
in 1907 after Kodály had returned to Budapest from Paris in 1907 with
a selection of the French composer's work in his trunk. While in Paris
(where he also met Romain Rolland and Jules Écorcheville) Kodály
had made an intensive study of Debussy, particularly of *Pelléas*, and

having earlier embarked on his collecting of Hungarian folk-music doubtless discovered for himself then what an astonished Bartók was to discover for himself later—that pentatonic and modal scale-formations were as much a part of Debussy's style as of his country's indigenous folk-song. Impressionism certainly left its mark on Kodály's harmonic thinking and to a lesser extent his orchestration (there is here a notable parallel with Vaughan Williams) but he never went through a truly Impressionist phase and, being a lesser talent than Bartók, never produced anything to equal, in Impressionist terms, 'Floraison' or the opening of the sixth door in *Bluebeard's Castle*.

The Impressionist influence in Kodály's work may be observed at close range in two sets of piano pieces, both of which date from before 1920—*Nine Piano Pieces*, op 3, and *Seven Piano Pieces*, op 11. Before discussing these, however, mention should be made of a single piece, again for piano, written shortly after the composer's return from Paris in 1907—the *Meditation on a Theme by Claude Debussy*, easily the sort of tribute that might have been included in the *Tombeau de Debussy* some years later (the theme comes from the second movement of the String Quartet). After a brooding introduction with little glinting splashes of whole-tone scale above a heaving bass-line, *quasi arpa* undulating chords in 6/4 (as in Holst's 'Venus' and Schmitt's *Tragédie de Salomé*) support a long lyrical derivation from the original motif. Although the Impressionist harmony has not yet been perfectly assimilated into Kodály's idiom, there is evidence that when it has been it will not seek to deny the supremacy of melody, which (as in the even earlier Adagio for violin and piano) is already beginning to show signs of folk-music inflexions. In no 2 of the *Nine Piano Pieces* the melodic line on several occasions flowers into a melisma over a chord of superimposed fifths, all of which derive from folk-sources (Ex. 42) —yet the result is pure Impressionism. In no 3 the folk-like melody in the tenor is encircled by rippling sextolets in a manner which hails from the great progenitors of Impressionism—Liszt, Grieg, Wagner (the 'Rainbow Bridge')—but the constant shifts in harmonic perspective, the long-held pedal-points, internal and external, as well as the perpetual hum of the ostinato, all contribute to a weirdly-glimmering, almost hypnotic, effect which again links the world of Debussy with that of the East European and oriental folk-melos. In no 7 of the same set the added-note chords over a rolling *ostinato* of fifths represents a rollicking, extrovert adaptation of Impressionist harmony to

Ex. 42
Kodály, No. 2 of Nine Pieces

'realist' subject-matter in a way similar to the technique of *Petrushka*.

No 3 of the *Seven Piano Pieces* is avowedly French in inspiration, since it quotes the well-known line from Verlaine, 'il pleure dans mon cœur comme il pleut sur la ville' and the pattering raindrops are reflected in the glancing off-beat open fifth chords in the right hand which offset the chromatic melancholy of the melody in the left. No 4, 'Epitaph', makes more conspicuous use of Impressionist technique with whole-tone figuration and a central section based on parallel chords, but most interesting of all are nos 2, 6 and 7, in which the modal contours and melismas of Hungarian folk-song are fetchingly blended with Impressionist harmony—for instance, at the climax of no 2 the Székely folk-song is pounded out in octaves 'con passione' over a descending sequence of seventh chords, and in the coda of no 6 the melody dies away in the distance (as in Debussy's 'Voiles') beneath upward-winging shivers of whole-tone sound. The ending of no 7 suggests a tolling of bells with deep-breathed open-fifth chords in bass and treble being answered, through their reverberations, by the same melodic phrase a semitone higher in the uppermost region of the treble. To enhance the aura of mystery the whole-tone phrase of the opening returns to have the very last word, with the familiar Impressionist direction 'laissez vibrer'.

HIM

Kodály's orchestral music shows less sustained awareness of Impressionism, but the depiction of the Viennese musical clock in *Háry János* (a basically pentatonic amalgam of tubular bells, celesta, piano, high brass and high woodwind) undoubtedly owes something to the Impressionist sound-world. In the first movement Kodály achieves an impressive climax through sustaining his melody in the tenor of the orchestra beneath a steadily-growing superstructure of rising parallel chords and whole-tone woodwind figuration, and the opening and closing pages of the 'Song' feature long stretches of melismatic writing (principally for flute and clarinet) over static, long-suspended string chords. A similar technique obtains in the *Peacock Variations*—in the ninth variation, and even more in the fourteenth. Here the folk-tune becomes the basis of long, flowing, freely-developing melodic lines on a solo flute accompanied by muted string tremolos and harp glissandi— *l'Après-midi d'un Paon*. As the variation progresses, piccolo, second flute and the two clarinets weave further strands of pentatonic and whole-tone melismas into the fabric, and then a *diminuendo* sets in, a night-music-like fade-out. No more convincing example of the compatibility of Impressionism and primitivism could be found than this piece; the one perfectly complements and enhances the other.[1] Impressionist harmony is responsible for much of the individuality of the *Psalmus Hungaricus*; the repeated added-note chords for harp and pizzicato strings in the lyrical Adagio section clearly bespeak their origin.

---

1. In this connection attention must be drawn to the work of the Hungarian naturalized-American composer Miklós Rózsa. For all his Germanic affiliations (he was educated at Leipzig and has always been content to work within classical formal disciplines) his style has remained firmly rooted in Magyar peasant music and some of his best work has come into being as a result of this combination of a folk-song foundation with the harmonic and textural methods of Impressionism— see for instance the fourth variation in the *Theme, Variations and Finale*, and the 'Pastorale' from the *Three Hungarian Sketches*—a languid evocation of the *puszta* very similar in design to the ninth variation of the *Peacock*, yet composed three or four years earlier. Also the slow movements of the Piano Concerto, Piano Sonata, Violin Concerto, Double Concerto, the *Notturno Ungherese*, and the music for the films, *The Thief of Bagdad* and *Jungle Book*—the latter based on the same Kipling classic which inspired Koechlin's series of orchestral works. The score for the Van Gogh 'biopic' *Lust for Life* demonstrates yet again just how readily Impressionist elements can be assimilated within a folk-song-orientated style.

I 2

IN NORTH AMERICA

Impressionism proved a vital musical force in the United States both before and after the First World War. Although at the turn of the century the greater proportion of the composers-in-residence boasted a pious upbringing in German conservatories, from about 1902 onwards —the year of the first American performance of *L'Après-midi d'un Faune* in Boston—the eyes of many began to turn towards the French school, and American composers started to go in increasing numbers to France to study. By the early '20s something of what we may, by analogy with the Russian phenomenon, term a Franco-American *entente cordiale* had sprung up, due largely to the enormous popularity enjoyed by American jazz and popular music in Parisian circles, and reciprocally, the amount of strength gathered by American composers in all fields—'serious', popular and jazz—from the language of French Impressionism.

A large amount of music in the Debussian idiom was written in America between 1900 and 1930 by 'serious' composers and only a small percentage of it can be considered here. In terms of sheer originality—it is doubtful whether he was ever directly affected by Debussy at all—there is nothing to surpass those works in the Charles Ives canon which may loosely be regarded as impressionistic. Ives's forthright, unpretentious and fearlessly academic outlook had several points in common with Debussy's, principally a desire for untrammelled freedom of musical expression. He sought to embrace musically every one of the multiple facets of existence and was not excessively concerned with 'niceness', 'rightness' and conventional notions of musical propriety and comeliness. Debussy's philosophy was far less radical than Ives's; there was a certain norm of harmonic dissonance beyond which he would not venture, and every experience, event or sensation which caught his muse's attention had to be passed directly through the refiner's fire of his sensibility. With Ives, on the other hand, the raw bleeding chunks of life which served him as inspiration tended to remain raw bleeding chunks in the completed works of art. Much of his music may be described as impressionistic in the sense that it consists of a chaotic jumble of impressions, a hodge-podge of disparate fragments, reminiscences, quotations from popular melody, allusions to composers as incompatible as Bach and Sankey. Among such compositions may be named *The Fourth of July*, the *Robert Browning Overture*, the first two movements of *Three Places in New England*, 'Decoration day' from the *Holidays* Symphony and the second movement of the Fourth Symphony. But in certain instances Ives's recollections gathered unto themselves that 'haze of distance and beauty', as Jefferies described it, through which fleeting impressions are at once enhanced and placed in clearer perspective. To this category of Impressionism Ives made a number of signal contributions. Chief among them are two of his loveliest orchestral works—'The Housatonic at Stockbridge', no 3 of *Three Places in New England* (a water-piece), and *Central Park in the Dark* (a night-piece).

'The Housatonic at Stockbridge' reflects the mood of a beautiful poem by Robert Underwood Johnson:

> Contented river! In thy dreamy realm
> The cloudy willow and the plumy elm . . .
> Thou beautiful! From every dreamy hill
> What eye but wanders with thee at thy will
> Imagining thy silver course unseen
> Convoyed by two attendant streams of green . . .
> Ah! There's a restive ripple, and the swift
> Red leaves—September's firstlings—faster drift.

An Impressionist autumn landscape: notice the insistence upon 'dreaming' and the sensitive merging of colours ('cloudy willow'—silver, green), then a suggestion of motion ('a restive ripple') and a point of colour contrast ('red leaves'). Ives said that the music was inspired by an early-morning walk he and his wife took one Sunday in summer: 'We walked in the meadows along the river and heard the distant singing from the church across the river. The mists had not entirely left the river and the colours, the running water, the banks and trees were something one would always remember.' The sound of distant

singing is conveyed impressionistically by a beautiful melody shared
between horn and cor anglais which has something of the nostalgic
flavour of a Celtic folk-tune (Ex. 43). However, the most unmistakably

Ex. 43
Ives, 'The Housatonic at Stockbridge' (*Three Places in New England*)

impressionistic element in the sound-picture is the responsibility of the
upper strings, muted, which play their basically whole-tone figurations
more or less independently of the rest of the orchestra and evoke a
hovering white stillness. Ex. 43 is from a voice and piano transcription
made by Ives in which he himself admitted that it was virtually impossible to reproduce the intended string effect on the piano. 'It was
intended that the strings be listened to separately or subconsciously—as
a kind of distant background of mists seen through the trees or over a
river valley, their parts bearing little or no relation to the tonality of
the tune.' After this atmospheric opening these natural sounds of
running water and rustling leaves gradually gain in intensity until a
terrifying climax is reached, as if the peacefully-flowing river had
turned into a monstrous raging torrent. The nightmare vision is
abruptly dispelled, however, and the music ends exquisitely on muted
strings, suspended on an unresolved chord of the dominant ninth.

Strings are used in an essentially similar way in the nocturne, *Central*

Park in the Dark. The nocturnal circumambient air, the starry vault of the heavens staring impassively down, are both evoked in the series of inconsequentially-drifting, non-metric, non-rhythmic, non-melodic string polychords and, again playing independently of the brass, wind and pianos, remains impervious to the varied disturbances (Wilfrid Mellers has defined them as 'car hooters, subway roars, yelling news-vendors, jazz bands and theatre hubbub') which seem to be attempting to disrupt them with ever-increasing aggressiveness. However, after a frenetic outburst of tantrums they appear to relinquish their efforts and the impressionistic string chords are heard proceeding on their way in the same sublimely glacial calm, as aloof and remote as ever.

Other Impressionist work of Ives is no less individual, and much of it can be found in his volume of *114 Songs*. All the time-honoured Impressionist preoccupations are here in evidence—night, dreams, mist, water and bells, and distance. 'Remembrance', for example, bears a quotation from Wordsworth's 'Solitary reaper':

> That music in my heart I bore
> Long after it was heard no more.

and evokes 'the sound of distant horn borne o'er shadowed lake'. This vocal line is echoed in the piano part, which consists for the rest entirely of arpeggiated open fifths—except for the final cadence where the far-away horn call is left suspended in sweet dissonance, rather like the ending of 'The Housatonic at Stockbridge'. 'Grantchester', a setting of Rupert Brooke's poem (an odd choice for a 'Connecticut Yankee', one might think, but little about Ives is predictable or orthodox), contains an actual quotation from *L'Après-midi d'un Faune*, in the manner of Dukas's *La Plainte, au loin, du Faune*, at the words 'and clever men have seen a Faun a-peeping through the green, and felt the Classics were not dead, To glimpse a Naiad's reedy head or hear the Goat-foot piping low'. Yet the most strikingly impressionistic passage is not at all Debussian. It evokes the drowsy reverie of the poet, lying in the grass and whiling away the sleepy hours under the wide sunny Cambridge sky 'until the centuries blend and blur . . . in Grantchester'. Ives's outer parts here move in contrary motion, steadily, chromatically, linked together by a trance-inducing ostinato in the tenor. In James Fenimore Cooper's 'Afterglow' the composer's intentions are overtly impressionistic. The music would exist in space, not in time; there is no regularity of stress or phrasing and the piano part is directed to be played 'as indistinctly as possible and both pedals used almost

constantly'. None the less the song is not in fact very successful in that
the harmony is too self-consciously and obviously experimental. One
can almost sense the composer working painstakingly from chord to
chord at the piano, hoping to make fire by rubbing together old dry
sticks of dissonance in every conceivable combination. Much less
contrived is 'Thoreau' (adapted from the Second Piano Sonata,
Concord) designed to evoke the faint sound of the Concord bell, which
transported into the wilderness where the poet is meditating, 'acquires a
certain vibratory hum as if the pine needles in the horizon were the
strings of a lyre which it swept'; and 'Mists' has a beautifully atmospheric beginning and ending in which the mists are conjured up, very
effectively, by augmented triads in treble and bass moving contrari-
wise over a pedal (Ex. 44).

Ex. 44
Ives, *Mists*

Dreams in the form of childhood recollections were a favourite
theme with Ives, and 'Tom sails away' and 'Down East' both conjure up
an Impressionist haze through which vague, dimly-perceived, long-
forgotten scenes are brought gradually into clearer focus, only to
recede again into a mist. For bells, too, Ives had a special predilection;
the slight but charming 'Evening bells' is a relatively conventional
stylization, but 'Walking' is more idiosyncratic—here the air is filled
with bell-reverberations from the village church, and although they are
referred to in the text on only two occasions, fourths and fifths in
various permutations dominate the substance of the accompaniment
and so suggest their ever-present hum. Tubular bells frequently find
their way into Ives's orchestral scores. The final movement of the
Third Symphony is faded out to a peal of muffled bells, and the same

device is put to great effect in 'Decoration day' where the disparate elements in the main body of the piece—the march to Wooster cemetery, the dirge ('Adeste Fideles') and 'Taps'—are all merged confusedly in a haze of obsessively tolling bells. Another favourite Impressionist device—the wordless chorus—is the protagonist in the coda of one of Ives's most impressive achievements, the finale of the Fourth Symphony. After a shattering climax with rock-steady descending bass and noble trumpet chorale, always underlaid by the inexorably marching tread of the separate percussion orchestra, the orchestral textures, colouristically enhanced by wordless chorus and theremin, begin to sing and hum a music of the spheres; they gradually dissolve into glittering particles of sonic dust until the percussion alone remains, marching onwards into infinity. This awe-inspiring vision is akin to that of Holst's 'Neptune'; both composers, roused to absorbed contemplation of the limitless vistas of time and space, found the techniques of Impressionism ideally suited to an expression of their wonderment.

In terms of sheer originality no other American post-Impressionist composer (if we may so dub Ives in the context of this study) quite scaled these heights. Much of the music written in the Impressionist idiom by American composers more or less contemporary with Ives has been well described by Mellers as 'genuinely sensitive, but also precious and parasitic'. For instance, Edward Burlinghame Hill was an ardent propagandist on behalf of French music; in 1924 he published one of the first comprehensive studies of contemporary French composers. An Impressionist cast of thought betrays itself in his symphonic poems *Lancelot and Guinevere* and *Lilacs*, and his refined sensibility is well in evidence in the *Prelude for Orchestra*, commissioned by the Kussevitsky Memorial Foundation on the occasion of the composer's eightieth birthday in 1953. It is basically the work of a romantic traditionalist subtly tinctured by Impressionism.

Emerson Whithorne and John Alden Carpenter made more substantial contributions. Like so many American composers, they were especially fascinated by cityscapes, and Whithorne's best known work, the suite *New York Nights and Days* for piano, is an evocation of certain aspects of the New York scene in the early '20s. Most obviously indebted to Debussy is the second piece, 'Chimes of Saint Patrick', which, like 'La Cathédrale Engloutie', attempts to blend the sonorities of bells, organ and Gregorian chant; but Whithorne has not Debussy's mastery of his raw material and the elements do not properly coalesce. The most successful part is the introduction with its bitonally-clashing major sixths and minor sevenths and the subtly evocative use of the tritone in the bass. 'Pell Street' ('Chinatown') is a gamelan stylization using the Chinese pentatonic scale; 'On the ferry' evokes a misty autumn morning on the Columbia river with strident hooters and whistles and snatches of popular song drifting in and out of the rhythmic chugging of paddle-wheels; 'Times Square' is an Impressionist metropolitan nocturne, a bewildering kaleidoscope of flashing lights, seething streams of humanity and various popular tunes of the day falling unannounced into the score and being just as unceremoniously booted out of it. However, the most beautiful example of Whithorne's impressionistic style is undoubtedly *The Rain*, in which the sound of pattering raindrops is captured almost as successfully as in 'Jardins sous la pluie'.

In John Alden Carpenter's best-known work, the Diaghilev ballet *Skyscrapers*, Impressionist influences have yielded to the lyrical dynamism of a Prokofiev strongly laced with American pop and jazz inflexions (it has noticeable affinities with *The Age of Steel*, which it anticipates by some five years). However, there is a variety of other compositions to prove that the roots of Carpenter's style lie in Impressionism. He was evidently fascinated by gamelan sonorities and by Chinese poetry and art, and there are generally some traces of this preoccupation even in those works not specifically oriental in inspiration. In the orchestral suite *Adventures in a Perambulator*, for instance, the recurrent theme which represents the occupier of the vehicle (i.e. the composer) is very clearly of gamelan origin though not wholly pentatonic. Elsewhere in this work—in 'En voiture', 'The lake' and 'Dreams' —the Impressionism is a familiar Franco-Russian confection of no special interest; it is hard to believe that in certain passages the composer is not alluding directly to *L'Après-midi d'un Faune* or to *Sheherezade*, although there are no quotation marks in the score. A different proposition is the collection of pieces entitled *Water Colours*. These are four settings of ancient Chinese poets for soprano and piano: gamelan-like pentatonic sonorities are naturally much in evidence, especially in the scintillating 'To a young gentleman' but the real gem of the set is the first song, 'On a screen' to a text by Li-Po:

> A tortoise I see on a lotus-flower resting
> A bird 'mid the reeds and rushes is nesting,
> A light skiff, propelled by some boatman's fair daughter,
> Whose song dies away o'er the fast flowing water.

IIM

The Post-Impressionists

The music is simple and beautiful; it has all the serenity and limpidity of a Kao K'o-kung landscape, with a pleasing contrast between the mutedly chromatic harmonic inflexions at 'a bird 'mid the reeds' and the diatonic transparency of 'a light skiff propelled . . .'. Similar qualities are to be found in the first, second and fifth of his *Diversions* for piano, exquisitely-wrought pieces devoid of stereotype; no 1 in particular is as perfect an Impressionist miniature as 'On a Screen'. Mention should also be made of the opening and closing sections of the amusing ballet-score *Krazy Kat* (based on George Herriman's comic-strip characters) in which Krazy is portrayed asleep by means of dreamily-rising pentatonic fourths and re-echoing horn-calls; and also of the symphonic poem *Sea Drift*, inspired by the same group of Whitman poems which had already prompted Delius's fine choral work of the same name and Vaughan Williams's *Sea Symphony*. There are occasional echoes of *La Mer*, but its Impressionism is unashamedly harnessed in the service of romantic nostalgia. The shoreline it delineates is essentially Wagnerian, not Debussian.

Of all the composers who, like Whithorne and Carpenter, wrote directly under the aegis of Impressionism—and there were many of them, including Charles M. Loeffler (*A Pagan Poem*, *La Mort de Tintagiles*, after Maeterlinck) Louis Gruenberg (the symphonic poems *The Enchanted Isle* and *The Hill of Dreams*) and Marion Bauer (*Sun Splendour* for orchestra, *Orientale* for soprano and orchestra)—the most highly thought of today is undoubtedly Charles Tomlinson Griffes, who died prematurely in 1920 at the age of 36. From an early age he showed himself responsive to colour and later came to associate certain colours with definite keys—that he eventually came under the influence of Scriabin is not surprising. He was also a gifted artist. He could draw well with pen and ink, was an excellent painter of water-colour landscapes and later worked in copper etchings. With these inclinations a response to Impressionism was almost a foregone conclusion; in common with so many of his contemporaries and predecessors, a penchant for an Orientalism of a vaguely Russian cast lost no time in declaring itself, although it was later to be transmuted into a mysticism which undoubtedly reflected Scriabin's influence. Works which came about as a result of this amalgam include the tone poem *The Pleasure Dome of Kubla Khan* and the justly-celebrated *Poem* for flute and orchestra, an elegantly-poised, gracefully-written essay in which post-romantic, impressionistic and oriental elements are held in perfect equilibrium.

His *Five Poems of Ancient China and Japan*, for voice and piano, and the Japanese dance-drama *Sho-Jo* have obvious oriental affiliations, but the *Roman Sketches* for piano are conveniently representative not only of Griffes's finely-tempered fluency in the handling of Impressionist idioms but also of his ability to graft on to them unassertive but telling intimations of a distinctive musical personality. Each sketch is prefaced by verses of William Sharp: no 1, the well-known 'The white peacock', seeks to create the atmosphere of tropical splendour against which moves the peacock through the noontide, 'white as a snowdrift illumined by sunlight'. The sunlight floods the garden, the pomegranate rears its glory of blossoms, the oleander dreams, the heat 'lies pale blue in the hollows', the 'dream-flowers' nod their heads. Small wonder that after the Scriabinesque opening ('languidamente e molto rubato') the music dreams itself into a polychrome haze of exotic Impressionism with a profusion of ninths and descending chromatic arabesque. Wilfrid Mellers has claimed that 'only a certain wildness at the climaxes sounds personal, American rather than French', and this 'wildness' seems a natural outgrowth of the conventional type of Romantic red-bloodedness which is found in the central section of *L'Après-midi d'un Faune*. 'The white peacock' is a beautiful but essentially derivative piece of music and so is no 3, 'The fountains of the Aqua Paola', clearly modelled on *Jeux d'Eau*. A more personal note is struck in 'Nightfall', in which the dissonant minor seconds in bar 2 anticipate the impressionistic clusters of Bartók (e.g. the 'Night Music' in *Out of Doors*); but by far the most original piece is the last of the series, 'Clouds'. The gliding sequence of chords with which Griffes sets the scene is reminiscent of the opening of 'Nuages', except that whereas Debussy's skies are leaden and grey, William Sharp's are golden and white, and Griffes's chords are not sober thirds and fifths but liberally spiced with added notes—and in this skyscape there is an agitation of storms in the offing. At 'più mosso' on p. 4 there begins to break through that wildness of which Mellers speaks in connection with 'The white peacock' and just before the main climax there is a strange and intriguing use of the parallel-chord technique (Ex. 45). In the coda reminiscences of earlier motifs return 'molto lontano' over a pedal of open fifths, asserting the reality of non-movement against the illusion of movement in the upper part.

This brief and of necessity highly selective account[1] of the Impressionist movement in America cannot be concluded without some mention of the keenness with which its repercussions were felt, not in

Ex. 45
Griffes, 'Clouds' (*Roman Sketches*)

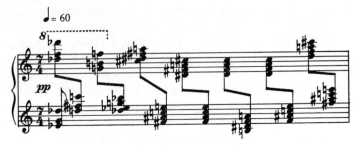

the 'classical' field but in the alien environments of popular music and jazz. It must be remembered that the demarcation-lines between pop, jazz and 'classical' music are much less rigidly defined in America than anywhere else, with innumerable composers and performers active and flourishing on either side of the barrier, if there is a barrier. Thus it came about that the superficies of Impressionist harmony—the blatantly sensuous appeal of its ninths, elevenths, thirteenths and added-sixths and their strikingly emotive properties—were early exploited by musicians seeking to re-actify the jaded harmonic taste-buds of *fin-de-siècle* commercial music. Debussy (and also Cyril Scott, another acknowledged source) wrote short and relatively straight-forward piano pieces which could easily be ransacked, and Impressionist harmony passed into the common-or-garden vernacular of the Tin-Pan-Alley song-plugger, Broadway arranger or vaudeville pianist and thence into the lingua franca of the jazz-band. There has always been a measure of cross-fertilization between the parallel streams of American popular music and jazz, and if the rhythmic and melodic idiosyncrasies of jazz gave a kind of strychnine injection to styles of composition for the pop-song market and musical theatre, jazz in reciprocation drew heavily on the harmonic bricks-and-mortar of Broadway commercial-ism in its endeavour to increase and develop its expressive scope.

On no jazz composer has the influence of Impressionism been more profound than on the man generally acknowledged to be the greatest creative spirit so far produced by the medium—Duke Ellington. Not that he merely uses Impressionist harmony—this alone would not qualify him as an Impressionist—but in his expressive intent, in style, idiom and technique he is far more indebted to French Impressionism than to any other form of European art. It is significant that Ellington started his life as a student of painting and by all accounts made considerable progress in this direction before taking up music in its place, and certainly the titles of many of his compositions betray a preoccupation with colours and scents—*Black and Tan Fantasy*, *Transbluency*, *In a Magenta Haze*, the lovely nocturne *Mood Indigo*, *On a Turquoise Cloud*, *Sepia Panorama*, *Black, Brown and Beige*, *Perfume Suite*.[2] We are constantly finding, transmogrified into the Negro vernacular, echoes of the languorous, dreamy type of mood-evocation which Debussy and Delius made particularly their own: *Dusk*, *Moon Mist*, *Misty Mornin'*, *Warm Valley*, *In a Blue Summer Garden*, *Sultry Sunset*. There is here a specific link with Delius (one must allow the composer his little joke in the penultimate item in the above list) in that these and all such pieces are not merely atmospheric abstractions like 'Nuages' or 'Les sons et les parfums tournent dans l'air du soir'; they are imbued with a strong vein of personal melancholy made explicit in, for example, *Solitude*, *Awful Sad*, *Reminiscin' in Tempo*, *Lonesome Lullaby*, *In a Sentimental Mood*, *Minnehaha*. In the latter Ellington uses a solo voice, in true Delian fashion, to spin an extra strand of colour into the rich warmly sensuous haze of reeds and brass. Ellington's Impressionism is definitely of the Delian rather than the Debussian variety; in other words abstract pictorialism yields its monopoly to the contemplation of natural phenomena under the aspect of mutability (the same of course applies to his Impressionist cityscapes—he is a city man born and bred, who often hears his music in the very heart of noise—such as *Harlem Air-Shaft* and *New York City Blues*). Ex. 46 is from the opening of *Sultry Sunset* and shows a sinuous melodic line curling nostalgically around a wash of self-indulgently chromatic harmony; timbre and harmony here pool their resources, as in so much Impressionist music, to create an appropriately languid atmosphere.

However, even these brief examples indicate that Ellington's Impressionism is no mere pasteboard imitation of Delius's. Despite misleading titles such as *Creole Rhapsody*, Ellington, unlike Delius, is not fundamentally a rhapsodist; in fact his mood-impressions are more akin in their terseness and concision to a Grieg lyric piece. Correspondingly, chromatic discipline in Ellington's harmony is more severe, with tonal schemes sharply etched and rigidly adhered to—there is no drifting endlessly in chains of unresolved discords, and while the norm of dissonance is higher than in Delius, inversions of chords are generally avoided, with a resultant increase in linear stability. Furthermore, these minuscule tone poems of atmosphere and mood constitute but one of

Ex. 46
Ellington, *Sultry Sunset*

the many facets of Ellington's creativity. His music is as highly personal
as Delius's and as subtly different from the latter's as Delius's is from
Debussy's, or Debussy's from Ravel's. In fact, although in later years he
numbered *In a Summer Garden*, *La Mer* and *Daphnis et Chloé* among his
favourite 'serious' compositions, it is improbable that he was acquainted
with them at first hand during the years in which his style was evolving.
It is far more likely that he acquired elements of Impressionist harmony
and scoring through Will Vodery, chief arranger for the Ziegfeld
follies—the same Will Vodery whose band made an impression on the
young Constant Lambert when it appeared in London in 1924. Lambert was one of the first to foster a genuine appreciation of jazz in
general in this country and of Duke Ellington's merits as a composer in
particular; he was also a great Francophile, early aware of the signi-

ficance of Impressionism as a vitally disruptive force in *fin-de-siècle* music and of the interconnection between Debussy, Delius and jazz.

Another professional arranger and orchestrator who later began to compose was Ferde Grofé, best known for his original scoring of Gershwin's *Rhapsody in Blue*. Grofé's *Grand Canyon* and *Mississippi* suites are typical of the lighter variety of nature-Impressionism, drawing freely on elements of Delius, Debussy and Ravel with the occasional admixture of jazz inflexions, producing an agreeable but by no means artistically significant confection (see especially 'Sunrise' and 'The painted desert' in *Grand Canyon*, 'Father of waters' and 'Old creole days' in *Mississippi*; another excellent example of the genre is the Canadian Robert Farnon's *Canadian Impressions*, particularly 'A la claire fontaine' and the beautiful 'Lake of the woods'). As far as Gershwin himself is concerned several people have noted a curious dream-like aura surrounding that most popular of all metropolitan travelogues, *An American in Paris*. Certainly the city seems to be here seen as a kaleidoscopic succession of sharply-defined but essentially fleeting images, one following the other with bewildering rapidity; the very vividness and superabundance of colour, in fact, creates a slightly unreal effect, and in the passage which immediately precedes the magnificent central blues ('andante ma con ritmo deciso') recollections of earlier themes move sleepily beneath a haze of bitonal harmony and enhance the impression of a momentary lull in the dream sequence. It is interesting to note that when the score was adapted for the purposes of a film-ballet bearing the same title (with Gene Kelly), the décor was based on the styles of the post-Impressionist painters—Utrillo, le Douanier Rousseau, Toulouse-Lautrec, Raoul Dufy—except for the sequence danced to the episode described above, in which Manet and Monet were the dominant influences. The colours here were various pastel shades of blue, with a red rose supplying the solitary splash of bright colour. Throughout the film ballet, colour and music were very closely and fascinatingly interwoven, the one exactly complementing the other.

---

1. Whilst it is unrealistic to speak of any Impressionist influence upon Aaron Copland's work, it is nevertheless interesting that he often uses Debussian open fourths and fifths (sometimes superimposed) to reflect space, stillness and distance

—cf. the opening to the *Lincoln Portrait* (the illimitable prairies), the prairie music in *Billy the Kid*, the opening of *Quiet City*, 'Conversation at the Soda fountain' in *Our Town*, 'Night thoughts' in *Music for a Great City*. Similarly Bernard Herrmann in his great dramatic cantata *Moby Dick* falls quite naturally into progressions of superimposed fifths to suggest depths of water when setting Ahab's second monologue ('it was a clear steel blue day') during which the captain 'leaned over the side and watched how his shadow in the water sank and sank to his gaze, the more and the more that he strove to pierce the profundity'. Early in the same work Herrmann uses a *Waldweben*-like undulating motion to evoke the glimmer of the evening sun over the waters ('Yonder, by the ever-brimming goblet's rim') and in the first act of his opera *Wuthering Heights* beautifully catches the mood of the Yorkshire moors in summer by purely impressionistic means—a bursting lyrical forward urge, modally-flavoured wood-wind arabesque, bejewelled, prismatic orchestral textures, 'complexe mais pas compliqué'.

2. It was startling to hear Ellington, in an interview given during the interval of a London concert in October 1971, using the same metaphor as Delius to describe his abhorrence of academic analysis of his work. Delius said to Eric Fenby: 'When you see a lovely rose you treasure it as it is, you don't pull it to pieces to appreciate its beauty and find out where its delicious perfume comes from. So it should be with music.' Ellington to Stanley Dance: 'If you take a flower to bits, you've got no flower.'

SELECT BIBLIOGRAPHY

Introduction

COOPER, Martin, *French Music from the death of Berlioz to the death of Fauré* (London 1951)

DAVIES, Laurence, *Gallic Muse* (London 1967)

DAWES, Frank, *Debussy Piano Music* (BBC Music Guides, London 1969)

GOMBRICH, E. H., *Story of Art* (London 1967)

LAMBERT, Constant, *Music Ho! A Study of Music in Decline* (London 1934)

LOCKSPEISER, Edward, *Debussy: his life and mind* (vol. I, London 1962; vol. II, London 1965)

LOCKSPEISER, Edward, *Debussy* (London 1963)

LOCKSPEISER, Edward, *Music and Painting – a study in comparative ideas from Turner to Schoenberg* (London 1973)

WEBER, Edith (Ed.), *Debussy et L'Evolution de la Musique au XXe Siècle* (*Proceedings of the international conference held in Paris on the occasion of the Debussy Centenary,* 1962, Paris 1965)

Chapter 1: Chopin and Liszt

ABRAHAM, Gerald, *100 Years of Music* (London 1964)

ABRAHAM, Gerald, *Chopin's Musical Style* (London 1939)

WALKER, Alan (Ed.), *Frédéric Chopin, Profiles of the Man and His Music* (London 1966)

WALKER, Alan (Ed.), *Franz Liszt: The Man and His Music* (London 1970)

Chapter 2: Grieg

ABRAHAM, Gerald (Ed.), *Grieg—a symposium* (London 1948)

Chapter 3: The Russian Nationalists

ABRAHAM, Gerald (Ed.), *Music of Tchaikovsky* (London 1969)

ABRAHAM, Gerald (Ed.), *Studies in Russian Music* (London 1935)

ABRAHAM, Gerald (Ed.), *On Russian Music* (London 1939)

GARDEN, Edward, *Balakirev: A Critical Study of his Life and Music* (London 1967)

Chapter 4: Wagner in France

DAVIES, Laurence, *César Franck and his circle* (London 1970)
DEMUTH, Norman, *César Franck* (London 1949)
GUTMAN, Robert W., *Richard Wagner: The Man, his Mind and his Music* (New York 1968)
MYERS, Rollo, *Emmanuel Chabrier and his Circle* (London 1969)

Chapter 5: In France

DEANE, Basil, *Albert Roussel* (London 1961)
DREW, David, 'Modern French Music', in Hartog, Howard (Ed.), *European Music in the 20th Century* (London 1957)
KOECHLIN, Charles, *Debussy* (Paris 1927)
MYERS, Rollo, *Ravel: Life and Works* (London 1960)
MYERS, Rollo, 'Debussy and French Music', *Music Times* October, 1967, 899–901
MELLERS, W. H., *Studies in Contemporary Music* (London 1948)
O'LOUGHLIN, Niall, 'Koechlin and Debussy', *Musical Times* November 1967 993–6

Chapter 6: In England

BACHARACH, A. L. (Ed.), *British Music of Our Time* (London 1946)
BAX, Arnold, *Farewell my Youth* (London 1943)
DAY, James, *Vaughan Williams* (London 1961)
DICKINSON, A. E. F., *Vaughan Williams* (London 1963)
FENBY, Eric, *Delius* (London 1971)
FENBY, Eric *Delius as I knew him* (London 1935, rev. ed. 1966)
HOLST, Imogen, *The Music of Gustav Holst* (London 1968)
HOWES, Frank, *English Musical Renaissance* (London 1966)
LONGMIRE, John, *John Ireland, Portrait of a Friend* (London 1969)
PIRIE, Peter J., 'Debussy and English Music', *Musical Times* July 1967, 599–601
PIRIE, Peter J., *Frank Bridge* (London 1971)

Chapter 7: In Austria and Germany

HENDERSON, Robert, 'Debussy and Schoenberg', *Musical Times* March 1967, 222–6
STUCKENSCHMIDT, H. H., 'L'influence de Debussy—Autriche et Allemagne', in Weber (Ed.) *Debussy et l'evolution de la musique au XXe siècle* (Paris 1965)

Chapter 8: In Spain

STARKIE, Walter, article on Mompou in Grove's *Dictionary of Music and Musicians* (5th ed., London 1954)
CHASE, Gilbert, *The Music of Spain* (2nd ed., New York 1959)
TREND, J. B., *Manuel de Falla and Spanish Music* (London 1935)

Chapter 9: In Italy

CARNER, Mosco, 'Debussy and Puccini', *Musical Times* June 1967, 502–5
WATERHOUSE, J. C. G., 'Debussy and Italian Music', *Musical Times* May 1968, 414–18

Chapter 10: In Russia

BOWERS, F., *Scriabin* (Tokyo/London 1971)
LAMBERT, Constant, 'Debussy as key-figure' in *Music Ho! A Study of Music in Decline* (London 1934)
NOBLE, Jeremy, 'Debussy and Stravinsky', *Musical Times* January 1967, 22–5

Chapter 11: In Hungary

CROSS, Anthony, 'Debussy and Bartok', *Musical Times* February 1967, 125–31
YOUNG, Percy M., *Zoltan Koddly* (London 1964)

Chapter 12: In North America

JAMES, Burnett, 'The Impressionism of Duke Ellington' (in *Essays on Jazz*) (London 1961)
MELLERS, Wilfred, *Music in a New Found Land* (London 1964)
RAAD, Virgina, 'L'influence de Debussy—Amerique', in Weber (Ed.), *Debussy et l'evolution de la musique au XXe siècle* (Paris 1965)

INDEX

Main page references are italicized